F47-94 BK Bud July 94

NORTH CAROLINA
STATE BOARD OF COMMUNITY COLLEGES
LIBRARIES
SOUTHEASTERN COMMUNITY COLLEGE

P9-DZA-958

For Reference

Not to be taken from this room

SOUTHEASTERN COMMUNITY
COLLEGE LIBRARY
WHITEVILLE, NC 28472

SLAVERY

OPPOSING VIEWPOINTS®

Other Books in the American History Series:

E
441
.8636
1992
c.2

SOUTHEASTERN COMMUNITY
COLLEGE LIBRARY
WHITEVILLE, NC 28472

SLAVERY

OPPOSING VIEWPOINTS®

David L. Bender, *Publisher*
Bruno Leone, *Executive Editor*

Teresa O'Neill, *Series Editor*
John C. Chalberg, Ph.D., professor of history,
  Normandale Community College, *Consulting Editor*

William Dudley, *Book Editor*

For Reference

Not to be taken from this room

AMERICAN HISTORY SERIES

No part of this book may be reproduced or used in any form or by any means, electrical, mechanical, or otherwise, including, but not limited to, photocopy, recording, or any information storage and retrieval system, without prior written permission from the publisher.

Library of Congress Cataloging-in-Publication Data

Slavery : opposing viewpoints / William Dudley, book editor.
     p.   cm. — (American history series)
  Includes bibliographical references (p.) and index.
  ISBN 1-56510-013-1 (lib. bdg. : acid-free paper) : — ISBN 1-56510-012-3 (pbk. : acid-free paper) :
  1. Slavery—United States—History—Sources. I. Dudley, William, 1964- . II. Series: American history series (San Diego, Calif.)
E441.S636 1992
973'.0496—dc20   92-21796
                                                CIP

Cover photos (clockwise from top): Library of Congress, The Bettmann Archive, National Archives, and Library of Congress. The following publishers have generously given permission to use excerpts from copyrighted works: From *Lay My Burden Down: A Folk History of Slavery*, edited by B.A. Botkin, © 1945 by B.A. Botkin. Reprinted by permission of Curtis Brown, Ltd. From "The Moral Legacy of the Founding Fathers" by John Hope Franklin, *The University of Chicago Magazine* 67 (4): 10-13, © 1975, The University of Chicago Magazine. Reprinted by permission. From *Slavery and Its Consequences*, edited by Robert A. Goldwin and Art Kaufman, © 1988 by the American Enterprise Institute for Public Policy Research, Washington, D.C. Reprinted with permission.

Grateful acknowledgment is also given to the Massachusetts Historical Society and the Virginia State Library Archives.

© 1992 by Greenhaven Press, Inc., PO Box 289009,
San Diego, CA 92198-9009

Contents

Foreword

Aboard the *Arbella* as it lurched across the cold, gray Atlantic, John Winthrop was as calm as the waters surrounding him were wild. With the confidence of a born leader, Winthrop gathered his Puritan passengers around him. It was time to offer a sermon. England lay behind them, and years of strife and persecution for their religious beliefs were over, he said. But the Puritan abandonment of England, he reminded his followers, did not mean that England was beyond redemption. Winthrop wanted his followers to remember England even as they were leaving it behind. Their goal should be to create a new England, one far removed from the authority of the Anglican church and King Charles I. In Winthrop's words, their settlement in the New World ought to be a model society, a city upon a hill. He hoped his band would be able to create a just society in America for corrupt England to imitate.

Unable to find either peace or freedom within their home country, these Puritans were determined to provide England with a living example of a community that valued both. Across the hostile Atlantic Ocean would shine the bright light of a just, harmonious, and God-serving society. England may have been beset by sin and corruption, but Winthrop and the colonists believed they could still save England—and themselves. Together, they would coax out of the rocky New England soil not only food for their tables but many thriving communities dedicated to achieving harmony and justice.

On June 8, 1630, John Winthrop and his company of refugees had their first glimpse of what they came to call New England. High on the surrounding hills stood a welcoming band of fir trees whose fragrance drifted to the *Arbella* on a morning breeze. To Winthrop, the "smell off the shore [was] like the smell of a garden."

This new world would, in fact, often be compared to the Garden of Eden. In it, John Winthrop would have his opportunity to start life over again. So would his family and his shipmates. So would all those who would come after them. Victims of conflict in old England hoped to find peace in New England.

Winthrop, for one, had experienced much conflict in his life. As a Puritan, he was opposed to Catholicism and Anglicanism, both of which, he believed, were burdened by distracting rituals and distant hierarchies. A parliamentarian by conviction, he despised Charles I, who had spurned Parliament and created a private army to do his bidding. He believed in individual responsibility and fought against the loss of religious and political freedom. A gentleman landowner, he feared the rising economic power of a merchant class that seemed to value only money. Once Winthrop stepped aboard the *Arbella*, he hoped conflict would not be a part of his American future.

But his Puritan religion told Winthrop that human beings are fallen creatures and that perfection, whether communal or individual, is unachievable on this earth. Therefore, he was presented with a dilemma: On the one hand, his religion demanded that he attempt to live a perfect life in an imperfect world. On the other hand, it told him that he was destined to fail.

Soon after Winthrop disembarked from the *Arbella*, he came face-to-face with this maddening dilemma. He found himself presiding not over a utopia—an ideal community—but over a colony caught up in disputes as troubling as any that he had confronted in his English past.

John Winthrop, it seems, was not the only Puritan with a dream of perfection, with a vision of a heaven on earth. Others in the community saw the dream differently. They wanted greater political and religious freedom than their leader was prepared to grant. Often, Winthrop was able to handle this conflict diplomatically. He expanded, for example, participation in elections and allowed the voters of Massachusetts Bay greater power.

But religious conflict was another matter because it was a conflict of competing visions of the Puritan utopia. In Roger Williams and Anne Hutchinson, two of his fellow colonists, John Winthrop faced rivals unprepared to accept his definition of the perfect community. To Williams, perfection demanded that he separate himself from the Puritan institutions in his community and create an even "purer" church. Winthrop, however, disagreed and exiled Williams to Rhode Island. Hutchinson presumed that she could interpret God's will without a minister. Again, Winthrop did not agree. Hutchinson was tried on charges of heresy, convicted, and banished from Massachusetts.

John Winthrop's Massachusetts colony was the first, but far from the last, American attempt to build a unified, peaceful community that, in the end, only provoked discord. This glimpse at its history reveals what Winthrop confronted: the unavoidable presence of conflict in American life.

American Assumptions

From America's origins in the early seventeenth century, Americans have often held several interrelated assumptions about their country. First, people believe that to be American is to be free. Second, because Americans did not have to free themselves from

9

feudal lords or an entrenched aristocracy, conflict is often considered foreign to American life. Finally, America has been seen as a perpetual haven from the troubles and disputes that are found in the Old World.

John Winthrop, for one, lived his life as though all of these assumptions were true. But the opposing viewpoints presented in the American History Series should reveal that for many Americans, these assumptions were and are myths. Indeed, for numerous Americans, liberty has not always been guaranteed, and conflict has been a necessary, sometimes welcome aspect of their life. To these Americans, the United States is less a sanctuary than it is one more battleground for old and new ideas.

Our American landscape has been torn apart again and again by a great variety of clashes—theological, ideological, political, economic, geographical, racial, gender-based, and class-based. But to discover such a landscape is not necessarily to come upon a hopelessly divided country. If the editors desire to prove anything during the course of this series, it is not that America has been destroyed by conflict but rather that America has been enlivened, enriched, and even strengthened by exchanges between Americans who have disagreed with one another.

Observers of American life, however, often see a country in which its citizens behave as though all of the basic questions of life have been settled. Over the years, they see generation after generation of Americans who seem to blithely agree with one another. In the nineteenth century, French traveler Alexis de Tocqueville called the typical American a "venturesome conservative." According to Tocqueville, this American was willing to risk money in the marketplace but otherwise presented the drab front of someone who thought, dressed, and acted just like everyone else. To Tocqueville, Americans were individualistic risk takers when it came to playing the game of capitalism but were victims of public opinion (which he defined as the "tyranny of the majority") when it came to otherwise expressing themselves.

In the twentieth century, sociologist David Riesman has registered his agreement with Tocqueville. He has defined the modern American as "other-directed." Perhaps willing to leap into the economic arena, this American is unwilling to take risks in the marketplace of ideas. The result is either silence or assent, either because this person is unsure of his or her own beliefs or because the mass media dictate beliefs—or a bit of both. The other-directed American is fearful of standing apart from the crowd.

The editors of this series would like to suggest that Tocqueville and Riesman were too narrow in their assessment of Americans. They have found innumerable Americans who have been willing to take the trouble to disagree.

Thomas Jefferson was one of the least confrontational of Americans, but he boldly and irrevocably enriched American life with his individualistic views. Like John Winthrop before him, he had a notion of an American Eden. Like Winthrop, he offered a vision of a harmonious society. And like Winthrop, he not only became enmeshed in conflict but eventually presided over a people beset by it. But unlike Winthrop, Jefferson believed this Eden was not located in a specific community but in each individual American. His Declaration of Independence from Great Britain could also be read as a declaration of independence for each individual in American society.

Jefferson's Ideal

Jefferson's ideal world was composed of "yeoman farmers," each of whom was roughly equal to the other in society's eyes, each of whom was free from the restrictions of both government and his fellow citizens. Throughout his life, Jefferson offered a continuing challenge to Americans: advance individualism and equality or see the death of the American experiment. Jefferson believed that the strength of this experiment depended upon a society of autonomous individuals and a society without great gaps between rich and poor. His challenge to his fellow Americans to create—and sustain—such a society has itself produced both economic and political conflict.

A society whose guiding document is the Declaration of Independence is a society assured of the freedom to dream—and to disagree. We know that Jefferson himself hated conflict, whether personal or political. His tendency was to avoid confrontations of any sort, to squirrel himself away and write rather than to stand up and speak his mind. It is only through his written words that we can grasp Jefferson's utopian dream of a society of independent farmers, all pursuing their private dreams and all leading lives of sufficient prosperity.

This man of wealth and intellect lived an essentially happy life in accord with his view that Americans ought to have the right to pursue "happiness." But Jefferson's public life was much more troublesome. From the first rumblings of the American Revolution in the 1760s to the North-South skirmishes of the 1820s that ultimately produced the Civil War, Jefferson was at or near the center of American political history. The issues were almost too many—and too crucial—for one lifetime. Jefferson had to choose between supporting or rejecting the path of revolution. During and after the ensuing war, he was at the forefront of the battle for religious liberty. After endorsing the Constitution, he opposed the economic plans of Alexander Hamilton. At the end of the century, he fought the infamous Alien and Sedition Acts, which limited civil liberties. As president, he opposed the Federalist court, conspiracies to divide the union, and calls for a new war against England.

Throughout his life, Thomas Jefferson, slaveholder, pondered the conflict between American freedom and American slavery. And from retirement at his Monticello retreat, he frowned at the rising spirit of commercialism that he feared was dividing Americans and destroying his dream of American harmony.

No matter the issue, however, Thomas Jefferson invariably supported the rights of the individual. Worried as he was about the excesses of commercialism, he accepted them because his main concern was to live in a society where liberty and individualism could flourish. To Jefferson, Americans had to be free to worship as they desired. They also deserved to be free from an overreaching government. To Jefferson, Americans should also be free to possess slaves.

Harmony, an Elusive Goal

Before reading the articles in this anthology, the editors ask readers to ponder the lives of John Winthrop and Thomas Jefferson. Each held a utopian vision, one based upon the demands of community and the other on the autonomy of the individual. Each dreamed of a country of perpetual new beginnings. Each found himself thrust into a position of leadership and found that conflict could not be avoided. And each lived long enough to face and express many opposing views. Harmony, whether communal or individual, was a forever elusive goal.

The opposing visions of Winthrop and Jefferson have been at the heart of many differences among Americans from many backgrounds through the whole of American history. Moreover, their visions have provoked important responses that have helped shape American society, the American character, and many an American battle.

Is the theme of community versus the individual the single defining theme in American history? No, but it is a recurring theme that provides us with a useful point of departure for showing that Americans have been more rambunctious and contentious than Tocqueville or Riesman found them to be, that blandness has not been the defining characteristic for all Americans.

In this age of mass media, the danger exists that the real issues that divide Americans will be, at best, distorted or, at worst, ignored. But by thinking honestly about the past, the real issues and real differences have often been of critical, even of life-and-death, importance to Americans. And they continue to be so today.

The editors of the American History Series have done extensive research to find representative opinions on the issues included in these volumes. They found numerous outstanding opposing viewpoints from people of all times, classes, and genders in American history. From those, they selected commentaries that best fit the nature and flavor of the period under consideration. Every attempt was made to include the most important and relevant viewpoints in each chapter. Obviously, not every notable viewpoint could be included. Therefore, a bibliography has been provided at the end of each book to aid readers in seeking out for themselves additional information.

The editors are confident that as this series reveals past conflicts, it will help revitalize the reader's views of the American present. In that spirit, the American History Series is dedicated to the proposition that American history is more complicated, more fascinating, and more troubling than John Winthrop, Thomas Jefferson, Alexis de Tocqueville, or David Riesman ever dared to imagine.

John C. Chalberg
Consulting Editor

Introduction

"None of the elements in the history of slavery in America are without ambiguity."

Denmark Vesey, a free black man living in the South, had long dreamed of overthrowing the hated slave system. He knew that any plan for a slave rebellion would have to be foolproof to stand even a remote chance of success. And Vesey had a plan that he believed just might succeed because it relied on simplicity, shrewdness, and the considerable power of his own personality. Vesey's first priority was to minimize the number of active coconspirators, which would minimize the number of potential betrayers. This small group would be deployed in a series of late-night raids on local arsenals. The captured weapons would be distributed to the rest of the slaves involved in the plot. Finally, the freshly armed black masses would be unleashed to attack and kill their white oppressors.

The year was 1822, nearly a decade before the brief but bloody rebellion of Nat Turner in Virginia. It was also a good ten years before Northern abolitionists began to organize and call for an end to slavery. The immediate target of the Denmark Vesey Conspiracy was Charleston, South Carolina. Vesey's timing proved to be less than perfect, but his chosen setting offered great possibilities. The city of Charleston was in the heart of the black belt of the American South, and Charleston had not yet seen any need to impose strict surveillance over its blacks. Instead, a fairly casual system of control was in place to monitor both slaves and free blacks. It was this system that Vesey hoped to take advantage of—and ultimately destroy. If secrecy could be maintained until the vital weapons were obtained, Vesey would be able to arm a large army of vengeful recruits eager to attack. Secrecy was essential. Surreptitious whispers could destroy the plot. And a city the size of Charleston was always rife with whisperers.

Denmark Vesey was close to embodying the ideal leader of a slave revolt. A mulatto and a free man, Vesey had developed extensive contacts outside the walls of slavery. Through the African Church of Charleston, he had come to know members of free black congregations in the North. This growing network provided Vesey with a sense of hope and some money. Furthermore, within the African Church, Vesey was able to preach freedom and gain a following among Charleston's black population without attracting attention from the city's whites.

A literate man, Vesey had access to Northern newspapers. By reading them, he had been able to follow the debates surrounding the 1820 controversy over the admission of Missouri to the Union. The issue of slavery's expansion was at the heart of that controversy. At least a few Northern congressmen had hinted at the unthinkable in the heat of the fight over what to do about slavery in Missouri and territories to the west: if the institution of slavery was this troublesome and divisive, they suggested, perhaps the time was approaching when it should be brought to an end. Such an opinion was a decidedly minority viewpoint in both North and South in the third decade of the nineteenth century. But it gave Denmark Vesey one more source of hope—and one more reason to strike quickly. After all, he reasoned, a powerful abolitionist movement might soon lead to a backlash, prodding the South to tighten the grip on its human property.

Vesey was a giant of a man with a mighty grip of his own. He made it clear to his followers that he would personally thrash anyone who might be tempted, for whatever reason, to reveal the conspiracy. The problem of betrayal within the slave community was a genuine one. That some slaves preferred the benefits of the system to the cost of overthrowing it was a reality Vesey could not afford to ignore. He also had to take into account the general fear of punishment from angry and self-righteous masters. Therefore, Vesey vowed, if any black coconspirator revealed his plot, he would out-terrorize the white terrorists. He would mete out his version of justice to any informers before the white authorities could destroy him.

Leaks Spoiled Vesey's Plans

Using a combination of charisma and coercion, Vesey moved. ahead with his planned uprising. A Saturday night in late spring was selected because many rural slaves would be in Charleston to help their masters prepare for the Sunday market. But the rebellion did not take place on the scheduled Saturday, and not on a hastily arranged earlier date. For not once, but twice, black informers revealed Vesey's plans. No matter how carefully he plotted, Vesey was unable to prevent the leaks he feared.

As a result of the two betrayals, the Vesey Conspiracy never became the Vesey Rebellion, successful or otherwise. Instead, on July 26, 1822, the authorities in Charleston (after rejecting the pleas of the governor of South Carolina) executed Vesey and nearly two dozen of his followers. And the two betrayers were freed by their grateful owners. One used his emancipation to work toward the eventual purchase of freedom for his wife. The other became a black slave owner who sold off, one by one, the members of a slave family he had bought to make a profit.

The story of the aborted Denmark Vesey uprising asks the students of American slavery to confront a number of opposing views: black versus white, white versus white, and black versus black. While the history of American slavery can generally be said to be the history of white oppression of blacks, it is not the history of a unified white population enslaving an equally monolithic black population. Historical accuracy demands that we look beyond the obvious.

Whether we are discussing blacks or whites, we are dealing with what historian Eugene Genovese has called the "history of the inarticulate." During the colonial and early national periods of American history, literacy was a rare quality on both sides of the racial divide. And not all of those who were able to read and write left documents for historians to examine. In addition, nothing even approaching reliable polling data exists for the antebellum years. We are left, therefore, with bits and pieces of evidence, with the hard data of census reports and the various thoughts recorded in diaries, letters, songs, and stories. Most of the evidence is what might be called impressionistic evidence, which is based on individual impressions and feelings rather than on facts. It is frustratingly incomplete and terribly imprecise. Such evidence must be used with great care and common sense.

Not All Whites, Blacks, Acted the Same

What the evidence does show unequivocally is that not all blacks possessed the same version of reality and not all whites thought—or acted—in the same way.

In the first place, only a minority of whites actually owned slaves. At the time of the Civil War, for example, less than one-half of the white adult males of the fifteen slave states possessed one or more slaves. Of those who were slave owners, their attitudes toward and treatment of their slaves varied widely. Not all slaveholders were as prone to violence, for example, as the fictional Simon Legree of Harriet Beecher Stowe's *Uncle Tom's Cabin*.

Regarding the slaves, we know that over half resided on plantations, defined as farms on which twenty or more slaves toiled. But even here, not all slaves performed the same work or lived in the same manner. Typically, the life and work of a field hand did not resemble those of a house slave. In fact, slave owners consciously maintained divisions among their slaves by favoring the house slaves and by using black slave drivers to oversee their field slaves. Finally, not all slaves or former slaves were as educated, cosmopolitan, or rebellious as Denmark Vesey.

Eugene Genovese, a prominent historian of American slavery, has put forward the notion of paternalism to explain how the slave system functioned. Defined as a system of reciprocal obligations, paternalism presumed less than total control by the white owner and some room for maneuvering on the part of the black slave. Slave owners could not rely on the lash alone, either to keep slaves in line or to force labor from them. And the slaves understood that they could control some elements of their lives, whether at work or away from it. Those owners who prized stability and predictability often permitted slave marriages, which were technically illegal, and sometimes accepted the slaves' judgment about the proper pace of the workday.

Using another technique of indirect paternalistic control, slaveholders extended a version of Christianity to the slave community. Slaveholders hoped slaves might be less inclined to revolt or run away if they were taught that rebellion was an un-Christian act.

All of this is meant to suggest that the better than two hundred years of American slavery cannot be neatly reduced to either-or, black-white, or North-South oppositions. From its inception to its demise, slavery was a complex form of tyranny that called forth a variety of responses from its practitioners and its victims.

When they arrived in the early seventeenth century, the first British people to settle in the South hoped to avoid this form of tyranny altogether. These people wanted to prove their superiority to the hated Spanish, who had introduced slavery into the Western Hemisphere with the arrival of Columbus in the late fifteenth century. As a result, plans for colonial Virginia included at least the outline of a utopian experiment where people of many races might live together harmoniously. Within half a century, by the 1660s, that experiment was in tatters and black slavery was in place, but many white Virginians remained uncomfortable with slavery.

Early Colonial Attitudes

Thomas Jefferson, for example, regarded slavery as a necessary evil. A slaveholder himself, Jefferson understood that he and his fellow Virginia slaveholders benefited financially and culturally from the sweat of their black labor force. Nonetheless, Jefferson did not shrink from describing the system as a "school for vice and tyranny." He worried considerably about its effects on the young, although he was most concerned about those young people who happened to be white. As a fledgling politician, Jefferson introduced measures to permit his fellow Virginians to emancipate their own slaves. He also wrote the Northwest Ordinance of 1787, which banned slavery in the territory acquired from Great Britain following the American Revolution. Later, however, as a retired politician and ex-president, Jefferson refused to free his own slaves, counseled young white Virginia slaveholders against the voluntary emancipation of theirs, and favored the expansion of slavery into the western territories. What had once been the two minds of Thomas Jefferson had slowly hardened into one.

The same might be said of the entire white South. Frightened by Nat Turner's violent 1831 rebellion and angered by the effrontery of the Northern abolitionists who presumed to know what was moral for the entire nation, Southern slaveholders began to assert that slavery was, in fact, a "positive good." By the early 1830s, politicians such as John C. Calhoun and intellectuals such as George Fitzhugh had established themselves as outspoken defenders of slavery—and as articulate American racists. Arguing that slavery was of positive good for whites because it gave them more time for leisure and cerebral work and for blacks because it operated as a kind of welfare system for inferior people, they sought to eliminate both doubt and debate on the subject.

Attitudes During the American Revolution

Sectional differences on the subject of slavery can be found at least as early as the Revolution. At that time, Northerners fretted that Southerners were more interested in protecting their slaves than in fighting the British. More than a few articulate Northerners were disgusted by the spectacle of Southerners (including George Washington) desperately seeking to retrieve their involuntary work force from the clutches of the departing British soldiers.

Debate over the Articles of Confederation and the Constitution adopted in Philadelphia in 1787 produced North-South tensions as well as praise for and condemnation of slavery. For example, at the Philadelphia Convention, Gouverneur Morris of Pennsylvania denounced slavery as a "nefarious institution, the curse of heaven on the states where it prevailed." George Mason of Virginia declared that "every master of slaves is born a petty tyrant. . . . I hold it essential that the general government should have the power to prevent the increase of slavery."

North-South differences were illuminated once again at the convention when the issue was determining congressional representation. The debate revealed an ironic reversal: Northerners insisted that slaves were property and therefore should not affect representation, while Southerners argued that slaves were human beings and ought to be counted as such. The result was the infamous Three-Fifths Compromise, which established each slave as three-fifths of a person for the purpose of allotting representatives to Congress. This determination also reflected the drafters' estimate of the relative worth of slaves.

Serious sectional differences between North and South did not surface again until the debate in 1818 and 1819 surrounding the admission of Missouri to statehood. By this point, the Union contained eleven slave states and eleven free states. The Missouri request to enter the Union threatened to upset this balance. The result, known as the Missouri Compromise, was the joint admission of Missouri as a slave state and Maine as a free state. In addition, a line was drawn across the American West. North of the line, any new states would be free of slavery, and states to the south would be slave states.

That compromise, of course, did not permanently settle the North-South dispute over the expansion of slavery. The Civil War is proof of that. But the issue of slavery's expansion as well as the subsequent rise of the abolitionist movement did shift the focus of debate. By the early 1830s, tensions within the South and within the minds of individual Southerners had given way to friction between North and South.

Rebellions Were Few in Number

Tension within the slave community remained much more constant. Open slave rebellions were rare occurrences in the general history of slavery. The slaves found few opportunities to plot rebellion. Only a few significant uprisings occurred in the long history of American slavery. That the Denmark Vesey Conspiracy and the Nat Turner rebellion occurred within a relatively short time span is an accident of history rather than testimony to the gathering of militant black forces against slavery. The relative absence of armed uprisings, however, should not be taken as evidence of the slaves' collective acceptance of their plight. The slaves, after all, could express their objections to their bondage in more ways than one.

Resistance was a daily reality. Armed rebellion required careful preparations, significant numbers, and impossibly good luck. But resistance could be a successful and spontaneous act of individual defiance. Its expression could be as subtle as feigned illness or as violent as arson or the poisoning of a hated master. It might be the desperate flight to be with a loved one enslaved on another plantation or the flight to a free state. Resistance might even be learning to read and write, planning a work slowdown, or putting foreign objects in the master's coffee.

By examining materials as divergent as slave songs, letters, and memoirs, we can begin to grapple with the complexity of the slave system and the various slave responses to it. The result of that examination should give the reader a heightened awareness of the many opposing views both inside the slave community and outside it. General agreement on the proposition that slavery was a monstrous evil should not imply that there was unanimity of opinion and unified action among those who were compelled to live under it. Because few slaves were like Denmark Vesey does not mean that most slaves were accomplices to that monstrous evil.

Betrayed though he was, Denmark Vesey would have attested to the truth of that statement. Forever worried that his plot might be revealed, he was forever confident that the slave masses would revolt at his command.

Determined to find trustworthy allies, Vesey's task was to judge—and retain—the loyalty of his recruits. Searching for that elusive margin of maneuverability, each slave's task was to judge —and stretch—the limits of the system. Our task is to read—and judge—these opposing views of the slaves, the slaveholders, and the internal and external critics of the entire system. The story of the failed conspiracy of Denmark Vesey demonstrates that none of the elements in the history of slavery in America are without ambiguity.

John C. Chalberg
Consulting Editor

CHAPTER 1

Slavery in Early America

Chapter Preface

The institution of slavery has played an important part in the economic and political development of the United States since colonial times. The slave trade brought riches to the port cities of Boston, New York, Charleston, and others. Slave labor was important in developing the plantation agriculture of the South. Finally, the institution of slavery—and the growing arguments over it—played an important role in developing the ideals of freedom that led to the American Revolution. The viewpoints in this chapter point to some of the early debates over slavery and shed understanding on the impact slavery and slaves had on the development of the United States.

When the first Africans landed in 1619 in Jamestown, Virginia, one year before the Pilgrims arrived in Plymouth, the African-New World slave trade was decades old. Tens of thousands of Africans had been transported to Brazil and the Caribbean islands. Indeed, of the estimated 9.6 million Africans brought to the New World between 1510 and 1870, only about 427,000, or 4.5 percent, landed in what is now the United States.

The historical development of slavery in the colonies is not fully clear. Most historians agree that at first blacks in the colonies seemed to have a status similar to that of white indentured servants; they could expect to be freed after a fixed term of years rather than being held for life. In part this system made economic sense, for the high mortality rates and short life expectancies made the more expensive lifetime slave a bad investment. However, as mortality rates fell, laws in the colonies were passed classifying blacks as slaves with no legal rights. By 1670 the legal status of slavery was firmly established in all the colonies.

The establishment of slavery in America was not only a matter of economics, but one of racism as well. Historian Irwin Unger, in examining the evolution of American slavery, writes:

> Racial attitudes as well as economics played a part in establishing slavery in North America. However harshly they were treated, white indentured servants were not without rights. As fellow Europeans, they could not be severely mistreated or abused with impunity. Woman servants could not be exploited sexually. If the master of an indentured servant violated the custom of the country or the terms of the contract, he or she could be sued by the servant. Except in the earliest period, Africans enjoyed no such rights. The English were prejudiced against the physical characteristics of Africans and viewed them as lesser

beings. Brutally torn away from all that was familiar, brought among strangers, surrounded by other captives who did not speak their language, and confronted with an alien landscape and an unfamiliar climate, blacks were in no position to protect themselves.

As the value of African workers increased they gradually ceased to be treated as indentured servants. First they became "servants for life," and then subject of ever more elaborate "slave codes" that defined their legal position in detailed ways and placed severe restrictions on their movements and conduct. Under these codes they become "chattel property," to be bought, sold, inherited, and bequeathed like houses, horses, or plows. By the end of the seventeenth century the distinction between black slaves and white servants had become sharply defined: Servants were humans; slaves were things.

The slave trade increased in the eighteenth century, and by 1759 about 325,000 blacks (almost all of them slaves) resided in the colonies. They comprised about one-fifth of the total colonial population. Approximately 12,000 blacks lived in New England, 25,000 in the middle colonies, and the remainder in the southern colonies. Most of the slaves outside the South were employed as day laborers, household servants, or artisans. Slaves in the South largely worked as field hands growing tobacco, indigo, and rice.

Opposition to slavery developed slowly. The earliest known written protest against slavery was produced in 1688 by a small gathering of Quakers, a religious sect. Religious arguments were a primary focus of early debate against slavery. Antislavery writers such as John Woolman and Samuel Sewall dwelled on whether slavery was moral and whether the Bible justified the practice.

At the time of the American Revolution, a new perspective on the slavery debate appeared—the idea of natural rights, which are possessed by all people and which cannot be taken away by any government. The concept of natural rights was an essential part of American arguments for independence from Great Britain. It reached its most famous expression in Thomas Jefferson's Declaration of Independence, in which he wrote "We hold these truths to be self-evident, that all men are created equal, that they are endowed by their Creator with certain unalienable Rights, that among these are Life, Liberty and the pursuit of Happiness."

Jefferson also wrote a passage condemning slavery in the Declaration of Independence, but it was struck out by the Continental Congress in the final draft. This conflict of natural rights ideology and the institution of slavery was quickly seized upon by antislavery writers, who argued that American revolutionaries were hypocrites.

Historian Edmund S. Morgan has written that this combination was more than a strange anomaly. He argues that slavery was essential to the evolution of political thought in the colonies, especially in Virginia, the home of George Washington, Thomas Jefferson, Patrick Henry, and other famous revolutionary leaders—and slaveholders. Slavery provided white Virginians a close example of what it was like not to have any liberty or natural rights. Also, by substituting black slaves for white indentured servants, the institution of slavery reduced the population of landless and impoverished whites in Virginia, who were often a threat to law and order. Many whites were able to become independent, if not wealthy, owners of at least small parcels of land. This reduced class tensions between rich and poor whites, enabling them to share ideals of political equality. Morgan writes:

> A free society divided between large landholders and small was much less riven by antagonisms than one divided between landholders and landless, masterless men. With the freedman's expectations, sobriety, and status restored, he was no longer a man to be feared. That fact, together with the presence of a growing mass of alien slaves, tended to draw the white settlers closer together and to reduce the importance of the class difference between yeoman farmer and large plantation owner. . . .
>
> As the tide of slavery rose between 1680 and 1720 Virginia moved toward a government in which the yeoman farmer had a larger share. . . . And in its chambers Virginians developed the ideas they so fervently asserted in the Revolution: ideas about taxation, representation, and the rights of Englishmen.

Thus Morgan concludes that slavery was an important, even indispensable, component of the social environment of the American colonies that led to the development of the ideals of the American Revolution. These ideals—liberty and equality—ironically led the United States to later question and ultimately abolish slavery.

VIEWPOINT 1

"It would conduce more to the Welfare of the Province, to have White Servants for a Term of Years, than to have Slaves for Life."

Slavery Is Immoral

Samuel Sewall (1652-1730)

As slavery was being established in the American colonies, open debates over the institution were sporadic and local. What historian Larry E. Tise identifies as the earliest antislavery and proslavery tracts published in colonial America were written at the start of the eighteenth century by two Massachusetts Puritan judges.

The following viewpoint was written by Samuel Sewall, a judge on the Massachusetts Superior Court who later became Chief Justice. Sewall was one of the judges who condemned several people to death in the 1692 Salem witch trials, actions about which he later confessed error and remorse. He is also well known for his detailed diary, an important source of information on colonial life for historians.

In 1700 Sewall became involved in a legal dispute with another judge, John Saffin, over the fate of a black slave Saffin refused to set free despite the terms of a contract calling for the slave's release. In defense of his position, Sewall wrote a pamphlet, *The Selling of Joseph a Memorial* which was first published in Boston in 1700 and later reprinted in the *Proceedings of the Massachusetts Historical Society* (vol. VII, 1863-1864, Boston). Sewall calls slavery an evil and immoral practice. Relying heavily on scripture in his reasoning, Sewall refutes several proslavery arguments, including the argument that the Africans are a cursed race, that they are lawful captives of wars, and that the Bible sanctions slavery.

Forasmuch *as* Liberty *is in real value next unto* Life: *None ought to part with it themselves, or deprive others of it, but upon most mature consideration.*

The Numerousness of Slaves at this Day in the Province, and the Uneasiness of them under their Slavery, hath put many upon thinking whether the Foundation of it be firmly and well laid; so as to sustain the Vast Weight that is built upon it. It is most certain that all Men, as they are the Sons of *Adam*, are Co-heirs, and have equal Right unto Liberty, and all other outward Comforts of Life. God *hath given the Earth [with all its commodities] unto the Sons of Adam, Psal., 115, 16. And hath made of one Blood all Nations of Men, for to dwell on all the face of the Earth, and hath determined the Times before appointed, and the bounds of their Habitation: That they should seek the Lord. Forasmuch then as we are the Offspring of* God, &c. *Acts* 17. 26, 27, 29. Now, although the Title given by the last Adam doth infinitely better Men's Estates, respecting God and themselves; and grants them a most beneficial and inviolable Lease under the Broad Seal of Heaven, who were before only Tenants at Will; yet through the Indulgence of God to our First Parents after the Fall, the outward Estate of all and every of their Children, remains the same as to one another. So that Originally, and Naturally, there is no such thing as Slavery. *Joseph* was rightfully no more a Slave to his Brethren, than they were to him; and they had no more Authority to *Sell* him, than they had to *Slay* him. And if *they* had nothing to do to sell him; the *Ishmaelites* bargaining with them, and paying down Twenty pieces of Silver, could not make a Title. Neither could *Potiphar* have any better Interest in him than the *Ishmaelites* had. *Gen.* 37, 20, 27, 28. For he that shall in this case plead *Alteration of Property*, seems to have forfeited a great part of his own claim to Humanity. There is no proportion between Twenty Pieces of Silver and Liberty. The Commodity itself is the Claimer. If *Arabian* Gold be imported in any quantities, most are afraid to meddle with it, though they might have it at easy rates; lest it should have been wrongfully taken from the Owners, it should kindle a fire to the Consumption of their whole Estate. 'Tis pity there should be more Caution used in buying a Horse, or a little lifeless dust, than there is in purchasing Men and Women: Whereas they are the Offspring of God, and their Liberty is,

... Auro pretiosior Omni. [To Each More Precious than Gold]

And seeing God hath said, *He that Stealeth a Man, and Selleth him, or if he be found in his Hand, he shall surely be put to Death.* Exod. 21, 16. This Law being of Everlasting Equity, wherein Man-Stealing is ranked among the most atrocious of Capital Crimes:

26

What louder Cry can there be made of that Celebrated Warning.

Caveat Emptor! [Buyer Beware!]

And all things considered, it would conduce more to the Welfare of the Province, to have White Servants for a Term of Years, than to have Slaves for Life. Few can endure to hear of a Negro's being made free; and indeed they can seldom use their Freedom well; yet their continual aspiring after their forbidden Liberty, renders them Unwilling Servants. And there is such a disparity in their Conditions, Colour, and Hair, that they can never embody with us, & grow up in orderly Families, to the Peopling of the Land; but still remain in our Body Politick as a kind of extravasat Blood. As many Negro Men as there are among us, so many empty Places are there in our Train Bands, and the places taken up of Men that might make Husbands for our Daughters. And the Sons and Daughters of *New England* would become more like *Jacob* and *Rachel*, if this Slavery were thrust quite out of Doors. Moreover it is too well known what Temptations Masters are under, to connive at the Fornication of their Slaves; lest they should be obliged to find them Wives, or pay their Fines. It seems to be practically pleaded that they might be lawless; 'tis thought much of, that the Law should have satisfaction for their Thefts, and other Immoralities; by which means, *Holiness to the Lord* is more rarely engraven upon this sort of Servitude. It is likewise most lamentable to think, how in taking Negroes out of *Africa*, and selling of them here, That which God has joined together, Men do boldly rend asunder; Men from their Country, Husbands from their Wives, Parents from their Children. How horrible is the Uncleanness, Mortality, if not Murder, that the Ships are guilty of that bring great Crouds of these miserable Men and Women. Methinks when we are bemoaning the barbarous Usage of our Friends and Kinsfolk in *Africa*, it might not be unreasonable to enquire whether we are not culpable in forcing the *Africans* to become Slaves amongst ourselves. And it may be a question whether all the Benefit received by *Negro* Slaves will balance the Accompt of Cash laid out upon them; and for the Redemption of our own enslaves Friends out of *Africa*. Besides all the Persons and Estates that have perished there.

Objections and Answers

Obj. 1. *These Blackamores are of the Posterity of Cham, and therefore are under the Curse of Slavery.* Gen. 9, 25, 26, 27.

Ans. Of all Offices, one would not beg this; viz. Uncall'd for, to be an Executioner of the Vindictive Wrath of God; the extent and duration of which is to us uncertain. If this ever was a Commission; How do we know but that it is long since out of Date? Many have found it to their Cost, that a Prophetical Denunciation of Judgment against a Person or People, would not warrant them to inflict that evil. If it would, *Hazael* might justify himself in all he did against his master, and the *Israelites* from 2 *Kings* 8, 10, 12.

Slavery Is Unjust Oppression

An Exhortation & Caution to Friends Concerning Buying or Keeping of Negroes was possibly the first printed protest against slavery. It was published in 1693 by George Keith. Keith, who was born in Scotland and lived in America from 1685 to 1704, was active in the Quaker movement.

The Lord hath commanded, saying, *Thou shalt not oppress an hired Servant that is poor and needy, whether he be of thy Brethren, or of the Strangers that are in thy Land, within thy Gates, least he cry against thee unto the Lord, and it be sin unto thee; Thou shalt neither vex a stranger nor oppress him, for ye were strangers in the Land of* Egypt, *Deut.* 24. 14, 15. *Exod.* 12. 21. But what greater Oppression can there be inflicted upon our Felow Creatures, than is inflicted on the poor Negroes! they being brought from their own Country against their Wills, some of them being stollen, others taken for payment of Debt owing by their Parents, and others taken Captive in War, and sold to Merchants, who bring them to the *American* Plantations, and sell them for Bond-Slaves to them that will give most for them; the Husband from the Wife, and the Children from the Parents; and many that buy them do exceedingly afflict them and oppress them, not only by continual hard Labour, but by cruel Whippings, and other cruel Punishments. . . .

Surely the Lord doth behold their Oppressions & Afflictions, and will further visit for the same by his righteous and just Judgments, except they break off their sins by Repentance, and their Iniquity by shewing Mercy to these poor afflicted, tormented miserable Slaves!

But it is possible that by cursory reading, this Text may have been mistaken. For *Canaan* is the Person Cursed three times over, without the mentioning of *Cham*. Good Expositors suppose the Curse entailed on him, and that this Prophesie was accomplished in the Extirpation of the *Canaanites*, and in the Servitude of the *Gibeonites*. . . . Whereas the Blackamores are not descended of *Canaan*, but of *Cush*. Psal. 68, 31. *Princes shall come out of Egypt* [Mizraim]. *Ethiopia* [Cush] *shall soon stretch out her hands unto God.* Under which Names, all *Africa* may be comprehended; and their Promised Conversion ought to be prayed for. *Jer.* 13, 23. *Can the Ethiopian change his Skin?* This shows that Black Men are the Posterity of *Cush*. Who time out of mind have been distinguished by their Colour. . . .

Obj. 2. *The* Nigers *are brought out of a Pagan Country, into places*

28

where the Gospel is preached.

Ans. Evil must not be done, that good may come of it. The extraordinary and comprehensive Benefit accruing to the Church of God, and to *Joseph* personally, did not rectify his Brethren's Sale of him.

Obj. 3. *The Africans have Wars one with another: Our Ships bring lawful Captives taken in those wars.*

Ans. For aught is known, their Wars are much such as were between *Jacob's* Sons and their Brother *Joseph.* If they be between Town and Town; Provincial or National: Every War is upon one side Unjust. An Unlawful War can't make lawful Captives. And by receiving, we are in danger to promote, and partake in their Barbarous Cruelties. I am sure, if some Gentlemen should go down to the *Brewsters* to take the Air, and Fish: And a stronger Party from *Hull* should surprise them, and sell them for Slaves to a Ship outward bound; they would think themselves unjustly dealt with; both by Sellers and Buyers. And yet 'tis to be feared, we have no other Kind of Title to our *Nigers. Therefore all things whatsoever ye would that men should do to you, do you even so to them: for this is the Law and the Prophets.* Matt. 7, 12.

Obj. 4. Abraham *had Servants bought with his Money and born in his House.*

Ans. Until the Circumstances of *Abraham's* purchase be recorded, no Argument can be drawn from it. In the mean time, Charity obliges us to conclude, that He knew it was lawful and good.

It is Observable that the *Israelites* were strictly forbidden the buying or selling one another for Slaves. *Levit.* 25. 39. 46. *Jer.* 34. 8-22. And God gaged His Blessing in lieu of any loss they might conceit they suffered thereby, *Deut.* 15. 18. And since the partition Wall is broken down, inordinate Self-love should likewise be demolished. God expects that Christians should be of a more Ingenuous and benign frame of Spirit. Christians should carry it to all the World, as the *Israelites* were to carry it one towards another. And for Men obstinately to persist in holding their Neighbours and Brethren under the Rigor of perpetual Bondage, seems to be no proper way of gaining Assurance that God has given them Spiritual Freedom. Our Blessed Saviour has altered the Measures of the ancient Love Song, and set it to a most Excellent New Tune, which all ought to be ambitious of Learning. *Matt.* 5. 43. 44. *John* 13. 34. These *Ethiopians,* as black as they are, seeing they are the Sons and Daughters of the First *Adam,* the Brethren and Sisters of the Last Adam, and the Offspring of God; They ought to be treated with a Respect agreeable.

Viewpoint 2

"It is to be feared that those Negroes that are free, if there be not some strict course taken with them by Authority, they will be a plague to this Country."

Slavery Is Moral

John Saffin (1632-1710)

John Saffin was a wealthy landowner and Massachussetts judge. In 1700 he became embroiled in a legal dispute when he refused to give a black slave his freedom. He viewed Samuel Sewall's tract *The Selling of Joseph a Memorial* as a personal affront, and in 1701 published a reply which was reprinted in *Notes on the History of Slavery in Massachussetts* by George H. Moore (New York: D. Appleton & Co., 1866). This tract is notable in that many of its arguments appear repeatedly in later pro-slavery literature. Saffin asserts that slavery is necessary to maintain order in society and that freeing the slaves would leave the colonies with an unwanted population of free blacks. He uses biblical citations to prove that the Bible sanctions slavery, and he claims that Africans benefit from slavery by being exposed to Christianity. Saffin concludes with a poem that derides the Negro character.

A Brief and Candid Answer to a late Printed Sheet,
Entituled, The Selling of Joseph

That Honourable and Learned Gentleman, the Author of a Sheet, Entituled, *The Selling of Joseph*, A Memorial, seems from thence to draw this conclusion, that because the Sons of *Jacob* did very ill in selling their Brother *Joseph* to the *Ishmaelites*, who were Heathens, therefore it is utterly unlawful to Buy and Sell Negroes, though among Christians; which Conclusion I presume is not well drawn from the Premises, nor is the case parallel; for it was unlawfull for the *Israelites* to sell their Brethren upon any account, or pretence whatsoever during life. But it was not unlawful for the Seed of *Abraham* to have Bond men, and Bond women either born in their House, or bought with their Money, as it is written of *Abraham, Gen.* 14.14 & 21.10 & *Exod.* 21.16 & *Levit.* 25.44, 45, 46 v. After the giving of the Law: And in *Josh.* 9.23. That famous Example of the *Gibeonites* is a sufficient proof where there [is] no other.

Different Orders of Men

To speak a little to the Gentleman's first Assertion: *That none ought to part with their Liberty themselves, or deprive others of it but upon mature consideration*; a prudent exception, in which he grants, that upon some consideration a man may be deprived of his Liberty. And then presently in his next Position or Assertion he denies it, *viz.: It is most certain, that all men as they are the Sons of* Adam *are Coheirs, and have equal right to Liberty, and all other Comforts of Life*, which he would prove out of *Psal.* 115.16. *The Earth hath he given to the Children of Men.* True, but what is all this to the purpose, to prove that all men have equal right to Liberty, and all outward comforts of this life; which Position seems to invert the Order that God hath set in the World, who hath Ordained different degrees and orders of men, some to be High and Honourable, some to be Low and Despicable; some to be Monarchs, Kings, Princes and Governours, Masters and Commanders, others to be Subjects, and to be Commanded; Servants of sundry sorts and degrees, bound to obey; yea, some to be born Slaves, and so to remain during their lives, as hath been proved. Otherwise there would be a meer parity among men, contrary to that of the Apostle, I *Cor. 12 from the 13 to the 26 verse*, where he sets forth (by way of comparison) the different sorts and offices of the Members of the Body, indigitating that they are all of use, but not equal, and of like dignity. So God hath set different Orders and Degrees of Men in the World, both in Church and Common weal. Now, if this Position of parity should be true, it would then follow that the ordinary Course of Divine Providence of God in the World should be wrong, and unjust, (which we must not dare to think, much less to affirm) and all the sacred Rules, Precepts and Commands of the Almighty which he hath given the Son of Men to observe and keep in their respective Places, Orders and Degrees, would be to no purpose; which unaccountably derogate from the Divine Wisdom of the most High, who hath made nothing in vain, but hath Holy Ends in all his Dispensations to the Children of men.

In the next place, this worthy Gentleman makes a large Discourse concerning the Utility and Conveniency to keep the one, and inconveniency of the other; respecting white and black Servants, which conduceth most to the welfare and benefit of this

Province: which he concludes to be white men, who are in many respects to be preferred before Blacks; who doubts that? doth it therefore follow, that it is altogether unlawful for Christians to buy and keep Negro Servants (for this is the Thesis) but that those that have them ought in Conscience to set them free, and so lose all the money they cost (for we must not live in any known sin) this seems to be his opinion; but it is a Question whether it ever was the Gentleman's practice? But if he could perswade the General Assembly to make an Act, That all that have Negroes, and do set them free, shall be Re imbursed out of the Publick Treasury, and that there shall be no more Negroes brought into the Country; 'tis probable there would be more of his opinion; yet he would find it a hard task to bring the Country to consent thereto; for then the Negroes must be all sent out of the Country, or else the remedy would be worse than the Disease; and it is to be feared that those Negroes that are free, if there be not some strict course taken with them by Authority, they will be a plague to this Country.

Again, If it should be unlawful to deprive them that are lawful Captives, or Bondmen of their Liberty for Life being Heathens; it seems to be more unlawful to deprive our Brethren, of our own or other Christian Nations of the Liberty, (though but for a time) by binding them to Serve some Seven, Ten, Fifteen, and some Twenty Years, which oft times proves for their whole Life, as many have been; which in effect is the same in Nature, though different in the time, yet this was allow'd among the *Jews* by the Law of God; and is the constant practice of our own and other Christian Nations in the World: the which our Author by his Dogmatical Assertions doth condemn as Irreligious; which is Diametrically contrary to the Rules and Precepts which God hath given the diversity of men to observe in their respective Stations, Callings, and Conditions of Life, as hath been observed.

Slavery and the Bible

And to illustrate his Assertion our Author brings in by way of Comparison the Law of God against man Stealing, on pain of Death: Intimating thereby, that Buying and Selling of Negro's is a breach of that Law, and so deserves Death: A severe Sentence: But herein he begs the Question with a *Caveat Emptor*. For, in that very Chapter there is a Dispensation to the People of *Israel*, to have Bond men, Women and Children, even of their own Nation in some case; and Rules given therein to be observed concerning them; Verse the 4*th*. And in the before cited place, *Levit*. 25.44, 45, 46. Though the *Israelites* were forbidden (ordinarily) to make Bond men and Women of their own Nation, but of Strangers they might: the words run thus, verse 44. *Both thy Bond men, and thy*

Bond maids which thou shalt have shall be of the Heathen, that are round about you: of them shall you Buy Bond men and Bond maids, &c. See also, *I Cor.* 12.13. Whether we be Bond or Free, which shows that in the times of the New Testament, there were Bond men also, etc.

In fine, The sum of this long Haurange, is no other, than to compare the Buying and Selling of Negro's unto the Stealing of men, and the Selling of *Joseph* by his Brethren, which bears no proportion therewith, nor is there any congrueity therein, as appears by the foregoing Texts.

The Bible Supports Slavery

Richard Nisbet was a planter from the West Indies who had moved to America. In 1773 in Philadelphia he published a pamphlet titled Slavery Not Forbidden by Scripture. *The work defended slavery, emphasizing its scriptural justification and the inferiority of blacks to whites.*

Slavery, like all other human institutions, may be attended with its particular abuses, but that is not sufficient totally to condemn it, and to reckon every one unworthy the society of men who owns a negro.

If precedent constitutes law, surely it can be defended, for it has existed in all ages. The scriptures, instead of forbidding it, declare it lawful. The divine legislator, Moses, says—"Both thy bond-men and thy bond-maids, which thou shalt have, shall be of the heathen that are round about you: of them shall ye buy bond-men and bond-maids. Moreover, of the children of the strangers that do sojourn among you, of them shall ye buy, and of their families that are with you, which they beget in your land: and they shall be your possession. And ye shall take them as an inheritance for your children after you, to inherit them for a possession, they shall be your bond-men for ever."

Our Author doth further proceed to answer some Objections of his own framing, which he supposes some might raise.

Object. 1. *That these Blackamores are of the Posterity of* Cham, *and therefore under the Curse of Slavery. Gen. 9.25, 26, 27.* The which the Gentleman seems to deny, saying, *they were the Seed of Canaan that were Cursed,* etc.

Ans. Whether they were so or not, we shall not dispute: this may suffice, that not only the seed of *Cham* or *Canaan*, but any lawful Captives of other Heathen Nations may be made Bond men as hath been proved.

Obj. 2. *That the Negroes are brought out of Pagan Countreys into places where the Gospel is Preached.* To which he Replies, *that we must not doe Evil that Good may come of it.*

Ans. To which we answer, That it is no Evil thing to bring them out of their own Heathenish Country, where they may have the Knowledge of the True God, be Converted and Eternally saved.

African Wars

Obj. 3. *The* Affricans *have Wars one with another*; our Ships bring lawful Captives taken in those Wars.

To which our Author answer Conjecturally, and Doubtfully, *for ought we know*, that which may or may not be; which is insignificant, and proves nothing. He also compares the Negroes Wars, one Nation with another, with the Wars between *Joseph* and his Brethren. But where doth he read of any such War? We read indeed of a Domestick Quarrel they had with him, they envyed and hated *Joseph*; but by what is Recorded, he was meerly passive and meek as a Lamb. This Gentleman farther adds, *That there is not any War but is unjust on one side*, etc. Be it so, what doth that signify: We read of lawful Captives taken in the Wars, and lawful to be Bought and Sold without contracting the guilt of the *Agressors*; for which we have the example of *Abraham* before quoted; but if we must stay while both parties Warring are in the right, there would be no lawful Captives at all to be Bought; which seems to be rediculous to imagine, and contrary to the tenour of Scripture, and all Humane Histories on that subject.

Obj. 4. *Abraham had Servants bought with his Money, and born in his House. Gen.* 14.14. To which our worthy Author answers, *until the Circumstances of Abraham's purchase be recorded, no Argument can be drawn from it.*

Ans. To which we Reply, this is also Dogmatical, and proves nothing. He farther adds, *In the mean time Charity Obliges us to conclude, that he knew it was lawful and good.* Here the gentleman yields the case; for if we are in Charity bound to believe *Abraham's* practice, in buying and keeping *Slaves* in his house to be lawful and good: then it follows, that our Imitation of him in this his Moral Action, is as warrantable as that of his Faith; *who is the Father of all them that believe. Rom.* 4.16.

In the close of all, Our Author Quotes two more places of Scripture, *viz.; Levit.* 25.46, and *Jer.* 34, from the 8. to the 22. *v.* To prove that the people of Israel were strictly forbidden the Buying and Selling one another for *Slaves*: who questions that? and what is that to the case in hand? What a strange piece of Logick is this? Tis unlawful for Christians to Buy and Sell one another for slaves. *Ergo*, It is unlawful to Buy and Sell Negroes that are lawful Captiv'd Heathens.

And after a Serious Exhortation to us all to Love one another according to the Command of Christ. *Math.* 5.43, 44. This worthy Gentleman concludes with this Assertion, *That these Ethiopeans as*

Black as they are, seeing they are the Sons and Daughters of the first Adam; *the Brethren and Sisters of the Second* Adam, *and the Offspring of God; we ought to treat them with a respect agreeable.*

Loving All People Equally Is Impossible

Ans. We grant it for a certain and undeniable verity, That all Mankind are the Sons and Daughters of *Adam,* and the Creatures of God: But it doth not therefore follow that we are bound to love and respect all men alike; this under favour we must take leave to deny; we ought in charity, if we see our Neighbour in want, to relieve them in a regular way, but we are not bound to give them so much of our Estates, as to make them equal with our selves, because they are our Brethren, the Sons of *Adam,* no, not our own natural Kinsmen: We are Exhorted *to do good unto all, but especially to them who are of the Houshold of Faith, Gal.* 6.10. And we are to love, honour and respect all men according to the gift of God that is in them: I may love my Servant well, but my Son better; Charity begins at home, it would be a violation of common prudence, and a breach of good manners, to treat a Prince like a Peasant. And this worthy Gentleman would deem himself much neglected, if we should show him no more Defference than to an ordinary Porter: And therefore these florid expressions, the Sons and Daughters of the First *Adam,* the Brethren and Sisters of the Second *Adam,* and the Offspring of God, seem to be misapplied to import and insinuate, that we ought to tender Pagan Negroes with all love, kindness, and equal respect as to the best of men.

By all which it doth evidently appear both by Scripture and Reason, the practice of the People of God in all Ages, both before and after the giving of the Law, and in the times of the Gospel, that there were Bond men, Women and Children commonly kept by holy and good men, and improved in Service; and therefore by the Command of God, *Lev.* 24:44, and their venerable Example, we may keep Bond men, and use them in our Service still; yet with all candour, moderation and Christian prudence, according to their state and condition consonant to the Word of God.

The Negroes Character.

Cowardly and cruel are those Blacks *Innate,*
Prone to Revenge, Imp of inveterate hate.
He that exasperates them, soon espies
Mischief and Murder in their very eyes.
Libidinous, Deceitful, False and Rude,
The Spume Issue of Ingratitude.
The Premises consider'd, all may tell,
How near good Joseph *they are parallel.*

Viewpoint 3

"The ... use of negroes ...., if granted, would both induce great numbers of white people to come here, and also render us capable of subsisting ourselves by raising provisions upon our lands."

Slavery Should Be Allowed in Georgia

Citizens of Savannah (1738)

Georgia was unique among the original thirteen colonies in that it was founded as a "free" colony in which slavery was forbidden. Georgia was conceived as a place where religious refugees and impoverished debtor prisoners could settle, and also as a shield against Spanish encroachment on the colonies from Florida. Slavery was deemed to be harmful to both these goals, and slavery was prohibited by law in 1735.

The prohibition, however, was unpopular among many of the settlers in Georgia. In 1738 the residents of Savannah sent a petition to the trustees of Georgia. The colonists complained that they were unable to profitably farm the land and that Georgia's economy was being undercut by South Carolina and other colonies which could use Negro slave labor. The petitioners requested that slavery be allowed in Georgia. The petition, excerpted here, was reprinted in *The History of Georgia* by Hugh M'Call (Atlanta: A.B. Caldwell, 1909).

The plea was rejected. However, the economic pressures described in this viewpoint resulted in a flourishing illicit slave trade, and Georgia eventually legalized slavery in 1749.

To the honorable the trustees for establishing the colony of Georgia.
May it please your honors,

We, whose names are under-written, being all settlers, freehold-ers and inhabitants of the province of Georgia, and being sensible of the great pains and care exerted by you, in endeavoring to set-tle this colony, since it has been under your protection and man-agement, do unanimously join to lay before you, with the utmost regret, the following particulars. But, in the first place, we must beg leave to observe, that it has afforded us a great deal of con-cern and uneasiness, that former representations made to you of the same nature, have not been thought worthy of a due consid-eration, nor even of an answer. We have most of us settled in this colony, in pursuance of a description and representation of it by you, in Britain; and from the experience of residing here several years, do find, that it is impossible the measures hitherto laid down for making it a colony, can succeed. None of all those who have planted their lands, have been able to raise sufficient pro-duce to maintain their families, in bread kind only, even though as much application and industry have been exerted to bring it about, as could be done by men engaged in an affair, in which they believe the welfare of themselves and posterity so much de-pended, and which they imagine must require more than ordi-nary pains to make it succeed; so that by the accumulated ex-penses every year of provisions, clothing, medicines, &c. for themselves, families and servants, several of them have expended all their money, nay, even run considerably in debt, and so have been obliged to leave off planting, and making further improve-ments; and those who continue, are daily exhausting more and more of their money, and some daily increasing their debts, with-out a possibility of being reimbursed, according to the present constitution. This being now the general state of the colony, it must be obvious, that people cannot subsist by their land accord-ing to the present establishment; and this being a truth resulting from trial, patience and experience, cannot be contradicted by any theoretical scheme of reasoning. The land then, according to the present constitution, not being able to maintain the settlers here, they must unavoidably have recourse to, and depend upon trade; but to our woful experience likewise, the same causes that prevent the first, obstruct the latter; for though the situation of this place is exceedingly well adapted to trade, and if it were en-couraged might be much more improved by the inhabitants, yet the difficulties and restrictions which we hitherto have, and at present do labor under, debar us of that advantage. Timber is the only thing we have here which we can export, and notwithstand-ing we are obliged to fall it in planting our land, yet we cannot

Slavery Justified

George Whitefield was a noted evangelist and preacher and an associate of evangelist John Wesley. In the following excerpt from a letter to Wesley written in 1751, Whitefield offers several justifications for slavery.

As for the lawfulness of keeping slaves, I have no doubt, since I hear of some that were bought with Abraham's money, and some that were born in his house. I also can not help thinking, that some of these servants mentioned by the apostles in their epistles were, or had been, slaves. It is plain that the Gibeonites were doomed to perpetual slavery; and, though liberty is a sweet thing to such as are born free, yet to those who may never know the sweets of it, slavery perhaps may not be so irksome. However this be, it is plain, to a demonstration, that hot countries can not be cultivated without Negroes. What a flourishing country might Georgia have been, had the use of them been permitted years ago! How many white people have been destroyed for the want of them, and how many thousands of pounds spent to no purpose at all? Though it is true, that they are brought in a wrong way, from their own country, and it is a trade not to be approved of, yet as it will be carried on whether we will or not, I should think myself highly favored if I could purchase a good number of them, in order to make their lives comfortable, and lay a foundation for breeding up their posterity in the nurture and admonition of the Lord.

manufacture it fit for foreign market, but at double the expense of other colonies; as for instance, the river of May, which is but twenty miles from us, with the allowance of negroes, load vessels with that commodity at one half of the price that we can do; and what should induce persons to bring ships here, when they can be loaded with one half of the expense so near us? therefore the timber on the land is only a continual charge to the possessors of it, though of very great service in all the northern colonies, where negroes are allowed, and consequently labor cheap. We do not in the least doubt, but that in time, silk and wine may be produced here, particularly the former; but since the cultivation of lands with white servants only, cannot raise provision for our families, as before mentioned, therefore it is likewise impossible to carry on these manufactures according to the present constitution. It is very well known that Carolina can raise every thing that this colony can, and they having their labor so much cheaper, will always ruin our market, unless we are in some measure on a footing with them; and as in both, the lands are worn out in four or five years, and then fit for nothing but pasture, we must always be at a great deal more expense than they in clearing new land for planting. . . .

We do from a sincere regard to its welfare, and in duty, both to you and ourselves, beg leave to solicit your immediate consideration to the two following chief causes of these our misfortunes, and the deplorable state of the colony; and which, we are certain, if granted, would be an infallible remedy to both:

First. The want of a free title or fee simple to our lands, which if granted, would occasion great numbers of new settlers to come amongst us, and likewise encourage those who remain here, cheerfully to proceed in making further improvements, as well to retrieve their sunk fortunes, as to make provision for their posterity.

Second. The want and use of negroes with proper limitations, which if granted, would both induce great numbers of white people to come here, and also render us capable of subsisting ourselves by raising provisions upon our lands, until we could make some produce from it for exportation, and in some measure to balance our importation. We are very sensible of the inconveniencies and mischiefs that have already and do daily arise from an unlimited use of negroes; but we are as sensible that these might be prevented by a proper limitation, such as, so many to each white man, or so many to such a quantity of land, or in any other manner which your honors shall think most proper. By granting us, gentlemen, these particulars, and such other privileges as his majesty's most dutiful subjects in America enjoy, you will not only prevent our impending ruin, but we are fully satisfied also, will soon make this the most flourishing colony possessed by his majesty in America, and your memories will be perpetuated to all future ages, our latest posterity sounding your praises as their first founders, patrons and guardians: but if, by denying us those privileges, we ourselves and families are not only ruined, but even our posterity likewise; you will always be mentioned as the cause and authors of all their misfortunes and calamities; which we hope will never happen.

We are with all due respect,
 your honors most dutiful,
  and obedient servants.
Savannah in Georgia, December 9th, 1738.

VIEWPOINT 4

"It is shocking to human Nature, that any Race of Mankind, and their Posterity, should be sentenced to perpetual Slavery."

Slavery Should Not Be Allowed in Georgia

Citizens of Darien (1739)

The question of whether to legalize slavery was a divisive issue in the early history of Georgia, a colony in which slavery had been banned by its trustees in England. In 1738 a petition calling for slavery was sent to the trustees by a group of Georgia settlers in Savannah. In 1739 a group of Scots settlers in the small town of Darien, Georgia, sent a counter-petition to Georgia's governor-general James Oglethorpe. This petition, excerpted here, was later published in the *Colonial Records of the State of Georgia* (Atlanta: 1905).

The people from Darien presented several arguments against the introduction of slavery. Some of their objections are practical, such as the argument that the work to overlook the slaves would exceed in cost any benefit slave labor might bring. Some of the arguments are moral and humanitarian, condemning the shocking nature of slavery.

Despite these objections, slavery was legalized in Georgia in 1749.

We are informed, that our Neighbors of Savannah have petitioned your Excellency for the Liberty of having Slaves. We hope, and earnestly entreat, that before such Proposals are hearkened unto, your Excellency will consider our Situation, and of what dangerous and bad Consequence such Liberty would be of to us,

40

for many Reasons;

I. The Nearness of the Spaniard, who have proclaimed Freedom to all Slaves who run away from their Masters, makes it impossible for us to keep them without more Labour in guarding them, that what we would be at to do their Work.

II. We are laborious, and know that a White Man may be by the Year more usefully employed than a Negro.

III. We are not rich, and becoming Debtors for Slaves, in case of their running away or dying, would inevitably ruin the poor Master, and he become a greater Slave to the Negro Merchant, than the Slave he bought could be to him.

Slavery and Christianity

John Martin Bolzius was a minister in Georgia who actively preached and campaigned against the introduction of slavery into that colony. In this excerpt from a letter to George Whitefield written in 1745, a fellow preacher who was planning to purchase slaves to help build and run an orphanage, Bolzius responds to Whitefield's argument that slavery can be beneficial to slaves by introducing them to Christianity.

Your Last Argument for Negroes was, as I remember, that you intended to bring them to the Knowledge of Christ.

But, Sir, my Heart wishes, that first the White people in the Colony and Neighbourhood may be brought to the Saving and Experimental Knowledge of Christ. As long as they are for this World, and take Advantage of the poor black Slaves, they will increase the Sins of the Land to a great Heighth. If a Minister had a Call to imploy his Strength and time to Convert Negroes, he has in Carolina a Large Field. Don't believe, Sir, the Language of those persons, who wish the Introduction of Negroes under pretence of promoting their Spiritual Happiness.

IV. It would oblige us to keep a Guard-duty at least as severe as when we expected a daily Invasion; and if that was the Case, how miserable would it be to us, and our Wives and Families, to have an Enemy without, and more dangerous ones in our Bosom!

V. It's shocking to human Nature, that any Race of Mankind, and their Posterity, should be sentenced to perpetual Slavery; nor in Justice can we think otherwise of it, than they are thrown amongst us to be our Scourge one Day or another for our Sins; and as Freedom to them must be as dear as to us, what a Scene of Horror must it bring about! And the longer it is unexecuted, the bloody Scene must be the greater. We therefore, for our own sakes, our Wives and Children, and our Posterity, beg your Consideration, and intreat, that instead of introducing Slaves, you'll put us in the way to get us some of our Countrymen, who with their Labour in time of Peace, and our Vigilance, if we are invaded, with the Help of those, will render it a difficult thing to hurt us, or that Part of the Province we possess. We will for ever pray for your Excellency, and are, with all Submission,

    Your Excellency's most obliged
    humble Servants

VIEWPOINT 5

"I do hereby further declare all indented servants, Negroes, or others (appertaining to Rebels) free, that are able and willing to bear arms."

Slaves Should Be Freed to Fight the American Rebels

John Murray, fourth earl of Dunmore (1732-1809)

Not all who would free the slaves acted from humanitarian or egalitarian motives. The first general emancipation of slaves in America was decreed in 1775 during the American Revolution by a colonial governor who wished to use the freed slaves to fight the colonists.

Lord Dunmore was colonial governor of Virginia from 1771 to 1775. While he was relatively popular at the beginning of his term, growing unrest between the colonies and Great Britain culminated in armed clashes that drove him from his post. On November 7, 1775, writing from a British warship stationed off the Virginia coast, Dunmore issued a proclamation promising freedom to indentured servants and Negro slaves who would join the British army. Historians differ on how many slaves took up his offer, with estimates ranging from eight hundred to fifteen hundred. The slaves participated in military raids along the Virginia coast, and Dunmore's proclamation caused great fear and consternation among the planters of Virginia. Great Britain, however, was itself divided on how to use the slaves against the colonists, and Dunmore's proclamation did not result in a general slave uprising. Dunmore's forces were eventually decimated by smallpox and did not play a major military part in the Revolutionary War. Dunmore returned to England and later became governor of the Bahamas. The petition, reprinted here in its entirety, was reprinted in *American Archives*, edited by Peter Force (Washington, DC, 1840).

PROCLAMATION BY THE GOVERNOUR OF VIRGINIA.

As I have ever entertained hopes that an accommodation might have taken place between *Great Britain* and this Colony, without being compelled, by my duty, to this most disagreeable, but now absolutely necessary step, rendered so by a body of armed men, unlawfully assembled, firing on His Majesty's Tenders; and the formation of an Army, and that Army now on their march to attack His Majesty's Troops, and destroy the well-disposed subjects of this Colony: To defeat such treasonable purposes, and that all such traitors, and their abettors may be brought to justice, and that the peace and good order of this Colony may be again restored, which the ordinary course of the civil law is unable to effect, I have thought fit to issue this my Proclamation, hereby declaring, that until the aforesaid good purposes can be obtained, I do, in virtue of the power and authority to me given, by His Majesty, determine to execute martial law, and cause the same to be executed throughout this Colony. And to the end that peace and good order may the sooner be restored, I do require every person capable of bearing arms to resort to His Majesty's standard, or be looked upon as traitors to His Majesty's crown and government, and thereby become liable to the penalty the law inflicts upon such offences—such as forfeiture of life, confiscation of lands, &c., &c.; and I do hereby further declare all indented servants, Negroes, or others (appertaining to Rebels) free, that are able and willing to bear arms, they joining His Majesty's Troops, as soon as may be, for the more speedily reducing this Colony to a proper sense of their duty to his Majesty's crown and dignity. I do further order, and require, all His Majesty's liege subjects to retain their quit-rents, or any other taxes due, or that may become due, in their own custody, till such time as peace may be again restored to this at present most unhappy Country, or demanded of them for their former salutary purposes, by officers properly authorized to receive the same.

Given under my hand, on board the Ship *William*, off Norfolk, the 7th day of November, in the sixteenth year of His Majesty's Reign.

GOD *Save the King*

VIEWPOINT 6

"Be not then, ye Negroes tempted by this proclamation to ruin yourselves."

Slaves Should Not Fight the American Rebels

Virginia Gazette (1775)

The 1775 emancipation proclamation of Lord Dunmore, the ex-governor of Virginia who promised freedom to black slaves willing to join his forces fighting the colonists, was bitterly attacked by many American planters. Ironically, the proclamation may have strengthened the resolve among white colonial leaders to declare independence from Great Britain. South Carolinian planter Edward Rutledge wrote that Dunmore's proclamation had done more "to work an eternal separation between Great Britain and the colonies, than any other expedient which could possibly have been thought of." Fear lay behind much of the reaction to Dunmore's proclamation. James Madison wrote that the prospect of Negro slaves siding with the British "is the only part in which this colony is vulnerable." Such a development did not, in fact, occur. An estimated five thousand blacks, both free and slave, fought in the Revolutionary War on both sides.

Part of the reaction to Dunmore's proclamation is found in the following viewpoint, taken from an editorial published in the *Virginia Gazette* on November 25, 1775. In this excerpt, the editor of the newspaper directs himself to blacks, arguing that they would be foolish to take Dunmore's offer. He notes that England has participated extensively in the slave trade, and he asserts that blacks might find themselves being sold to the West Indies.

45

A COPY of the above proclamation having fallen into my hands, I thought it was necessary, for the welfare of two sorts of people, that its public appearance should be attended with comments of the following nature. . . .

The second class of people, for whose sake a few remarks upon this proclamation seem necessary, is the *Negroes*. They have been flattered with their freedom. . . . To none . . . is freedom promised but to such as are able to do Lord *Dunmore* service. The aged, the infirm, the women and children, are still to remain the property of their masters, masters who will be provoked to severity, should part of their slaves desert them. Lord *Dunmore's* declaration, therefore . . . leaves by far the greater number at the mercy of an enraged and injured people. But should there be any amongst the Negroes weak enough to believe that *Dunmore* intends to do them a kindness, and wicked enough to provoke the fury of the Americans against their defenceless fathers and mothers, their wives, their women and children, let them only consider the difficulty of effecting their escape, and what they must expect to suffer if they fall into the hands of the Americans. . . . Long have the Americans, moved by compassion, and actuated by sound policy, endeavoured to stop the progress of slavery. Our Assemblies have repeatedly passed acts laying heavy duties upon imported Negroes, by which they meant altogether to prevent the horrid traffick; but their human intentions have been as often frustrated by the cruelty and covetousness of a set of English merchants, who prevailed upon the King to repeal our kind and merciful acts, little indeed to the credit of his humanity. Can it then be supposed that the Negroes will be better used by the English. . . . No, the ends of Lord *Dunmore* and his party being answered, they will either give up the offending Negroes to the rigour of the laws they have broken, or sell them in the West Indies, where every year they sell many thousands of their miserable brethren, to perish either by the inclemency of the weather, or the cruelty of barbarous masters. Be not then, ye Negroes tempted by this proclamation to ruin yourselves. I have given you a faithful view of what you are to expect; and I declare before GOD, in doing it, I have considered your welfare, as well as that of the country. Whether you will profit by my advice I cannot tell; but this I know, that whether we suffer or not, if you desert us, you most certainly will.

"With equal justice may negroes say, By the Immutable laws of nature, we are equally entitled to life, liberty and property with our lordly masters."

Slavery Violates Human Rights

David Cooper (1725-1795)

David Cooper was a New Jersey Quaker active in the antislavery movement. He is best known for two pamphlets attacking slavery, *A Mite Cast into the Treasury*, published in 1772, and *A Serious Address*, published in 1783 in Trenton, New Jersey. Both pamphlets sold widely; antislavery leader Anthony Benezet provided copies of *A Serious Address* to each member of Congress and the New Jersey State Assembly.

In *A Serious Address*, from which the following viewpoint is excerpted, Cooper refers to the natural human rights enumerated and defended in the Declaration of Independence and other writings of American revolutionary leaders. He argues that America is hypocritical in fighting for freedom from British rule while denying freedom to the slaves. He maintains that the right of liberty is meant for all people, and that unless blacks can be proved inhuman, their natural rights are violated by the continuation of slavery. Cooper's opinions were shared by others, for by 1804 all states from Pennsylvania northward had passed laws abolishing slavery, and several southern states had passed laws restricting the slave trade and making it easier for owners to free their own slaves.

It was a claim of freedom unfettered from the arbitrary control of others, so essential to free agents, and equally the gift of our beneficent Creator to all his rational children, which put fleets and armies into motion, covered earth and seas with rapine and carnage, disturbed the repose of Europe, and exhausted the treasure of nations. Now is the time to demonstrate to Europe, to the whole world, that America was in earnest, and meant what she said, when, with peculiar energy, and unanswerable reasoning, she plead the cause of human nature, and with undaunted firmness insisted, that *all mankind* came from the hand of their Creator *equally free.* Let not the world have an opportunity to charge her conduct with a contradiction to her solemn and often repeated declarations; or to say that her sons are not real friends to freedom; that they have been actuated in this awful contest by no higher motive than selfishness and interest, like the wicked servant in the gospel, who, after his Lord had forgiven his debt, which he was utterly unable to pay, shewed the most cruel severity to a fellow servant for a trifling demand, and thereby brought on himself a punishment which his conduct justly merited. Ye rulers of America beware! Let it appear to future ages, from the records of this day, that you not only professed to be advocates for freedom, but really were inspired by the love of mankind, and wished to secure the invaluable blessing to all; that, as you disdained to submit to the unlimited control of others, you equally abhorred the crying crime of holding your fellow men, as much entitled to freedom as yourselves, the subjects of your undisputed will and pleasure.

American Hypocrisy

However habit and custom may have rendered familiar the degrading and ignominious distinctions, which are made between people with a black skin and ourselves, I am not ashamed to declare myself an advocate for the rights of that highly injured and abused people; and, were I master of all the resistless persuasion of Tully and Demosthenes, could not employ it better, than in vindicating their rights as men, and forcing a blush on every American slaveholder, who has complained of the treatment we have received from Britain; which is no more to be equalled, with ours to negroes, than a barley corn is to the globe we inhabit. Must not every generous foreigner feel a secret indignation rise in his breast, when he hears the language of Americans upon any of their own rights as freemen being in the least infringed, and reflects that these very people are holding thousands and tens of thousands of their innocent fellow men in the most debasing and abject slavery, deprived of every right of freemen, except light and air? How similar to an atrocious pirate, setting in all the solemn pomp of a judge, passing sentence of death on a petty thief. Let us try the likeness by the standard of facts. The first settlers of these colonies emigrated from England, under the sanction of royal charters, held all their lands under the crown, and were protected and defended by the parent state, who claimed and exercised a control over their internal police, and at length attempted to levy taxes upon them, and, by statute, declared the colonies to be under their jurisdiction, and that they had, and ought to have, a right to make laws to bind them in all cases whatsoever. The American Congress in their declaration, July 1775, say,

> If it were *possible* for men who exercise their reason to believe that the Divine Author of our existence intended a *part* of the human race to hold an absolute property in, and an unbounded power over others, marked out by infinite goodness and wisdom, as the objects of a legal domination never rightly resistible, however severe and oppressive; the inhabitants of these colonies might at least require from the parliament of Great Britain some evidence, that this *dreadful authority* over them has been granted to that body. But a *reverence* for our *great Creator, principles of humanity*, and the dictates of *common sense*, must convince all those who reflect upon the subject, that government was instituted to promote the welfare of mankind, and ought to be administered for the attainment of that end.

Again they say,

> By this perfidy (Howe's conduct in Boston) *wives* are *separated* from their *husbands, children* from their *parents*, the aged and sick from their *relations* and *friends*, who wish to attend and *comfort* them.

> We most solemnly before God and the world declare, that exerting the utmost energy of those powers which our beneficent Creator hath graciously bestowed upon us, the arms we have been compelled by our enemies to assume, we will in defiance of every *hazard*, with unabated firmness and perseverance, employ for the preservation of our liberties, being with one mind resolved to die freemen rather than live *slaves*. . . .

Africa lies many thousand miles distant, its inhabitants as independent of us, as we are of them; we sail there, and foment wars among them, in order that we may purchase the prisoners, and encourage the stealing one another to sell them to us; we bring them to America, and consider them and their posterity for ever, our slaves, subject to our arbitrary will and pleasure; and if they imitate our example, and offer by force to assert their native freedom, they are condemned as traitors, and a hasty gibbet strikes terror on their survivors, and rivets their chains more secure.

The Principles of Humanity

Does not this forcible reasoning apply equally to Africans? Have we a better right to enslave them and their posterity, than Great Britain had to demand Three-pence per pound for an article of luxury we could do very well without? And Oh! America, will not a *reverence* for our *great Creator, principles of humanity,* nor the *dictates* of *common sense,* awaken thee to *reflect,* how far thy government falls short of impartially *promoting* the *welfare* of *mankind,* when its laws suffer, yea, justify men in murdering, torturing, and abusing their fellow men, in a manner shocking to humanity?

Equality Embraces All Races

James Forten, born a free black, was a sailmaker and one of Philadelphia's most prominent and wealthiest citizens in the early nineteenth century. In a collection of his letters entitled Letters from a Man of Colour on a Late Bill Before the Senate of Pennsylvania *and published in 1813, he spoke against slavery and in support of the rights of free blacks.*

WE hold this truth to be self-evident, that God created all men equal, and is one of the most prominent features in the Declaration of Independence, and in that glorious fabrick of collected wisdom, our noble Constitution. This idea embraces the Indian and the European, the Savage and the Saint, the Peruvian and the Laplander, the white Man and the African, and whatever measures are adopted subversive of this inestimable privilege, are in direct violation of the letter and spirit of our Constitution, and become subject to the animadversion of all, particularly those who are deeply interested in the measure.

How abundantly more aggravated is our conduct in these respects to Africans, in bringing them from their own country, and separating by sale these near connections, never more to see each other, or afford the least *comfort* or tender endearment of social life. But they are black, and ought to obey; we are white, and ought to rule.—Can a better reason be given for the distinction, that Howe's conduct is *perfidy* and ours innocent and blameless, and justified by our *laws*?

Thou wicked servant, out of thine own mouth shalt thou be judged.—Is a claim to take thy property without thy consent so galling, that thou wilt defy every hazard, rather than submit to it? And at the same time hold untold numbers of thy fellow men in slavery, (which robs them of every thing valuable in life) as *firmly rivetted* by *thee,* as thou art resolved to use the utmost energy of thy power, to preserve thy own freedom?

Have the Africans offered us the least *provocation* to make us their *enemies?*—Have their infants committed, or are they even *suspected* of any offence? And yet we leave them no alternative, but *servitude* or *death.*

The unenlightened Africans, in their own native land, enjoyed freedom, which was their birthright, until the more savage Christians transported them by thousands, and sold them for slaves in the wilds of America, to cultivate it for their lordly oppressors.

With equal justice may negroes say, By the *immutable laws of nature*, we are equally entitled to life, liberty and property with our lordly masters, and have never *ceded* to any power whatever, a *right* to deprive us thereof. . . .

Declarations of Rights

To the inhabitants of the colonies.
Weigh in the opposite balance, the endless miseries you and your descendants must endure, from an established arbitrary power.

Declaration of independence in Congress, 4th July, 1776.
We hold these truths to be self-evident, that *all men* are created *equal*, that they are endowed by their Creator with certain *unalienable rights*; that among these are *life, liberty,* and the *pursuit of happiness.*

Declaration of rights of Pennsylvania, July 15, 1776.
That *all men* are born *equally free* and *independent*, and have certain natural inherent and *unalienable rights*, among which are, the enjoying and defending *life* and *liberty*, acquiring, possessing and protecting *property*, and pursuing and obtaining happiness and safety.

Declaration of rights of Massachusets, Sept. 1, 1779.
All men are born *free* and *equal*, and have certain natural, essential, and *unalienable rights*; among which may be reckoned the right of enjoying and defending their *lives* and *liberties*; that of acquiring, possessing and protecting *property*; in fine, of seeking and obtaining *safety* and *happiness.*

Does this reasoning apply more forcibly in favour of a white skin than a black one? Why ought a negro to be less free than the subject of Britain, or a white face in America? Have we not all one Father? Hath not one God created us? Why do we deal treacherously every man against his brother? Mal.ii.10.

Do Americans reprobate this doctrine when applied to themselves? And at the same time enforce it with tenfold rigor upon others, who are indeed *pensioners* on their *bounty* for all they *possess*, nor can they *hold* a single enjoyment of life longer than they *vouchsafe* to *permit*?

You who have read a description of the inhuman scenes occasioned by the slave-trade, in *obtaining, branding, transporting, selling*, and keeping in *subjection* millions of human creatures; reflect a moment, and then determine which is the most *impious cause*: and after this, if neither the *voice of justice*, nor suggestions of *humanity*, can *restrain* your *hands* from being contaminated with the practice; cease to *boast* the Christian name from him, who commanded his followers "to do unto others as they would others should do unto them."

Who would believe the same persons, whose feelings are so exquisitely sensible respecting themselves, could be so callous toward negroes, and the *miseries* which, by their *arbitrary power*, they wantonly inflict.

Slavery Violates the Law of Nature

James Otis was an American political leader during the time of the American revolution, and an early advocate of the colonies' independence from Great Britain. In his pamphlet The Rights of the British Colonies Asserted and Proved, *published in 1764, Otis argued that all people, including black slaves, have the natural right of liberty.*

The colonists are by the law of nature freeborn, as indeed all men are, white or black. . . . Does it follow that 'tis right to enslave a man because he is black? Will short curled hair like wool instead of Christian hair, as 'tis called by those whose hearts are as hard as the nether millstone, help the argument? Can any logical inference in favor of slavery be drawn from a flat nose, a long or short face? Nothing better can be said in favor of a trade that is the most shocking violation of the law of nature, has a direct tendency to diminish the idea of the inestimable value of liberty, and makes every dealer in it a tyrant, from the director of an African company to the petty chapman in needles and pins on the unhappy coast. It is a clear truth that those who every day barter away other men's liberty will soon care little for their own.

If these solemn *truths* uttered at such an awful crisis, are *self-evident*: unless we can shew that the African race are not *men*, words can hardly express the amazement which naturally arises on reflecting, that the very people who make these pompous declarations are slave-holders, and, by their legislative, tell us, that these blessings were only meant to be the *rights* of *white men*, not of *all men*: and would seem to verify the observation of an eminent writer; "When men talk of liberty, they mean their own liberty, and seldom suffer their thoughts on that point to stray to their neighbours."

This was the voice, the language of the supreme council of America, in vindication of their rights as men, against imposition and unjust control: Yes, it was the voice of all America, through her representatives in solemn Congress uttered. How clear, full, and conclusive! "We hold these truths to be self-evident, that all men are created equal, and endowed by their Creator with the unalienable rights of life, liberty, and the pursuit of happiness." "By the immutable laws of nature *all men* are entitled to life and liberty." We need not now turn over the libraries of Europe for authorities to prove, that blacks are born equally free with whites; it is declared and recorded as the sense of America: Cease then ye cruel taskmasters, ye petty tyrants, from attempting to vindicate your having the same interest in your fellow men as in your cattle, and let blushing and confusion of face strike every American, who henceforth shall behold advertisements offering their brethren to sale, on a footing with brute beasts. . . .

Difficulties of Our Own Creation

It may be objected that there are many difficulties to be guarded against in setting of negroes free, and that, were they all to be freed at once, they would be in a worse condition than at present. I admit that there is some weight in these objections; but are not these difficulties of your own creating? And must the innocent continue to suffer, because we have involved ourselves in difficulties? Let us do justice as far as circumstances will admit, give such measure as we ask, if we expect Heaven to favour us with the continuance of our hard earned liberty. The work must be begun, or it can never be completed. "It is begun, and many negroes are set free." True, it is begun, but not in a manner likely to produce the desired *end*, the entire *abolition* of *slavery*. This is the business of the superintending authority, the main spring which gives motion to the whole political machine; which, were they to undertake in good earnest, I have no doubt but we should soon see a period fixed, when our land should no longer be polluted with slave-holders, nor give forth her increase to feed slaves: and indeed it hath been a matter of wonder to many, that that body, who have been so much employed in the study and defence of the *rights* of *humanity*, should suffer so many years to elapse without any effectual movement in this business. Had they, with the declaration of independence, recommended it to the different Legislatures to provide laws, declaring, that no person imported into, or born in America after that date, should be held in slavery; it would have been a step correspondent with our own *claims*, and, in time, have completed the work, nor can I see any impropriety, but what the nature of the case will justify, to have it still take place.

VIEWPOINT 8

"Slavery . . . is not repugnant to the law of nature."

Slavery Does Not Violate Human Rights

Theodore Parsons (1751-1779)

The doctrine of natural rights, which eventually became the basis for America's Declaration of Independence, dominated public and political discussion during the American Revolution. Many people used this doctrine to attack the institution of slavery. James Otis, in asserting the rights of the colonies, argued that "The colonists are by the law of nature free born, as indeed all men are, white and black."

In 1773 the commencement at Harvard University in Massachusetts featured a debate between two graduating senior students on the question of whether slavery is "agreable to the law of nature." Theodore Parsons took the position defending slavery. Parsons' father, a Congregational clergyman, had come under fire from his parishioners for owning slaves.

Excerpts from Parsons' arguments at the debate entitled "A Forensic Dispute on the Legality of Enslaving the Africans," (Boston, 1773), are reprinted here. He first defines natural law as what brings greatest happiness to the whole. He then links the argument of slavery with the question of equality, arguing that not all people are equal. Much as children are not equal to parents and thus are subject to parental authority, Parsons argues, blacks are not the equal of whites. Consequently, for blacks to be under the authority of whites is not inconsistent with natural law. He further asserts that black slaves in America are better off than if they had remained in Africa, where they were "destitute of every mean of improvement in social virtue." Parsons concludes that slavery benefits blacks, contributes to the happiness of everyone, and is thus consistent with natual law.

I am well aware of the difficulty of his task who attempts to defend a proposition of this nature. An heart replete with benevolence and compassion will hardly admit reasoning that involves principles seemingly incompatible with the happiness of *any*. Suffer me therefore to entreat you, that every tender sentiment, that even the feelings of humanity may be suspended, while we calmly attend to the voice of reason, which is the voice of nature's alwise and benevolent Author.

Degrees of Liberty

That Liberty to all is sweet I freely own; but still 'tis what, in a state of society at least, all cannot equally enjoy, and what even in a *free* government can be enjoyed in the most perfect sense by none. Such is the nature of society, that it requires various degrees of authority and subordination; and while the universal rule of right, *the happiness of the whole*, allows greater degrees of Liberty to some, the same immutable law suffers it to be enjoyed only in less degrees by others. And though my friend, I can most cordially join with you in the benevolent wish, that it were possible that these Africans, who I am free with you to call my brethren, and to whom, it is confessed, the principles of our civil constitution allow but a small degree of liberty, might enjoy it equally with us; yet 'till I am convinced it might comport with the rule above mentioned, to allow them more I am in duty bound to appear an advocate for those principles.

Let it therefore be remembered, that the question to be considered is, *"Whether the slavery, to which Africans are in this Province, by the permission of law, subjected, be agreeable to the law of nature?"*

Defining the Laws of Nature

It is, I presume, scarcely necessary to observe to you, that by the law of nature is intended that law which is the measure of all our moral actions, and by which their fitness and propriety, and consequently their justice or injustice, are to be determined. In other words, that law to which whatever action is in it's nature fit and proper, just and right, is agreable, and to which every action of an opposite nature is disagreable. This, then being intended by the law of nature, whether the justice of *African slavery*, if found agreable to this law, is defensible, will be needless to inquire. But it will be said, through this definition of the law of nature be admitted, we are still to be informed what those actions are, that are agreable to this law, and consequently right. I answer, whatever action in it's nature, concomitant circumstances being considered, tends to *happiness on the whole*, is agreable to this law, and every action of a contrary tendency is hereunto disagreable. And hence it will follow, that whatever practical principle of society, (which is to be considered as the action of the community) hath this tendency, is to be reputed just, and approved and adopted, and those of a contrary tendency consequently disapproved.

To demonstrate this, it will be necessary only to observe, that as nothing in nature can possibly be of the least consequence but happiness or misery, so the difference in the tendency of the practical principles of any society to the production of these, is the only thing that can possibly render some eligible, fit and proper, rather than others; and was it not for this distinction, it must forever remain a matter of perfect indifference, what practical principles were in any society adopted. But without stopping more fully to demonstrate the truth of this principle, it having been recognised as well by the generality of ethnic writers, as by the wisdom of all good governments, I shall proceed to enquire, how far it will operate to the determination of the present question.

And in the first place, I shall enquire into the agreement of the law of nature with the idea of slavery *in general*, in opposition to that principle of nature equality, which is so zealously contended for by the advocate for universal Liberty.

By slavery *in general* I mean the involuntary subordination of the will of one to that of another; whereby, independent of all compact, the actions of the former are in all things to be directed by the will of the latter. Now if slavery *in general*, according to this definition, be agreable to the law of nature, the principle of natural equality must fall, and in order to determine the question in dispute, it will be necessary only to apply the general principle to the case of the *African* subordination, whereby it will be easy to discern if there is any thing in the nature of their particular case not agreable hereto.

I am therefore now to shew, that slavery as above defined, is not repugnant to the law of nature, and therefore that the principle of natural equality cannot be true.

The Natural Right of Authority

That right of authority is to be found in some being involving subordination in others, independent of all voluntary contract on the part of the subordinate, is, as far as I know, universally acknowledged. Such is the right of the Governor of the universe to govern and direct the conduct of all finite existences, and such is the right of parents to govern and direct the conduct of their children. Now if it be found, that there is the same foundation for authority and subordination among different individuals of the human species, between whom no such relations as those above-mentioned do subsist, as there is for authority and subordination in those cases where it is acknowledged to be just, it will follow, that degrees of rightful authority in some, involving degrees of subordination in others, must be admitted among them likewise. In other words, if the *reason* and *foundation* of the *absolute* authority of the Governor of the universe over the creation, and the *limited* authority of parents over their children, be found to operate with equal strength in favor of a right of some individuals among mankind to exercise any degrees of authority over others, the exercise of such authority must be acknowledged just, i.e. agreable to the law of nature. And now to determine this question, it is necessary to inquire, in what the right of authority, in the cases abovementioned, is founded: And here the answer is obvious, in *the greatest good of the whole*. For since the Governor of the universe is possessed of power, wisdom, and goodness in perfection of degree, it is impossible but that the greatest happiness to the creation should be the result of his exercise of the most absolute sovereignty. And though this right of absolute authority in the Creator over his creatures be inseparable from the relation between Creator and creature, yet it is not founded simply in that relation, that is, in the idea of derived existence; but in the natural imperfection and dependance of the creature, and the natural perfection of the Creator, and the reason of the necessarily absolute subjection of the creature does not consist merely in his having *received existence*, but in his having received it from such a Being; a Being by the perfection of his nature qualified for the most perfect government, and under whose administration it is impossible but that the beforementioned immutable law of nature, the greatest happiness of the whole, should operate to effect. Agreable to this is the foundation of the natural authority of parents over their children; it by no means consisting in the notion of *derived existence*; but in the different qualifications of parents and children to execute this immutable law: For while parents so far excel their children in wisdom, and from natural affection are disposed to promote their happiness, it will follow, that more happiness will result to both, from the exercise of authority in parents, and subordination in children, than from the exercise of equal Liberty in each. And that this authority of parents over their children is derived from this source, and not from the natural relation subsisting between them, considered merely as parents and offspring, is moreover evident beyond all contradiction from this consideration, that whenever the parent is by any means disqualified, in the respects before mentioned, to direct the conduct of his child, the subordination of the child ceases.

Questioning Natural Equality

If this, which I think none will deny, be a just representation of the foundation in *nature* of authority and subordination; in order to justify involuntary slavery in *general*, in opposition to the notion of *natural* equality, it is necessary only to inquire, whether among different individuals, between whom there is no such natural relation as that of parent and offspring, there be not the same reason, ground, and foundation in nature for the exercise of authority in some, necessarily involving subordination in others, which there is in cases where such relation actually subsists. And concerning this, no one surely can remain a moment undetermined, who reflects with the least degree of attention, upon the vast inequality observable between different individuals of the human species, in point of qualification for the proper direction of conduct. Now whether this inequality be considered as arising from difference in natural capacity, difference in the means of improvement, or in disposition properly to employ such means: in a word, whether it arises from nature or education, or any other supposeable quarter, it matters not, while this is in fact the case, while some are actually found so far to excel others both in respect of wisdom and benevolence, both in the knowledge of the principles of propriety, and a disposition to practice such principles, that the general end, happiness, would be better promoted by the exercise of authority in the former, though necessarily involving subordination in the latter, than by the enjoyment of equal Liberty in each, the exercise of such authority must be right, and never the less so, though the individuals by such an œconomy subordinated, do not consent. It is fit that children should be subjected to the authority of their parents, whether they consent to such subjection or not; this is put beyond all possibility of doubt by the express declaration of wisdom which cannot err; not to mention the consent of all ages in their approbation of the principles of those civil societies which have warranted the exercise of such authority. Every law is applicable to all cases within the same reason; and since it cannot be denied that the reason of authority and subordination between parents and children, equally applies to the support of a distinction of the same kind among others not so related, it follows inevitably, that a distinction in the latter case is equally justifiable with one in the former; they are both supported by the same principle of natural law, and therefore must stand or fall together.

I have introduced these observations upon the foundation of the authority of the Governor of the universe over the creation, and of parents over their children, for the sake of example, rather than as necessary to support the general idea of inequality: I say as necessary, for while there is so manifestly great an inequality in the capacities and dispositions of mankind to direct their own as well as the conduct of others, to its only proper end, I think it demonstrable, that the principle of absolute equality could not be supported, even though we had no argument from fact by which it might be illustrated. And in truth, I think, before the principle of absolute equality can be maintained, it must be made to appear, that all mankind, in point of capacity and disposition to conduct properly, are equal.

A Natural Right to Be Slaves

George Fitzhugh was one of the most famous of all proslavery writers and intellectuals. In his works, including this excerpt from Cannibals All! or Slaves Without Masters *written after 1850, he argued that slavery as it had evolved in the South was a morally superior social system to the capitalism developing in the North, and that slaves were better off than the free yet poor laborers in the North and in Europe.*

We agree with Mr. Jefferson that all men have natural and inalienable rights. To violate or disregard such rights, is to oppose the designs and plans of Providence, and cannot "come to good." The order and subordination observable in the physical, animal, and human world show that some are formed for higher, others for lower stations—the few to command, the many to obey. We conclude that about nineteen out of every twenty individuals have "a natural and inalienable right" to be taken care of and protected, to have guardians, trustees, husbands, or masters; in other words, they have a natural and inalienable right to be slaves. The one in twenty are as clearly born or educated or some way fitted for command and liberty. Not to make them rulers or masters is as great a violation of natural right as not to make slaves of the mass. A very little individuality is useful and necessary to society—much of it begets discord, chaos and anarchy.

It now remains only to apply these general principles to the particular case of *Africans* in this country, and see what degree of authority the people here are thereby warranted to exercise over them; and if it shall appear in fact, that they are not reduced by the law of this land to a degree of subordination beyond what the law of nature abovementioned, the happiness of both, requires, it will follow undeniably, that the law by which they are thus subjected is just. . . .

The notion of equality, in the strict sense, had no foundation *in nature*; but as happiness is the only end of action, so superiority in wisdom, goodness, &c. is in the nature of things a proper foundation of authority. And as nature has made differences among creatures in these respects; so it is fit and proper, and agreable to nature's law, that different degrees of authority in point of direction of conduct should be exercised by them; and that in some cases, even among the human species, this difference is so important, as to render the exercise of authority justifiable, even without the consent of the governed: For this I have produced an example from fact, in the case of parents and children. . . . I now go on to say, as a consequence from the same acknowledged principle, that whenever such a connection of things takes place, that any number of men cannot, consistently with the good of the whole, have a residence in any community but in a state of involuntary subordination, and that their residence in such community notwithstanding such subordination, be in fact best for the whole, such subordination, though invountary, is no violation of the law of nature; but on the contrary to all intents and purposes correspondent thereto. This is a true conclusion from premises incontestible, principles universally acknowledged. . . . Subordination in this case comes fully within the reason of the subordination of children, rests on precisely the same foundation, and is therefore justifiable on precisely the same principles. For whether the necessity of such subordination arises from natural incapacity, or from any other quarter, it matters not, if this is in fact the case; if the interest of the whole does require it; let the causes or reasons of such requirement be what they may, such subordination is equally justifiable as in any other case whatever; not only in the case of children, but even in the case of consent; for the obligation to submission arising from consent, is founded in the general obligation to fulfil contracts; which obligation is ultimately founded in the good of society.

The State of the Africans

Now fully within this predicament lies, as I conceive, the particular case of *Africans* in this country. That it is only a state of limited subordination (I say *limited*, for it is to be remembered, that the authority of those to whom they are subordinate, is restricted by the superior authority of law, to which we are all subordinate, and which provides that they, as well as others, shall be treated according to the general principles of humanity) that these people can *consistently* enjoy a residence among us is, I suppose, acknowledged by all. And whether it is not better for them to reside here, notwithstanding such subordination, even regard being had to *their* interest only, than in their native country, no one can doubt, at least no one, who has a tolerably adequate conception of their misery, and wretchedness there. Figure to yourself my friend, you are not unacquainted with *African* history, figure to yourself the delightful situation of a natural inhabitant of *Africa*. View him necessarily destitute of every mean of improvement in social virtue, of every advantage for the cultivation of those principles of humanity, in which alone consists the dignity of the rational nature, and from which only source spring all that pleasure, that happiness of life, by which the human species is distinguished from the other parts of the animal creation. Consider his situation as a candidate for an eternal existence; view him as necessarily ignorant of every principle of that religion, through the happy influence of which alone the degenerate race of Adam can rationally form the most distant expectation of future felicity. View him moreover in a state of the most abject slavery, a slavery of the worst kind, a slavery of all others most destructive of human happiness,—an entire subjection to the tyrannizing power of lust and passion,—wholly devoted to the governing influence of those irregular propensities, which are the genuine offspring of depraved nature, when unassisted by philosophy or religion. Behold him actually clothed in all that brutal stupidity, that savage barbarity which naturally springs from such a source. Add to this, his condition of perpetual insecurity, arising from the state of hostility and war that forever rages in those inhospitable climes; and consider the treatment he is to expect, whom the fortune of war has subjected to the power of his enraged foe, whose natural cruelty is perpetually sharpened, and whose desire of revenge is continually cherished, by a sense of his own danger. . . . without it: But who I beseech you, ever thought the consent of a child, an ideot, or a madman necessary to his subordination? Every whit as immaterial is the consent of these miserable Africans, whose real character seems to be a compound of the three last mentioned. What can avail his consent, who through ignorance of the means necessary to promote his happiness, is rendered altogether incapable of choosing for himself? And as the consent of such a being could by no means involve subordination in a case where it would be otherwise improper, so the want of it can be no bar in a case where it would not. In all such cases it is undoubtedly the duty of those, whom providence has favored with the means of improvement in understanding, and the wisdom resulting from such improvement, to make use of their discretion in directing the conduct of those who want it.

I am sensible that I have already dwelt too long upon this argument; you will however in this connexion, permit me to add, that were involuntary subjection, in all cases, contrary to the law of nature, it is impossible to suppose, that the Governor of the universe, whose wisdom is infinite, and whose will is eternally and immutably coincident with, and *when revealed to us*, the *measure* of, this law, should ever have expressly tolerated it in any particular instance. . . .

Were it necessary or expedient, it would be easy to shew, by comparison, in a great variety of instances not mentioned, the superiority of a slave in this country, in point of condition, to a natural inhabitant of *Africa*. And though it be too true, that these unhappy creatures are in many particular cases, cruelly treated, yet, while their importation is to them a redemption from a condition on the whole so much more miserable, we must, as I said before, justify the government in tolerating such importation.

CHAPTER 2

Life Under Slavery

Chapter Preface

Between 1830 and 1860, a time of increasing national divisions over slavery, numerous accounts of slave life were published. These accounts of life under slavery almost invariably had either abolitionist or proslavery agendas. Those focusing on the cruelty of slavery were a staple of the abolitionist movement's campaign to persuade Americans to abolish the institution. Conversely, proslavery writers sought to portray slavery as humane and civilizing and certainly better than being a peasant in Europe or an industrial worker in the North. While many arguments for slavery rested on racist beliefs, and virtually no one today defends slavery as a "positive good," separating propaganda from fact in determining just what life was like under slavery is a task that still causes controversy among historians.

Making generalizations about slave life is complicated by the fact that slaves in the antebellum South lived under a wide variety of circumstances and held a variety of positions, including household servant, wagon driver, iron foundry worker, and skilled artisan. Nine out of ten slaves, however, worked as farm laborers, growing cotton, tobacco, rice, and other products. About half of these laborers worked on large plantations of twenty slaves or more, while the others worked on smaller and poorer farms, often alongside their masters.

Patterns of life on these plantations were roughly similar. Slaves worked from dawn to dusk under the supervision of their masters or of white or black overseers. At night they were often kept under curfew in their cabins, which were frequently inspected to ensure that slaves did not leave them. Slaves had no right to leave their home without the permission of their owner, and those found away from home were treated as runaways and subjected to punishment. Owners had unlimited legal right to decide and administer punishment to their human property, and flogging was commonly used. Most slaves were illiterate. Recalcitrant slaves were sold. Marriages among slaves had no legal standing, and families were often broken up by the selling of one or more of their members.

Historian Richard Shenkman writes that the historical evidence points to the oppressiveness of slavery, notwithstanding some accounts of its humaneness:

> That southerners actually thought blacks liked slavery is widely believed but dubious. . . . While planters may have harbored

genuine familial feelings for their slaves, they frequently lived in fear of them. . . . Southern legislators, alert to the dangers all around them, enacted reams of laws designed to keep slaves in check. It should be evident that laws forbidding the teaching of slaves to read and write, for instance, would hardly have been necessary if whites had really thought blacks were content and happy.

Shenkman goes on to argue that writings defending slavery may have been motivated by the Southerners' need to justify slavery in the face of abolitionist attacks.

One important consideration historians note in examining the treatment of slaves is the paradoxical fact that slaves were both people and property. According to the legal codes slaves were mere property, to be disposed of as the owner saw fit. However, as historian Robert Kelley writes:

To begin with the most fundamental fact: Slaves were not *things*. Whatever the law said, they were in reality human beings. A plow could not be evasive at work tasks, or burn down the barn, or escape—nor would it bleed when whipped, or develop for self-protection an elaborate courteous politeness when dealing with a master. An intricate complex of informal customs and "rights" sprang up because the slave was a person.

Because the slave owner ultimately needed the cooperation of his slaves, he relied sometimes on kindly concern as well as discipline. In some instances, slave owners, in addition to providing for their material welfare, granted their slaves autonomy for creating their own lives and community by allowing and promoting slave marriages, granting slaves private garden plots, and allowing more freedom for religious and social gatherings. Thus, the acts of kindness and the sense of family portrayed by defenders of slavery were not necessarily fiction. They were instead part of a paternalistic system that, as historian Eugene D. Genovese writes, "afforded a fragile bridge across the intolerable contradictions inherent in a society based on racism, slavery, and class exploitation that had to depend on the willing reproduction and productivity of its victims."

Despite the fact that some slaves were able to create a tolerable life and community for themselves, the fact remains that slaves lived without legal protection and at the whim of their masters. Perhaps the last word should belong to a slave interviewed in 1937 remembering his days of slavery:

What I likes best, to be slave or free? Well, it's this way. In slavery I owns nothing and never owns nothing. In freedom I's own the home and raise the family. All that cause me worriment, and in slavery I had no worriment, but I takes the freedom.

VIEWPOINT 1

"No human institution, in my opinion, is more manifestly consistent with the will of God than domestic slavery."

Slavery Is Just

George McDuffie (1790-1851)

While slavery was abolished in the northern part of the United States by the early 1800s, it became even more economically entrenched in the South. The invention of the cotton gin in 1793 greatly increased the demand for slave labor on southern cotton plantations. Increasingly, slavery was viewed as a North vs. South issue.

The following viewpoint is taken from a speech presented to the South Carolina legislature in 1835 by George McDuffie, Democratic governor of South Carolina from 1834 to 1836. The speech was reprinted in the book *American History Leaflets, Colonial and Constitutional*, published in July 1893 and edited by Albert B. Hart and Edward Channing. In this speech, McDuffie strongly attacks Northern abolitionists who were printing and distributing antislavery literature. He stoutly defends the institution of slavery as a positive good rather than a necessary evil. He states that slavery is a moral institution that benefits both the slaves and society as a whole. Many of the ideas expressed in this speech were central to the southern defense of slavery.

Since your last adjournment, the public mind throughout the slaveholding states has been intensely, indignantly, and justly excited by the wanton, officious, and incendiary proceedings of certain societies and persons in some of the nonslaveholding states, who have been actively employed in attempting to circulate among us pamphlets, papers, and pictorial representations of the most offensive and inflammatory character, and eminently calculated to seduce our slaves from their fidelity and excite them to insurrection and massacre. These wicked monsters and deluded fanatics, overlooking the numerous objects in their own vicinity, who have a moral if not a legal claim upon their charitable regard, run abroad in the expansion of their hypocritical benevolence, muffled up in the saintly mantle of Christian meekness, to fulfill the fiendlike errand of mingling the blood of the master and the slave, to whose fate they are equally indifferent, with the smoldering ruins of our peaceful dwellings. . . .

For the institution of domestic slavery we hold ourselves responsible only to God, and it is utterly incompatible with the dignity and the safety of the state to permit any foreign authority to question our right to maintain it. It may nevertheless be appropriate, as a voluntary token of our respect for the opinions of our confederate brethren, to present some views to their consideration on this subject, calculated to disabuse their minds of false opinions and pernicious prejudices.

The Will of God

No human institution, in my opinion, is more manifestly consistent with the will of God than domestic slavery, and no one of His ordinances is written in more legible characters than that which consigns the African race to this condition, as more conducive to their own happiness, than any other of which they are susceptible. Whether we consult the sacred Scriptures or the lights of nature and reason, we shall find these truths as abundantly apparent as if written with a sunbeam in the heavens. Under both the Jewish and Christian dispensations of our religion, domestic slavery existed with the unequivocal sanction of its prophets, its apostles, and finally its great Author. The patriarchs themselves, those chosen instruments of God, were slaveholders. In fact, the divine sanction of this institution is so plainly written that "he who runs may read" it, and those overrighteous pretenders and Pharisees who affect to be scandalized by its existence among us would do well to inquire how much more nearly they walk in the ways of godliness than did Abraham, Isaac, and Jacob.

That the African Negro is destined by Providence to occupy this condition of servile dependence is not less manifest. It is marked on the face, stamped on the skin, and evinced by the intellectual inferiority and natural improvidence of this race. They have all the qualities that fit them for slaves, and not one of those that would fit them to be freemen. They are utterly unqualified, not only for rational freedom but for self-government of any kind. They are, in all respects, physical, moral, and political, inferior to millions of the human race who have for consecutive ages dragged out a wretched existence under a grinding political despotism, and who are doomed to this hopeless condition by the very qualities which unfit them for a better. It is utterly astonishing that any enlightened American, after contemplating all the manifold forms in which even the white race of mankind is doomed to slavery and oppression, should suppose it possible to reclaim the African race from their destiny.

The Capacity to Enjoy Freedom

The capacity to enjoy freedom is an attribute not to be communicated by human power. It is an endowment of God, and one of the rarest which it has pleased His inscrutable wisdom to bestow upon the nations of the earth. It is conferred as the reward of merit, and only upon those who are qualified to enjoy it. Until the "Ethiopian can change his skin," it will be in vain to attempt, by any human power, to make freemen of those whom God has doomed to be slaves by all their attributes.

Let not, therefore, the misguided and designing intermeddlers who seek to destroy our peace imagine that they are serving the cause of God by practically arraigning the decrees of His providence. Indeed, it would scarcely excite surprise if, with the impious audacity of those who projected the Tower of Babel, they should attempt to scale the battlements of heaven and remonstrate with the God of wisdom for having put the mark of Cain and the curse of Ham upon the African race instead of the European.

If the benevolent friends of the black race would compare the condition of that portion of them which we hold in servitude with that which still remains in Africa, totally unblessed by the lights of civilization or Christianity and groaning under a savage despotism, as utterly destitute of hope as of happiness, they would be able to form some tolerable estimate of what our blacks have lost by slavery in America and what they have gained by freedom in Africa. Greatly as their condition has been improved by their subjection to an enlightened and Christian people—the only mode under heaven by which it could have been accomplished—they are yet wholly unprepared for anything like a rational system of self-government. Emancipation would be a positive curse, depriving them of a guardianship essential to their happiness, and they may well say in the language of the Spanish proverb, "Save us from our friends and we will take care of our enemies."

If emancipated, where would they live and what would be their condition? The idea of their remaining among us is utterly visionary. Amalgamation is abhorrent to every sentiment of nature; and if they remain as a separate caste, whether endowed with equal privileges or not, they will become our masters, or we must resume the mastery over them. This state of political amalgamation and conflict, which the Abolitionists evidently aim to produce, would be the most horrible condition imaginable and would furnish Dante or Milton with the type for another chapter illustrating the horrors of the infernal regions. The only disposition, therefore, that could be made of our emancipated slaves would be their transportation to Africa, to exterminate the natives or be exterminated by them; contingencies either of which may well serve to illustrate the wisdom, if not the philanthropy, of these superserviceable madmen who in the name of humanity would desolate the fairest region of the earth and destroy the most perfect system of social and political happiness that ever has existed.

It is perfectly evident that the destiny of the Negro race is either the worst possible form of political slavery or else domestic servitude as it exists in the slaveholding states. The advantage of domestic slavery over the most favorable condition of political slavery does not admit of a question. . . .

The Conditions of Slaves

In all respects, the comforts of our slaves are greatly superior to those of the English operatives, or the Irish and continental peasantry, to say nothing of the millions of paupers crowded together in those loathsome receptacles of starving humanity, the public poorhouses. Besides the hardships of incessant toil, too much almost for human nature to endure, and the sufferings of actual want, driving them almost to despair, these miserable creatures are perpetually annoyed by the most distressing cares for the future condition of themselves and their children.

From this excess of labor, this actual want, and these distressing cares, our slaves are entirely exempted. They habitually labor from two to four hours a day less than the operatives in other countries; and it has been truly remarked, by some writer, that a Negro cannot be made to injure himself by excessive labor. It may be safely affirmed that they usually eat as much wholesome and substantial food in one day as English operatives or Irish peasants eat in two. And as it regards concern for the future, their condition may well be envied even by their masters. There is not upon the face of the earth any class of people, high or low, so perfectly free from care and anxiety. They know that their masters will provide for them, under all circumstances, and that in the extremity of old age, instead of being driven to beggary or to seek public charity in a poorhouse, they will be comfortably accommodated and kindly treated among their relatives and associates. . . .

In a word, our slaves are cheerful, contented, and happy, much beyond the general condition of the human race, except where those foreign intruders and fatal ministers of mischief, the emancipationists, like their arch-prototype in the Garden of Eden and actuated by no less envy, have tempted them to aspire above the condition to which they have been assigned in the order of Providence. . . .

All Is Peace

In this excerpt from Sociology for the South *published in 1854, George Fitzhugh argues for the moral superiority of slavery to capitalism.*

At the slaveholding South all is peace, quiet, plenty and contentment. We have no mobs, no trades unions, no strikes for higher wages, no armed resistance to the law, but little jealousy of the rich by the poor. We have but few in our jails, and fewer in our poor houses. We produce enough of the comforts and necessaries of life for a population three or four times as numerous as ours. We are wholly exempt from the torrent of pauperism, crime, agrarianism, and infidelity which Europe is pouring from her jails and alms houses on the already crowed North.

Reason and philosophy can easily explain what experience so clearly testifies. If we look into the elements of which all political communities are composed, it will be found that servitude, in some form, is one of the essential constituents. No community ever has existed without it, and we may confidently assert none ever will. In the very nature of things there must be classes of persons to discharge all the different offices of society, from the highest to the lowest. Some of those offices are regarded as degrading, though they must and will be performed; hence those manifold forms of dependent servitude which produce a sense of superiority in the masters or employers and of inferiority on the part of the servants. Where these offices are performed by members of the political community, a dangerous element is introduced into the body politic; hence the alarming tendency to violate the rights of property by agrarian legislation, which is beginning to be manifest in the older states, where universal suffrage prevails without domestic slavery, a tendency that will increase in the progress of society with the increasing inequality of wealth.

Slavery Preserves Social Order

No government is worthy of the name that does not protect the rights of property, and no enlightened people will long submit to such a mockery. Hence it is that, in older countries, different political orders are established to effect this indispensable object; and it will be fortunate for the nonslaveholding states if they are not, in less than a quarter of a century, driven to the adoption of a similar institution, or to take refuge from robbery and anarchy under a military despotism.

But where the menial offices and dependent employments of society are performed by domestic slaves, a class well defined by their color and entirely separated from the political body, the rights of property are perfectly secure without the establishment of artificial barriers. In a word, the institution of domestic slavery supersedes the necessity of an order of nobility and all the other appendages of a hereditary system of government. If our slaves were emancipated and admitted, bleached or unbleached, to an equal participation in our political privileges, what a commentary should we furnish upon the doctrines of the emancipationists, and what a revolting spectacle of republican equality should we exhibit to the mockery of the world! No rational man would consent to live in such a state of society if he could find a refuge in any other.

Domestic slavery, therefore, instead of being a political evil, is the cornerstone of our republican edifice. No patriot who justly estimates our privileges will tolerate the idea of emancipation, at any period, however remote, or on any conditions of pecuniary advantage, however favorable. I would as soon open a negotiation for selling the liberty of the state at once as for making any stipulations for the ultimate emancipation of our slaves. So deep is my conviction on this subject that, if I were doomed to die immediately after recording these sentiments, I could say in all sincerity and under all the sanctions of Christianity and patriotism, "God forbid that my descendants, in the remotest generations, should live in any other than a community having the institution of domestic slavery as it existed among the patriarchs of the primitive church and in all the free states of antiquity."

If the legislature should concur in these general views of this important element of our political and social system, our confederates should be distinctly informed, in any communications we may have occasion to make to them, that in claiming to be exempted from all foreign interference, we can recognize no distinction between ultimate and immediate emancipation. . . .

The Value of Cotton

And we have the less reason to look forward to this inauspicious result from considering the necessary consequences which would follow to the people of those states and of the whole commercial world from the general emancipation of our slaves. These consequences may be presented, as an irresistible appeal, to every rational philanthropist in Europe or America. It is clearly demonstrable that the production of cotton depends, not so much on soil and climate as on the existence of domestic slavery. In the relaxing latitudes where it grows, not one-half the quantity would be produced but for the existence of this institution; and every practical planter will concur in the opinion that if all the slaves in these states were now emancipated, the American crop would be reduced the very next year from 1,200,000 to 600,000 bales.

No great skill in political economy will be required to estimate how enormously the price of cotton would be increased by this change, and no one who will consider how largely this staple contributes to the wealth of manufacturing nations, and to the necessaries and comforts of the poorer classes all over the world, can fail to perceive the disastrous effects of so great a reduction in the quantity and so great an enhancement in the price of it. In Great Britain, France, and the United States, the catastrophe would be overwhelming, and it is not extravagant to say that for little more than 2 million Negro slaves, cut loose from their tranquil moorings and set adrift upon the untried ocean of at least a doubtful experiment, 10 million poor white people would be reduced to destitution, pauperism, and starvation.

An anxious desire to avoid the last sad alternative of an injured community prompts this final appeal to the interests and enlightened philanthropy of our confederate states. And we cannot permit ourselves to believe that our just demands, thus supported by every consideration of humanity and duty, will be rejected by states who are united to us by so many social and political ties, and who have so deep an interest in the preservation of that Union.

VIEWPOINT 2

"There is not a man on earth who does not believe that slavery is a curse."

Slavery Is Evil

Theodore Dwight Weld (1803-1895)

Theodore Dwight Weld was a leading figure in the American abolitionist movement. A revivalist preacher trained by evangelist Charles G. Finney, Weld and his followers traveled and lectured against slavery and distributed antislavery tracts throughout the country, including the South.

The following viewpoint is taken from *American Slavery as It Is*, a book written and compiled by Weld and his wife, Angelina Grimke, and sister-in-law Sarah Grimke and published in 1839. The Grimke sisters were themselves noted abolitionists and feminists. The book is primarily a compilation of articles and notices from Southern newspapers documenting the cruelties of slavery. It sold thousands of copies and is considered one of the most influential publications of the antislavery movement. The excerpt below includes Weld's introduction to the documents. It is a strident attack on the morality of slavery and the character of slaveholders. None of Weld's speeches have been recorded, but this viewpoint gives an idea of his effectiveness as a speaker against slavery.

Reader, you are impaneled as a juror to try a plain case and bring in an honest verdict. The question at issue is not one of law but of fact—What is the actual condition of the slaves in the United States? A plainer case never went to a jury. Look at it. TWENTY-SEVEN HUNDRED THOUSAND PERSONS in this country, men, women, and children, are in SLAVERY. Is slavery, as a condition for human beings, good, bad, or indifferent? We submit the question without argument. You have common sense, and conscience, and a human heart—pronounce upon it. You have a wife, or a husband, a child, a father, a mother, a brother, or a sister—make the case your own, make it theirs, and bring in your verdict.

The Verdict Is Guilty

The case of Human Rights against Slavery has been adjudicated in the court of conscience times innumerable. The same verdict has always been rendered—"Guilty"; the same sentence has always been pronounced, "Let it be accursed"; and human nature, with her million echoes, has rung it round the world in every language under heaven, "Let it be accursed. Let it be accursed." His heart is false to human nature who will not say "Amen." There is not a man on earth who does not believe that slavery is a curse. Human beings may be inconsistent, but human *nature* is true to herself. She has uttered her testimony against slavery with a shriek ever since the monster was begotten; and till it perishes amidst the execrations of the universe, she will traverse the world on its track, dealing her bolts upon its head, and dashing against it her condemning brand.

We repeat it, every man knows that slavery is a curse. Whoever denies this, his lips libel his heart. Try him; clank the chains in his ears and tell him they are for *him*. Give him an hour to prepare his wife and children for a life of slavery. Bid him make haste and get ready their necks for the yoke, and their wrists for the coffle chains, then look at his pale lips and trembling knees, and you have *nature's* testimony against slavery.

Two million seven hundred thousand persons in these states are in this condition. They were made slaves and are held such by force, and by being put in fear, and this for no crime! Reader, what have you to say of such treatment? Is it right, just, benevolent? Suppose I should seize you, rob you of your liberty, drive you into the field, and make you work without pay as long as you live—would that be justice and kindness, or monstrous injustice and cruelty?

Now, everybody knows that the slaveholders do these things to the slaves every day, and yet it is stoutly affirmed that they treat them well and kindly, and that their tender regard for their slaves restrains the masters from inflicting cruelties upon them. We shall go into no metaphysics to show the absurdity of this pretense. The man who *robs* you every day is, forsooth, quite too tender-hearted ever to cuff or kick you!

Gentle Oppression

True, he can snatch your money, but he does it gently lest he should hurt you. He can empty your pockets without qualms, but if your *stomach* is empty, it cuts him to the quick. He can make you work a lifetime without pay, but loves you too well to let you go hungry. He fleeces you of your *rights* with a relish, but is shocked if you work bareheaded in summer or in winter without warm stockings. He can make you go without your *liberty*, but never without a shirt. He can crush, in you, all hope of bettering your condition by vowing that you shall die his slave, but, though he can coolly torture your feelings, he is too compassionate to lacerate your back; he can break your heart, but he is very tender of your skin. He can strip you of all protection and thus expose you to all outrages, but if you are exposed to the *weather*, half-clad and half-sheltered, how yearn his tender bowels!

Slavery a National Shame

Born a slave and later freed, Frederick Douglass became one of the foremost black leaders of his time. His eloquent speeches and writings against slavery made him famous throughout the United States. His eloquence is evident in this excerpt from one of his lectures published in 1851.

While slavery exists, and the union of these States endures, every American citizen must bear the chagrin of hearing his country branded before the world, as a nation of liars and hypocrites; and behold his cherished national flag pointed at with the utmost scorn and derision. . . .

Let me say again, *slavery is alike the sin and the shame of the American people*: It is a blot upon the American name, and the only national reproach which need make an American hang his head in shame, in the presence of monarchical governments.

What! Slaveholders talk of treating men well, and yet not only rob them of all they get, and as fast as they get it, but rob them of *themselves*, also; their very hands and feet, and all their muscles, and limbs, and senses, their bodies and minds, their time and liberty and earnings, their free speech and rights of conscience, their right to acquire knowledge and property and reputation; and yet they who plunder them of all these would fain make us believe that their soft hearts ooze out so lovingly toward their slaves that they always keep them well-housed and well-clad, never push them too hard in the field, never make their dear backs smart, nor let their dear stomachs get empty.

But there is no end to these absurdities. Are slaveholders dunces, or do they take all the rest of the world to be, that they think to bandage our eyes with such thin gauzes? Protesting their kind regard for those whom they hourly plunder of all they have and all they get! What! When they have seized their victims and annihilated all their *rights*, still claim to be the special guardians of their *happiness!* Plunderers of their liberty, yet the careful suppliers of their wants? Robbers of their earnings, yet watchful sentinels round their interests, and kind providers of their comforts? Filching all their time, yet granting generous donations for rest and sleep? Stealing the use of their muscles, yet thoughtful of their ease? Putting them under drivers, yet careful that they are not hard-pushed? Too humane, forsooth, to stint the stomachs of their slaves, yet force their *minds* to starve, and brandish over them pains and penalties if they dare to reach forth for the smallest crumb of knowledge, even a letter of the alphabet!

It is no marvel that slaveholders are always talking of their *kind treatment* of their slaves. The only marvel is that men of sense can be gulled by such professions. Despots always insist that they are merciful. The greatest tyrants that ever dripped with blood have assumed the titles of "most gracious," "most clement," "most merciful," etc., and have ordered their crouching vassals to accost them thus. When did not vice lay claim to those virtues which are the opposites of its habitual crimes? The guilty, according to their own showing, are always innocent, and cowards brave, and drunkards sober, and harlots chaste, and pickpockets honest to a fault. . . .

False Testimonies

As slaveholders and their apologists are volunteer witnesses in their own cause and are flooding the world with testimony that their slaves are kindly treated; that they are well-fed, well-clothed, well-housed, well-lodged, moderately worked, and bountifully provided with all things needful for their comfort, we propose, first, to disprove their assertions by the testimony of a multitude of impartial witnesses, and then to put slaveholders themselves through a course of cross-questioning which shall draw their condemnation out of their own mouths.

We will prove that the slaves in the United States are treated with barbarous inhumanity; that they are overworked, underfed, wretchedly clad and lodged, and have insufficient sleep; that they are often made to wear round their necks iron collars armed with prongs, to drag heavy chains and weights at their feet while working in the field, and to wear yokes, and bells, and iron horns; that they are often kept confined in the stocks day and night for weeks together, made to wear gags in their mouths for hours or days, have some of their front teeth torn out or broken off that they may be easily detected when they run away; that they are frequently flogged with terrible severity, have red pepper rubbed into their lacerated flesh, and hot brine, spirits of turpentine, etc., poured over the gashes to increase the torture; that they are often stripped naked, their backs and limbs cut with

75

knives, bruised and mangled by scores and hundreds of blows with the paddle, and terribly torn by the claws of cats, drawn over them by their tormentors; that they are often hunted with bloodhounds and shot down like beasts, or torn in pieces by dogs; that they are often suspended by the arms and whipped and beaten till they faint, and, when revived by restoratives, beaten again till they faint, and sometimes till they die; that their ears are often cut off, their eyes knocked out, their bones broken, their flesh branded with red hot irons; that they are maimed, mutilated, and burned to death over slow fires. All these things, and more, and worse, we shall *prove*. Reader, we know whereof we affirm, we have weighed it well; *more and worse* WE WILL PROVE.

Library of Congress.

Slaveowners and overseers frequently resorted to flogging to subdue or punish slaves.

Mark these words, and read on; we will establish all these facts by the testimony of scores and hundreds of eyewitnesses, by the testimony of *slaveholders* in all parts of the slave states, by slaveholding members of Congress and of state legislatures, by ambassadors to foreign courts, by judges, by doctors of divinity, and clergymen of all denominations, by merchants, mechanics, lawyers, and physicians, by presidents and professors in colleges and professional seminaries, by planters, overseers, and drivers. We shall show, not merely that such deeds are committed but that they are frequent; not done in corners but before the sun; not in one of the slave states but in all of them; not perpetrated by brutal overseers and drivers merely but by magistrates, by legislators, by professors of religion, by preachers of the gospel, by governors of states, by "gentlemen of property and standing," and by delicate females moving in the "highest circles of society."

We know, full well, the outcry that will be made by multitudes, at these declarations; the multiform cavils, the flat denials, the charges of "exaggeration" and "falsehood" so often bandied, the sneers of affected contempt at the credulity that can believe such things, and the rage and imprecations against those who give them currency. We know, too, the threadbare sophistries by which slaveholders and their apologists seek to evade such testimony. If they admit that such deeds are committed, they tell us that they are exceedingly rare, and therefore furnish no grounds for judging of the general treatment of slaves; that occasionally a brutal wretch in the *free* states barbarously butchers his wife, but that no one thinks of inferring from that the general treatment of wives at the North and West.

Vapid Babblings

They tell us, also, that the slaveholders of the South are proverbially hospitable, kind, and generous, and it is incredible that they can perpetrate such enormities upon human beings; further, that it is absurd to suppose that they would thus injure their own property, that self-interest would prompt them to treat their slaves with kindness, as none but fools and madmen wantonly destroy their own property; further, that Northern visitors at the South come back testifying to the kind treatment of the slaves, and that the slaves themselves corroborate such representations. All these pleas, and scores of others, are bruited in every corner of the free states; and who that has eyes to see has not sickened at the blindness that saw not, at the palsy of heart that felt not, or at the cowardice and sycophancy that dared not expose such shallow fallacies. We are not to be turned from our purpose by such vapid babblings. . . .

The foregoing declarations touching the inflictions upon slaves are not haphazard assertions, nor the exaggerations of fiction conjured up to carry a point; nor are they the rhapsodies of enthusiasm, nor crude conclusions jumped at by hasty and imperfect investigation, nor the aimless outpourings either of sympathy or poetry; but they are proclamations of deliberate, well-weighed convictions, produced by accumulations of proof, by affirmations and affidavits, by written testimonies and statements of a cloud of witnesses who speak what they know and testify what they have seen; and all these impregnably fortified by proofs innumerable in the relation of the slaveholder to his slave, the nature of arbitrary power, and the nature and history of man. . . .

The barbarous indifference with which slaveholders regard the forcible sundering of husbands and wives, parents and children, brothers and sisters, and the unfeeling brutality indicated by the language in which they describe the efforts made by the slaves, in their yearnings after those from whom they have been torn away, reveals a "public opinion" toward them as dead to their agony as if they were cattle. It is well-nigh impossible to open a Southern paper without finding evidence of this. Though the truth of this assertion can hardly be called in question, we subjoin a few illustrations, and could easily give hundreds. . . .

Runaway Advertisements

From the *Southern Argus*, Oct. 31, 1837.
"Runaway—my negro man, Frederick, about 20 years of age. He is no doubt near the plantation of G.W. Corprew, Esq. of Noxubbee county, Mississippi, as *his wife belongs to that gentleman, and he followed her from my residence.* The above reward will be paid to any one who will confine him in jail and inform me of it at Athens, Ala.
"Athens, Alabama.

Kerkman Lewis."

From the *Savannah* (Ga.) *Republican*, May 24, 1838.
"$40 Reward.—Ran away from the subscriber in Savannah, his negro girl Patsey. She was purchased among the gang of negroes, known as the Hargreave's estate. She is no doubt lurking about Liberty county, at which place *she has relatives.*

Edward Houstoun, of Florida."

From the *Charleston* (S.C.) *Courier*, June 29, 1837.
"$20 Reward will be paid for the apprehension and delivery, at the work-house in Charleston, of a mulatto woman, named Ida. It is probable she may have made her way into Georgia, where she has *connections.*

Matthew Muggridge."

From the *Norfolk* (Va.) *Beacon*, March 31, 1838.
"The subscriber will give $20 for the apprehension of his negro woman, Maria, who ran away about twelve months since. She is known to be lurking in or about Chuckatuch, in the county of Nansemond, where *she has a husband*, and *formerly belonged.*

Peter Oneill."

Slavery Brutalizes Human Beings

Daniel A. Payne was a black educator and minister. He established a school in Charleston, South Carolina, for black children in 1826, but was forced to abandon it after legislation restricting the education of blacks was passed in 1834. He later became a Bishop of the African Methodist Episcopal Church and president of Wilberforce University in Ohio. This excerpt is taken from a speech Payne delivered that was printed in the Lutheran Herald and Journal *on August 1, 1839.*

Slavery brutalizes man. . . . This being God created but a little lower than the angels, and crowned him with glory and honor; but slavery hurls him down from his elevated position, to the level of brutes, strikes this crown of glory from his head and fastens upon his neck the galling yoke, and compels him to labor like an ox, through summer's sun and winter's snow, without remuneration. Does a man take the calf from the cow and sell it to the butcher? So slavery tears the child from the arms of the reluctant mother, and barters it to the soul trader for a young colt, or some other commodity! Does the bird catcher tear away the dove from his mate? So slavery separates the groaning husband from the embraces of his distracted and weeping wife! And are the beasts of the forest hunted, tortured and slain at the pleasure of the cruel hunter? So are the slaves hunted, tortured and slain by the cruel monster slavery!

From the *Macon* (Ga.) *Messenger,* Jan. 16, 1839.

"Ranaway from the subscriber, two negroes, Davis, a man about 45 years old; also Peggy, his wife, near the same age. Said negroes will probably make their way to Columbia county, as *they have children* living in that county. I will liberally reward any person who may deliver them to me.

Nehemiah King."

From the *Petersburg* (Va.) *Constellation,* June 27, 1837.

"Ranaway, a negro man, named Peter. *He has a wife* at the plantation of Mr. C. Haws, near Suffolk, where it is supposed he is still lurking.

John L. Dunn."

From the *Richmond* (Va.) *Whig,* Dec. 7, 1839.

"Ranaway from the subscriber, a negro man, named John Lewis. It is supposed that he is lurking about in New Kent county, where he professes to have *a wife.*

Hill Jones,
Agent for R.F. & P. Railroad Co."

From the *Richmond* (Va.) *Enquirer*, Feb. 20, 1838.

"$10 Reward for a negro woman, named Sally, 40 years old. We have just reason to believe the said negro to be now lurking on the James River Canal, or in the Green Spring neighborhood, where, we are informed, *her husband resides*. The above reward will be given to any person *securing* her.

Polly C. Shields.
Mount Elba, Feb. 19, 1838."

"$50 Reward.—Ranaway from the subscriber, his negro man Pauladore, commonly called Paul. I understand Gen. R. Y. Hayne *has purchased his wife and children* from H.L. Pinckney, Esq. and has them now on his plantation at Goosecreek, where, no doubt, the fellow is frequently *lurking*.

T. Davis."

"$25 Reward.—Ran away from the subscriber, a negro woman, named Matilda. It is thought she may be somewhere up James River, as she was claimed as *a wife* by some boatman in Goochland.

J. Alvis."

"Stop the Runaway!!!—$25 Reward. Ranaway from the Eagle Tavern, a negro fellow, named Nat. He is no doubt attempting to *follow his wife, who was lately sold to a speculator* named Redmond. The above reward will be paid by Mrs. Lucy M. Downman, of Sussex county, Va."

Multitudes of advertisements like the above appear annually in the Southern papers. Reader, look at the preceding list—mark the unfeeling barbarity with which their masters and *mistresses* describe the struggles and perils of sundered husbands and wives, parents and children, in their weary midnight travels through forests and rivers, with torn limbs and breaking hearts, seeking the embraces of each other's love. In one instance, a mother, torn from all her children and taken to a remote part of another state, presses her way back through the wilderness, hundreds of miles, to clasp once more her children to her heart; but, when she has arrived within a few miles of them, in the same county, is discovered, seized, dragged to jail, and her purchaser told, through an advertisement, that she awaits his order. But we need not trace out the harrowing details already before the reader.

VIEWPOINT 3

"Judging of them as you meet them in the streets, see them at work, or at church, . . . one must see that they are a happy people."

Slavery Is Not Oppressive

Nehemiah Adams (1806-1878)

Nehemiah Adams was a Congregationalist minister in Boston, Massachusetts. Adams had antislavery leanings and worked against the extension of slavery to the western territories. In 1853, for reasons of health he traveled for three months in the South. What he saw there caused him to question his views of slavery as an evil and oppressive institution.

Adams' observations were published by Boston publisher T.R. Marvin & B.B. Mussey in 1854 in the book *A South-Side View of Slavery*. The book became highly popular with those who argued in defense of slavery. In the excerpts printed here, Adams describes his observations of black slaves in the South and concludes that many of them live contented lives. He enumerates several advantages of the life of a slave, including freedom from starvation. Adams argues that while individual slavemasters may be cruel, many are not.

The writer has lately spent three months at the south for the health of an invalid. Few professional men at the north had less connection with the south by ties of any kind than he, when the providence of God made it necessary to become for a while a stranger in a strange land. He was too much absorbed by private circumstances to think of entering at all into a deliberate consideration of any important subject of a public nature; yet for this very reason, perhaps, the mind was better prepared to receive dispassionately the impressions which were to be made upon it. The impressions thus made, and the reflections which spontaneously arose, the writer here submits, not as a partisan, but as a Christian; not as a northerner, but as an American; not as a politician, but as a lover and friend of the colored race. . . .

I will relate the impressions and expectations with which I went to the south; the manner in which things appeared to me in connection with slavery in Georgia, South Carolina, and Virginia; the correction or confirmation of my northern opinions and feelings; the conclusions to which I was led; the way in which our language and whole manner toward the south have impressed me; and the duty which it seems to me, as members of the Union, we at the north owe to the subject of slavery and to the south, and with the south to the colored race. I shall not draw upon fictitious scenes and feelings, but shall give such statements as I would desire to receive from a friend to whom I should put the question, "What am I to believe? How am I to feel and act?". . .

How to say enough of preconceived notions respecting slavery, so as to compare subsequent impressions with them, and yet not enough to give southern friends room to exult and say that we all have false and exaggerated notions about slavery, is somewhat difficult. At the risk of disagreeable imputations, and with a desire to be honest and ingenuous, I will merely add, that there was one thing which I felt sure that I should see on landing, viz., the whole black population cowed down. This best expresses in a word my expectation. "I am a slave," will be indented on the faces, limbs, and actions of the bondmen. Hopeless woe, entreating yet despairing, will frequently greet me. How could it be otherwise, if slavery be such as our books, and sermons, and lectures, and newspaper articles represent? nay, if southern papers themselves, especially their advertisements, are to be relied upon as sources of correct impressions?

Arrival and First Impressions

The steam tug reached the landing, and the slaves were all about us. One thing immediately surprised me; they were all in good humor, and some of them in a broad laugh. The delivery of every trunk from the tug to the wharf was the occasion of some hit, or repartee, and every burden was borne with a jolly word, grimace, or motion. The lifting of one leg in laugh seemed as natural as a Frenchman's shrug. I asked one of them to place a trunk with a lot of baggage; it was done; up went the hand to the hat—"Any thing more, please sir?" What a contrast, I involuntarily said to myself, to that troop at the Albany landing on our Western Railroad! and on those piles of boards, and on the roofs of the sheds, and at the piers, in New York! I began to like these slaves. I began to laugh with them. It was irresistible. Who could have convinced me, an hour before, that slaves could have any other effect upon me than to make me feel sad? One fellow, in all the hurry and bustle of landing us, could not help relating how, in jumping on board, his boot was caught between two planks, and "pulled clean off;" and how "dis ole feller went clean over into de wotter," with a shout, as though it was a merry adventure.

Negro Slaves and English Paupers

Edmund Ruffin was an agriculturalist and a strong supporter of the Confederacy. His articles defending slavery were widely published in newspapers and periodicals throughout the South. This excerpt is from his book, The Political Economy of Slavery, *originally published in 1853.*

The negro slaves in the United States have increased from 300,000, the number originally imported from Africa, to nearly 4,000,000, or more than twelve for one. This is a sufficient evidence of their general good treatment, induced by the self-interest of the owners. If it were possible to designate, separately, the whole class of poor laborers in England, and to trace them and their descendants for two hundred years, it is most probable that the original number would be found diminished in as great proportion as that in which our negro slaves have increased—or reduced to less than one-twelfth part. Yet this widespread, miserable, and life-destroying hunger slavery and paper slavery in England is there called freedom by the fanatics and so-called philanthropists, who abhor, and call incessantly for God's vengeance upon, the negro slavery of this country!

One thing seemed clear; they were not so much cowed down as I expected. Perhaps, however, they were a fortunate set. I rode away, expecting soon to have some of my disagreeable anticipations verified. . . .

The city of Savannah abounds in parks, as they are called— squares, fenced in, with trees. Young children and infants were there, with very respectable colored nurses—young women, with bandanna and plaid cambric turbans, and superior in genteel appearance to any similar class, as a whole, in any of our cities. They could not be slaves. Are they slaves? "Certainly," says the friend at your side; "they each belong to some master or mistress.". . .

Everyday Life

Our fancies with regard to the condition of the slaves proceed from our northern repugnance to slavery, stimulated by many things that we read. The every-day life, the whole picture of society at the south, is not presented to us so frequently—indeed it cannot be, nor can it strike the mind as strongly—as slave auctions and separations of families, fugitives hiding in dismal swamps, and other things which appeal to our sensibilities. Whatever else may be true of slavery, these things, we say, are indisputable; and they furnish materials for the fancy to build into a world of woe.

Without supposing that I had yet seen slavery, it was nevertheless true that a load was lifted from my mind by the first superficial look at the slaves in the city.

It was as though I had been let down by necessity into a cavern which I had peopled with disagreeable sights, and, on reaching bottom, found daylight streaming in, and the place cheerful.

A better-looking, happier, more courteous set of people I had never seen, than those colored men, women, and children whom I met the first few days of my stay in Savannah. It had a singular effect on my spirits. They all seemed glad to see me. I was tempted with some vain feelings, as though they meant to pay me some special respect. I was all the more grateful, because for months sickness and death had covered almost every thing, even the faces of friends at home, with sadness to my eye, and my spirits had drooped. But to be met and accosted with such extremely civil, benevolent looks, to see so many faces break into pleasant smiles in going by, made one feel that he was not alone in the world, even in a land of strangers.

Taking a Whole Race by the Hand

How such unaffected politeness could have been learned under the lash I did not understand. It conflicted with my notions of slavery. I could not have dreamed that these people had been "down trodden," "their very manhood crushed out of them," "the galling yoke of slavery breaking every human feeling, and reducing them to the level of brutes." It was one of the pleasures of taking a walk to be greeted by all my colored friends. I felt that I had taken a whole new race of my fellow-men by the hand. I took care to notice each of them, and get his full smile and salutation; many a time I would gladly have stopped and paid a good price for a certain "good morning," courtesy, and bow; it was worth more than gold; its charm consisted in its being unbought, unconstrained, for I was an entire stranger. Timidity, a feeling of necessity, the leer of obliged deference, I nowhere saw; but the artless, free, and easy manner which burdened spirits never wear. It was difficult to pass the colored people in the streets without a smile awakened by the magnetism of their smiles. Let any one at the north, afflicted with depression of spirits, drop down among these negroes, walk these streets, form a passing acquaintance with some of them and unless he is a hopeless case, he will find himself in moods of cheerfulness never awakened surely by the countenances of the whites in any strange place. Involuntary servitude did not present itself to my eye or thoughts during the two weeks which I spent in Savannah, except as I read advertisements in the papers of slaves for sale. . . .

This illustration, taken from a periodical published in South Carolina in 1863, portrays the slave plantation as a place where whites and blacks live happily together.

Historical Pictures/Stock Montage.

The streets of southern cities and towns immediately struck me as being remarkably quiet in the evening and at night.

"What is the cause of so much quiet?" I said to a friend.

"Our colored people are mostly at home. After eight o'clock they cannot be abroad without a written pass, which they must show on being challenged, or go to the guard house. The master must pay fifty cents for a release. White policemen in cities, and in towns patrols of white citizens, walk the streets at night."

Here I receive my first impression of interference with the personal liberty of the colored people. The white servants, if there be any, the boys, the apprentices, the few Irish, have liberty; the colored men are under restraint.

But though I saw that this was a feature of slavery, I did not conclude that it would be well to dissolve the Union in order to abolish it. Apart from the question of slavery, it was easy to see that to keep such a part of the population out of the streets after a reasonable hour at night, preventing their unrestrained, promiscuous roving, is a great protection to them, as well as to the public peace. In attending evening worship, in visiting at any hour, a written pass is freely given; so that, after all, the bondage is theoretical, but still it is bondage. Is it an illustration, I asked myself, of other things in slavery, which are theoretically usurpations, but practically benevolent? . . .

The Children of the Slaves

But of all the touching sights of innocence and love appealing to you unconsciously for your best feelings of tenderness and affection, the colored young children have never been surpassed in my experience. Might I choose a class of my fellow-creatures to instruct and love, I should be drawn by my present affection toward them to none more readily than to these children of the slaves; nor should I expect my patience and affection to be more richly rewarded elsewhere. Extremes of disposition and character, of course, exist among them, as among others; but they are naturally as bright, affectionate, and capable as other children, while the ways in which your instructions impress them, the reasonings they excite, the remarks occasioned by them, are certainly peculiar. . . .

Going to meeting one Sabbath morning, a child, about eight years old, tripped along before me, with her hymn book and nicely-folded handkerchief in her hand, the flounces on her white dress very profuse, frilled ankles, light-colored boots, mohair mits, and sunshade, all showing that some fond heart and hand had bestowed great care upon her. Home and children came to mind. I thought of the feelings which that flower of the family perhaps occasioned. Is it the pastor's daughter? Is it the daughter of the lady whose garden I had walked in, but which bears no such plant as this? But my musings were interrupted by the child, who, on hearing footsteps behind, suddenly turned, and showed one of the blackest faces I ever saw. It was one of the thousands of intelligent, happy colored children, who on every Sabbath, in every southern town and city, make a northern visitor feel that some of his theoretical opinions at home, with regard to the actual condition of slavery, are much improved by practical views of it.

Labor and Privileges

Life on the cotton plantations is, in general, as severe with the colored people as agricultural life at the north. I have spent summers upon farms, however, where the owners and their hands excited my sympathy by toils to which the slaves on many plantations are strangers. Every thing depends upon the disposition of the master. It happened that I saw some of the best specimens, and heard descriptions of some of the very bad. In the rice swamps, malaria begets diseases and destroys life; in the sugar districts, at certain seasons, the process of manufacture requires labor, night and day, for a considerable time. There the different dispositions of the master affect the comfort of the laborers variously, as in all other situations.

But in the cotton-growing country, the labor, though extending in one form and another nearly through the year, yet taking each day's labor by itself, is no more toilsome than is performed by a hired field hand at the north; still the continuity of labor from February to the last part of December, with a slight intermission in midsummer, when the crop is "laid by," the stalks being matured, and the crop left to ripen, makes plantation life severe.

Some planters allow their hands a certain portion of the soil for their own culture, and give them stated times to work it; some prefer to allow them out of the whole crop a percentage equal to such a distribution of land; and some do nothing of the kind; but their hearts are made of the northern iron and the steel. It is the common law, however, with all who regard public opinion at the south, to allow their hands certain privileges and exemptions, such as long rest in the middle of the day, early dismission from the field at night, a half day occasionally, in addition to holidays, for which the colored people of all denominations are much indebted to the Episcopal church, whose festivals they celebrate with the largest liberty.

Slave Investments

They raise poultry, swine, melons; keep bees; catch fish; peddle brooms, and small articles of cabinet making; and, if they please, lay up the money, or spend it on their wives and children, or waste it for things hurtful, if there are white traders desperate enough to defy the laws made for such cases, and which are apt to be most rigorously executed. Some slaves are owners of bank and railroad shares. A slave woman, having had three hundred dollars stolen from her by a white man, her master was questioned in court as to the probability of her having had so much money. He said that he not unfrequently had borrowed fifty and a hundred dollars of her, and added, that she was always very strict as to his promised time of payment.

It is but fair, in this and all other cases, to describe the condition of things as commonly approved and prevailing; and when there are painful exceptions, it is but just to consider what is the public sentiment with regard to them. By this rule a visitor is made to feel that good and kind treatment of the slaves is the common law, subject, of course, to caprices and passions.

A strong public sentiment protects the person of the slave against annoyances and injuries. Boys and men cannot abuse another man's servant. Wrongs to his person are avenged. It amounts in many cases to a chivalric feeling, increased by a sense of utter meanness and cowardice in striking or insulting one who can not return insult for insult and blow for blow. Instances of this protective feeling greatly interested me. One was rather singular, indeed ludicrous, and made considerable sport; but it shows how far the feeling can proceed. A slave was brought before a mayor's court for some altercation in the street; the master privately requested the mayor to spare him from being chastised, and the mayor was strongly disposed to do so; but the testimony was too palpably against the servant, and he was whipped; in consequence of which the master sent a challenge to the mayor to fight a duel. . . .

Absence of Pauperism

Pauperism is prevented by slavery. This idea is absurd, no doubt, in the apprehension of many at the north, who think that slaves are, as a matter of course, paupers. Nothing can be more untrue.

Every slave has an inalienable claim in law upon his owner for support for the whole of life. He can not be thrust into an almshouse, he can not become a vagrant, he can not beg his living, he can not be wholly neglected when he is old and decrepit.

I saw a white-headed negro at the door of his cabin on a gentleman's estate, who had done no work for ten years. He enjoys all the privileges of the plantation, garden, and orchard; is clothed and fed as carefully as though he were useful. On asking him his age, he said he thought he "must be nigh a hundred;" that he was a servant to a gentleman in the army "when Washington fit Cornwallis and took him at Little York."

At a place called Harris's Neck, Georgia, there is a servant who has been confined to his bed with rheumatism thirty years, and no invalid has more reason to be grateful for attention and kindness. . . .

Thus the pauper establishments of the free States, the burden and care of immigrants, are almost entirely obviated at the south by the colored population. While we bow in submission to the duty of governing or maintaining certain foreigners, we can not any of us conceal that we have natural preferences and tastes as to the ways of doing good. In laboring for the present and future welfare of immigrants, we are subjected to evils of which we are ashamed to complain, but from which the south is enviably free. To have a neighborhood of a certain description of foreigners about your dwellings; to see a horde of them get possession of a respectable dwelling in a court, and thus force the residents, as they always do, to flee, it being impossible to live with comfort in close connection with them; to have all the senses assailed from their opened doors; to have your Sabbath utterly destroyed,—is not so agreeable as the presence of a respectable colored population, every individual of which is under the responsible oversight of a master or mistress, who restrains and governs him, and has a reputation to maintain in his respectable appearance and comfort, and keeps him from being a burden on the community....

Slaves Are Treated Well

George Fitzhugh was one of the most famous of all proslavery writers and intellectuals. In this excerpt from his book, Sociology of the South, *published in 1854, Fitzhugh claims that there is a natural affection between masters and their slaves.*

There is no rivalry, no competition to get employment among slaves, as among free laborers. Nor is there a war between master and slave. The master's interest prevents his reducing the slave's allowance or wages in infancy or sickness, for he might lose the slave by so doing. His feeling for his slave never permits him to stint him in old age. The slaves are all well fed, well clad, have plenty of fuel, and are happy. They have no dread of the future—no fear of want. A state of dependence is the only condition in which reciprocal affection can exist among human beings—the only situation in which the war of competition ceases, and peace, amity and good will arise. A state of independence always begets more or less of jealous rivalry and hostility. A man loves his children because they are weak, helpless and dependent. He loves his wife for similar reasons. When his children grow up and assert their independence, he is apt to transfer his affection to his grandchildren. He ceases to love his wife when she becomes masculine or rebellious; but slaves are always dependent, never the rivals of their master. Hence, though men are often found at variance with wife or children, we never saw one who did not like his slaves, and rarely a slave who was not devoted to his master.

The following case, that came to my knowledge, offers a good illustration of the views which many slaves take of their dependent condition. A colored woman with her children lived in a separate cabin belonging to her master, washing clothes for families in that place. She paid her master a percentage of her earnings, and had laid up more than enough to buy her freedom and that of her children. Why, as she might be made free, does she not use it rather?

She says that if she were to buy her freedom, she would have no one to take care of her for the rest of her life. Now her master is responsible for her support. She has no care about the future. Old age, sickness, poverty, do not trouble her. "I can indulge myself and children," she says, "in things which otherwise I could not get. If we want new things faster than mistress gets them for us, I can spare money to get them. If I buy my freedom, I cut myself off from the interests of the white folks in me. Now they feel that I belong to them, and people will look to see if they treat me well." Her only trouble is, that her master may die before her; then she will "have to be free."

Wages of Labor

One error which I had to correct in my own opinions was with regard to wages of labor. . . .

The accusation against slavery of working human beings without wages must be modified, if we give a proper meaning to the term *wages*. A stipulated sum per diem is our common notion of wages. A vast many slaves get wages in a better form than this—in provision for their support for the whole of life, with permission to earn something, and more or less according to the disposition of the masters and the ability of the slaves. A statement of the case, which perhaps is not of much value, was made by a slaveholder in this form: You hire a domestic by the week, or a laborer by the month, for certain wages, with food, lodging, perhaps clothing; I hire him for the term of life, becoming responsible for him in his decrepitude and old age. Leaving out of view the involuntariness on his part of the arrangement, he gets a good equivalent for his services; to his risk of being sold, and passing from hand to hand, there is an offset in the perpetual claim which he will have on some owner for maintenance all his days. . . .

The Features of Slavery

We have thus far looked at the slaves apart from the theory of slavery and from slave laws, and from their liability to suffering by being separated and sold. These features of slavery deserve to be considered by themselves; we can give them and things of that class a more just weight, and view the favorable circumstances of their condition with greater candor. This I have endeavored to do, describing every thing just as it struck me, leaving out of the question the evils of slavery, and abstract doctrines respecting it. . . .

Judging of them as you meet them in the streets, see them at work, or at church, or in their prayer meetings and singing meetings, or walking on the Sabbath or holidays, one must see that they are a happy people, their physical condition superior to that of very many of our operatives, far superior to the common Irish people in our cities, and immeasurably above thousands in Great

Britain. . . . It is obvious that if one can have all his present wants supplied, with no care about short crops, the markets, notes payable, bills due, be relieved from the necessity of planning and contriving, all the hard thinking being done for him by another, while useful and honorable employment fills his thoughts and hands, he is so far in a situation favorable to great comfort which will show itself in his whole outer man. Some will say, "This is the lowest kind of happiness." Yet it is all that a large portion of the race seek for; and few, except slaves, obtain it. Thus far I am constrained to say, that the relief which my feelings have experienced in going to the south and seeing the slaves at home is very great. Whatever else may be true of their condition, to whatever perils or sorrows, from causes not yet spoken of, they may be subjected, I feel like one who has visited a friend who is sick and reported to be destitute and extremely miserable, but has found him comfortable and happy. The sickness is there, but the patient is not only comfortable, but happy, if the ordinary proofs of it are to be taken. We may wonder that he should be; we may prove on paper that he can not be; but if the colored people of Savannah, Columbia, and Richmond are not, as a whole, a happy people, I have never seen any.

VIEWPOINT 4

"This system is one of robbery and cruel wrong, from beginning to end."

Slavery Is Oppressive

Peter Randolph (1825-1897)

Peter Randolph grew up a slave in Virginia. Emancipated with his fellow slaves upon his owner's death, Randolph settled in Boston and became a preacher. He published and sold *Sketches of a Slave Life,* based on his experiences as a slave, and he later wrote *From the Slave Cabin to the Pulpit: The Autobiography of Rev. Peter Randolph.*

Sketches of a Slave Life, originally published in 1847 and excerpted in this viewpoint, attempted to convince people of the cruelty of slavery and the necessity of its abolition. Randolph describes how slaves are mistreated by owners and overseers, and he attacks observers such as Nehemiah Adams for failing to see the truth about the cruelty of slavery.

The good Anti-Slavery men have very much to contend with, in their exertions for the cause of freedom. Many people will not believe their statements; call them unreasonable and fanatical. Some call them ignorant deceivers, who have never been out of their own home, and yet pretend to a knowledge of what is going on a thousand miles from them. Many call them dangerous members of society, sowing discord and distrust where there should be nought but peace and brotherly love. My Readers! give attention to the simple words of one who knows what he utters is truth; who is no stranger to the *beauties* of slavery or the *generosity* of the slaveholder. Spend a few moments in reading his statement in regard to the system of American slavery. Do not scoff or doubt. He writes what he does know, what he has seen and experienced; for he has been, for twenty-seven years of his life, a

92

slave; and he here solemnly pledges himself to TRUTH. Not once has he exaggerated, for he could not; the half of the woes and horrors of slavery, his feeble pen could not portray.

This system is one of robbery and cruel wrong, from beginning to end. It robs men and women of their liberty, lives, property, affections, and virtue, as the following pages will show. It is not only a source of misery to those in bonds, but those who fasten the chains are made wretched by it; for a state of war constantly exists between the master and servant. The one would enforce obedience to his every wish, however wrong and unjust; he would exact all the earnings of the slave, to the uttermost farthing. The latter feels the restraint and writhes under it; he sees the injustice, and at times attempts to assert his rights; but he must submit either to the command or the lash; obey implicitly he must.

The argument so often brought forward, that it would be for the interest of the owner to treat his slaves well, and of course he would not injure his own interests, may do for some, but not for the thinking and considerate. When does the angry tyrant reflect upon what, in the end, will be the best for him? To gratify his passion for the moment, to wreak out his revenge upon a helpless menial, is, at the time of excitement, his interest, and he will serve it well. . . .

Some will say, "The slaveholder cannot live without the negro; the climate will not permit the white man to toil there." Very well; admit it. Then let him grant to men their rights; make them free citizens; pay them justly for their honest toil, and see the consequences. All would be happier and better. Slavery enriches not the mind, heart, or soil where it abides; it curses and blights every thing it comes in contact with. Away, away with, tear up by the roots, these noxious weeds, which choke the growth of all fair plants, and sow in their stead the beauteous flowers of freedom, well watered by the pure waters of religion, and what a rich harvest will be yours!

Personal History

Before going into particulars relative to the horrors of slavery, I will give a little of my own history. I was owned, with eighty-one others, by a man named Edloe, and among them all, only myself could either read or write. . . .

My father did not belong to Edloe, but was owned by a Mr. George Harrison, whose plantation adjoined that of my master. Harrison made my father a slave-driver placing an overseer over him. He was allowed to visit my mother every Wednesday and every Saturday night. This was the time usually given to the slaves to see their wives. My father would often tell my mother how the white overseer had made him cruelly whip his fellows, until the blood ran down to the ground. All his days he had to follow this dreadful employment of flogging men, women and children, being placed in this helpless condition by the tyranny of his master. I used to think very hard of my father, and that he was a very cruel man; but when I knew that he could not help himself, I could not but alter my views and feelings in regard to his conduct. I was ten years old when he died.

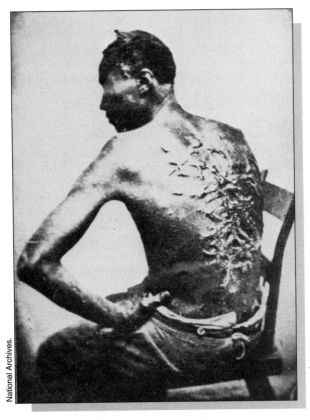

National Archives.

The hideous network of scars on the back of this former slave attests to the severe beatings many slaves endured.

When my father died, he left my mother with five children. We were all young at the time, and mother had no one to help take care of us. Her lot was very hard indeed. She had to work all the day for her owner, and at night for those who were dearer to her than life; for what was allowed her by Edloe was not sufficient for our wants. She used to get a little corn, without his knowledge, and boil it for us to satisfy our hunger. As for clothing, Edloe would give us a coarse suit once in three years; mother sometimes would beg the cast-off garments from the neighbors, to cover our nakedness; and when they had none to give, she would sit and cry over us, and pray to the God of the widow and fatherless for help and succor. At last, my oldest brother was sold from her, and carried where she never saw him again. She went mourning for him all her days, like a bird robbed of her young,—like Rachel bereft of her children, who would not be comforted, because they were not. She departed this life on the 27th of September, 1847, for that world "where the wicked cease from troubling, and the weary are at rest.". . . .

The Hours for Work

The slave goes to his work when he sees the daybreak in the morning, and works until dark at night. The slaves have their food carried to them in the field; they have one half hour to eat it in, in the winter, and one hour in the summer. Their time for eating is about eight in the morning, and one in the afternoon. Sometimes, they have not so much time given to them. The overseer stands by them until they have eaten, and then he orders them to work.

The slaves return to their huts at night, make their little fires, and lie down until they are awakened for another day of toil. No beds are given them to sleep on; if they have any, they find themselves. The women and the men all have to work on the farms together; they must fare alike in slavery. Husbands and wives must see all that happens to each other, and witness the sufferings of each. They must see their children polluted, without the power to prevent it. . . .

House Slaves

When the slave-master owns a great many slaves, ten or a dozen are always employed to wait on himself and family. They are not treated so cruelly as the field slaves; they are better fed and wear better clothing, because the master and his family always expect to have strangers visit them, and they want their servants to look well. These slaves eat from their master's table, wear broadcloth and calico; they wear ruffled-bosomed shirts, too,—such as Doctor Nehemiah Adams declares he saw while on his visit to the South, where he became so much in love with the "peculiar institution." These slaves, although dressed and fed better than others, have to suffer alike with those whose outward condition is worse. They are much to be compared to galvanized watches, which shine and resemble gold, but are far from being the true metal; so with these slaves who wait upon their masters at table—their broadcloth and calico look fine, but you may examine their persons, and find many a lash upon their flesh. They are sure of their whippings, and are sold the same as others.

Sometimes their masters change, and put them on the farm, that the overseers may whip them. Among those who wait upon the master, there is always one to watch the others, and report them to him. This slave is treated as well as his master, because it is for the master's interest that he does this. This slave he always carries with him when he visits the North; particularly such slaves as cannot be made to leave their master, because they are their master's watch-dog at home. So master can trust them. Before leaving, master always talks very kindly to them, and promises something very great for a present, if they are true to him until his return.

Slaves and the Irish People

Born a slave, Frederick Douglass escaped to freedom and became one of the foremost black leaders of his time. This excerpt is taken from a collection of his speeches entitled Lectures on American Slavery *and originally published in 1851.*

It is often said, by the opponents of the Anti-Slavery cause, that the condition of the people of Ireland is more deplorable than that of the American slaves. *Far* be it from me to underrate the sufferings of the Irish people. They have been long oppressed; and the same heart that prompts me to plead the cause of the American bond-man, makes it impossible for me *not* to sympathize with the oppressed of all lands. Yet I must say that there is no analogy between the two cases. The Irishman is poor, but he is *not* a slave. He *may* be in rags, but he is *not* a slave. He is still the master of his own body, and can say with the poet, "The hand of Douglass is his own."

These slaves know what they must say when asked as to their treatment at home, and of the treatment of their fellows. They leave their wives, their mothers, brothers and sisters, and children, toiling and being driven and whipped by the overseer, and tortured and insulted on every occasion.

Deception of the Slaveholder

All the slaves, as well as their owners, are addicted to drinking; so when the slaveholder wants to make a show of his niggers, (as he calls them,) he gives them rum to drink.

When the master knows a Northern man is to visit him, he gives orders to the overseer, and the overseer orders every slave to dress himself, and appear on the field. If the slaves have any best, they must put it on. Perhaps a man has worked hard, extra times all the year, and got his wife a fourpenny gown,—she must put it on, and go to the field to work. About the time the stranger is expected, a jug of rum is sent to the field, and every slave has just enough given him to make him act as if he was crazy.

When such a stranger as Rev. Dr. Adams appears with the master, he does not see the negroes, but the rum that is in them; and when he hears their hurrah, and sees their Jim-Crow actions, he takes it for granted that they are as happy as need be, and their condition could not be bettered.

The owner gives the visitor liberty to ask his "niggers" questions. He will ask them if they love their master, or wish to leave him. Poor slave will say, he would not leave his master for the world; but O, my reader! just let the poor slave get off, and he would be in Canada very soon, where the slaveholder dare not venture.

The slaves do not speak for themselves. The slaveholding master and his rum are working in their heads, speaking for slavery; and this is the way the slaveholder deceives his friend from the North.

Flogging

For whipping the slaves in Virginia, there are no rules. The slave receives from the slaveholder from fifty to five hundred lashes. The slave-owner would think fifty stripes an insult to the slave. If the slave is let off with fifty lashes, he must show a very good temper. Men, women, and children must be whipped alike on their bare backs, it being considered an honor to whip them over their clothes. The slaves are placed in a certain position when they are flogged, with sufficient management to hold them very still, so they cannot work their hands or feet, while they are "wooding them up," as they call it in Virginia.

Some of the slaves have to lie down on their stomachs, flat on the ground, and stretched out so as to keep their skin tight for the lash and thus lie until they receive as much as they choose to put on; if they move, they must receive so many lashes extra. When the slaveholder expects to give his slave five hundred lashes, he gives him about half at a time; then washes him down with salt and water, and then gives him the remainder of what he is to have. At such times, the slave-owner has his different liquors to drink, while he is engaged in draining the blood of the slave. So he continues to drink his rum and whip his victim. When he does not flog his victims on the ground, they are tied by their hands, and swung up to a great tree, just so the end of their toes may touch the ground. In this way, they receive what number of lashes they are destined to. The master has straw brought, that the blood may not touch his shoes. Ah, reader! this is true, every word of it. The poor slave is whipped till the blood runs down to the earth, and then he must work all day, cold or hot, from week's end to week's end. There are hundreds of slaves who change their skins nearly as often as they have a new suit of clothes. . . .

Food and Clothing

I shall now show what the slaves have to eat and wear. They have one pair of shoes for the year; if these are worn out in two months, they get no more that year, but must go barefooted the rest of the year, through cold and heat. The shoes are very poor ones, made by one of the slaves, and do not last more than two or three months. One pair of stockings is allowed them for the year; when these are gone, they have no more, although it is cold in Virginia for five months. They have one suit of clothes for the year. This is very poor indeed, and made by the slaves themselves on the plantation. It will not last more than three months, and then the poor slave gets no more from the slaveholder, if he go naked. This suit consists of one shirt, one pair of pants, one pair of socks, one pair of shoes, and no vest at all. The slave has a hat given him once in two years; when this is worn out, he gets no more from the slaveholder, but must go bareheaded till he can get one somewhere else. Perhaps the slave will get him a skin of some kind, and make him a hat.

The food of the slaves is this: Every Saturday night, they receive two pounds of bacon, and one peck and a half of corn meal, to last the men through the week. The women have one half pound of meat, and one peck of meal, and the children one half peck each. When this is gone, they can have no more till the end of the week. This is very little food for the slaves. They have to beg when they can; when they cannot, they must suffer. They are not allowed to go off the plantation; if they do, and are caught, they are whipped very severely, and what they have begged is taken from them. . . .

City and Town Slaves

The slaves in the cities (Petersburg, Richmond and Norfolk, in Virginia) do not fare so hard as on the plantations, where they have farming work to do. Most of the town and city slaves are hired out, to bring in money to their owners. They often have the privilege of hiring themselves out, by paying their owners so much, at stated times,—say once a week, or once a month. Many of them are employed in factories and work at trades. They do very well, for if they are industrious, they can earn considerably more than is exacted of them by their owners. All can dress well, have comfortable homes, and many can read and write. Many of them lay up money to purchase either their own freedom or that of some dear one. These slaves are not subjected to the lash as the poor creatures upon the plantations are, for their owners would feel (as every man should feel, in the true sense) their dignity fallen, their nobility sullied, by raising the whip over their human property.

Cruelty and Chance

Lydia Maria Child wrote numerous books, pamphlets, and articles for the abolitionist movement including the one that is excerpted here, An Appeal in Favor of That Class of Americans Called Africans, *published in 1836.*

The following occurred near Natchez, and was told to me by a highly intelligent man, who, being a diplomatist and a courtier, was very likely to make the best of national evils: A planter had occasion to send a female slave some distance on an errand. She did not return so soon as he expected, and he grew angry. At last he gave orders that she should be severely whipped when she came back. When the poor creature arrive, she pleaded for mercy, saying she had been so very ill, that she was obliged to rest in the fields; but she was ordered to receive another dozen lashes, for having had the impudence to speak. She died at the whipping-post; nor did she perish alone—a new-born baby died with her. The gentleman who told me this fact, witnessed the poor creature's funeral. It is true, the master was universally blamed and shunned for the cruel deed; but the laws were powerless.

I shall be told that such examples as these are of rare occurrence; and I have no doubt that instances of excessive severity are far from being common. I believe that a large proportion of masters are as kind to their slaves as they can be, consistently with keeping them in bondage; but it must be allowed that this, to make the best of it, is very stinted kindness. And let it never be forgotten that the negro's fate depends entirely on the character of his master; and it is a mere matter of chance whether he fall into merciful or unmerciful hands; his happiness, nay, his very life, depends on chance.

Slavery, as seen here by the casual observer, might be supposed not to be so hard as one would imagine, after all the outcry of philanthropists, who "sit in their chimney-corners amid the Northern hills, and conjure up demoniac shapes and fiendish spirits, bearing the name of slaveholders." But Slavery is *Slavery,* wherever it is found. Dress it up as you may, in the city or on the plantation, the human being must feel that which binds him to another's will. Be the fetters of silk, or hemp, or iron, all alike warp the mind and goad the soul.

The city slave may escape the evil eye and cruel lash of the overseer, but if he offend the all-important master, there is retribution for him. "Hand this note to Capt. Heart," (of Norfolk,) or "Capt. Thwing," (of Petersburg,)—and well does the shrinking slave know what is to follow. These last-mentioned gentlemen *give* their time to, and improve their talents by, laying the lash upon the naked backs of men and women!

Ah, my readers! take what side you will of slavery,—Dr. Adams's "South side," or the Abolitionist's North side,—there is but *one side*, and that is dark, *dark*. You may think you see bright spots, but look at the surroundings of those spots, and you will see nothing but gloom and darkness. While toiling industriously, and living with a dear family in comparative comfort and happiness, the city slave (whose lot is thought to be so easy) suddenly finds himself upon the auction-block, knocked down to the highest bidder, and carried far and forever from those dearer to him than life; a beloved wife, and tender, helpless children are all bereft, in a moment, of husband, father and protector, by a fate worse than death;—and for what? To gratify some spirit of revenge, or add to the weight of the already well-filled purse of some *Christian white man*, who professes ownership in his fellow-man. Wretch! you may command, for a season, the bones and sinews of that brother, so infinitely your superior; but, remember! that form is animated by a never-dying spirit; it will not always slumber; a God of infinite love and justice reigns over all, and beholds your unholy, inhuman traffic! Believe you, justice will triumph, the guilty shall not go unpunished on the earth; the righteous are to be recompensed, *much more the wicked and the sinner.*

"We had such a good time, and everybody cried when the Yankees cried out: 'Free.'"

A Positive Reminiscence of Slavery

Millie Evans (1849?—?)

Millie Evans was a slave in North Carolina from the time of her birth around 1849 until the Civil War. She was interviewed in 1936 as part of the slave narrative program of the Federal Writers' Project, which in the 1930s interviewed hundreds of ex-slaves between the ages of 75 and 100. B.A. Botkin, director of the project, later compiled and edited these narratives into a collection titled *Lay My Burden Down.*

In the following viewpoint, Evans describes her life under slavery. She emphasizes what she remembered as positive aspects of slave life, including the kindness of her masters and the difficulties she endured following emancipation.

Was born in 1849, but I don't know just when. My birthday comes in fodder-pulling time 'cause my ma said she was pulling up till 'bout a hour 'fore I was born. Was born in North Carolina and was a young lady at the time of surrender.

I don't 'member Old Master's name; all I 'member is that we call 'em Old Master and Old Mistress. They had 'bout a hundred niggers, and they was rich. Master always tended the men, and Mistress tended to us.

Better Living Then

Every morning 'bout four 'clock Old Master would ring the bell for us to git up by, and you could hear that bell ringing all over the plantation. I can hear it now. It would go ting-a-ling, ting-a-ling, and I can see 'em now stirring in Carolina. I git so lonesome when I think 'bout times we used to have. 'Twas better living back yonder than now.

I stayed with my ma every night, but my mistress raised me. My ma had to work hard, so every time Old Mistress thought we little black children was hungry 'tween meals she would call us up to the house to eat. Sometime she would give us johnnycake and plenty of buttermilk to drink with it. They had a long trough for us that they would keep so clean. They would fill this trough with buttermilk, and all us children would git round the trough and drink with our mouths and hold our johnnycake with our hands. I can just see myself drinking now. It was so good. There was so many black folks to cook for that the cooking was done outdoors. Greens was cooked in a big black washpot just like you boils clothes in now. And sometime they would crumble bread in the potlicker and give us spoons, and we would stand round the pot and eat. When we et our regular meals, the table was set under a chinaberry tree with a oilcloth tablecloth, and when they called us to the table they would ring the bell. But we didn't eat out of plates. We et out of gourds and had homemade wood spoons. And we had plenty to eat. Whooo-eee! Just plenty to eat. Old Master's folks raised plenty of meat, and they raise their sugar, rice, peas, chickens, eggs, cows, and just everything good to eat.

Every evening at three 'clock Old Mistress would call all us litsy bitsy children in, and we would lay down on pallets and have to go to sleep. I can hear her now singing to us pickaninnies. . . .

When I got big 'nough I nursed my mistress' baby. When the baby go to sleep in the evening, I would put it in the cradle and lay down by the cradle and go to sleep. I played a heap when I was little. We played Susanna Gal, jump rope, calling cows, running, jumping, skipping, and just everything we could think of. When I got big 'nough to cook, I cooked then.

The kitchen of the big house was built 'way off from the house, and we cooked on a great big old fireplace. We had swing pots and would swing 'em over the fire and cook and had a big old skillet with legs on it. We call it a oven and cooked bread and cakes in it.

Sundays

We had the best mistress and master in the world, and they was Christian folks, and they taught us to be Christian-like too. Every Sunday morning Old Master would have all us niggers to the house while he would sing and pray and read the Bible to us all. Old Master taught us not to be bad; he taught us to be good; he told us to never steal nor to tell false tales and not to do anything that was bad. He said: "You will reap what you sow, that you sow it single and reap double." I learnt that when I was a little child, and I ain't forgot it yet. When I got grown I went the Baptist way. God called my pa to preach and Old Master let him preach in the kitchen and in the back yard under the trees. On preaching day Old Master took his whole family and all the slaves to church with him.

We had log schoolhouses in them days, and folks learnt more than they does in the bricks today.

Down in the quarters every black family had a one- or two-room log cabin. We didn't have no floors in them cabins. Nice dirt floors was the style then, and we used sage brooms. Took a string and tied the sage together and had a nice broom outen that. We would gather broom sage for our winter brooms just like we gathered our other winter stuff. We kept our dirt floors swept as clean and white. And our bed was big and tall and had little beds to push under there. They was all little enough to go under the other and in the daytime we would push 'em all under the big one and make heaps of room. Our beds was stuffed with hay and straw and shucks, and, believe me, child, they sure slept good.

When the boys would start to the quarters from the field, they would get a turn of lider [lightwood] knots. I 'specks you knows 'em as pine knots. That was what we use for light. When our fire went out, we had no fire. Didn't know nothing 'bout no matches. To start a fire we would take a skillet lid and a piece of cotton and a flint rock. Lay the cotton on the skillet lid and take a piece of iron and beat the flint rock till the fire would come. Sometime we would beat for thirty minutes before the fire would come and start the cotton, then we would light our pine.

Up at the big house we didn't use lider knots but used tallow candles for lights. We made the candles from tallow that we took from cows. We had molds and would put string in there and leave the end sticking out to light and melt the tallow and pour it down around the string in the mold.

We use to play at night by moonlight, and I can recollect singing with the fiddle. Oh, Lord, that fiddle could almost talk, and I can hear it ringing now. Sometime we would dance in the moonlight too.

Raising Cotton

Old Master raised lots of cotton, and the womenfolks carded and spun and wove cloth, then they dyed it and made clothes. And we knit all the stockings we wore. They made their dye too, from different kinds of bark and leaves and things. They would take the bark and boil it and strain it up and let it stand a day, then wet the 'terial in cold water and shake it out and drop in the boiling dye and let it set 'bout twenty minutes, then take it out and hang it up and let it dry right out of that dye. Then rinse it in cold water and let it dry, then it would be ready to make.

I'll tell you how to dye. A little beech bark dyes slate color, set with copperas. Hickory bark and bay leaves dye yellow, set with chamber lye; bamboo dyes turkey red, set color with copperas. Pine straw dyes purple, set color with chamber lye. To dye cloth brown we would take the cloth and put it in the water where leather had been tanned and let it soak, then set the color with apple vinegar. And we dyed blue with indigo and set the color with alum.

If All Slaves Had Belonged to White Folks Like Ours

Harriet McFarlin Payne, born a slave in the 1850s, was interviewed in the 1930s as part of the Federal Writers' Project slave narrative program. Her narrative is taken from the book Lay My Burden Down, *published in 1989 and edited by B.A. Botkin.*

My mammy and daddy belonged to Colonel Jesse Chaney, much of a gentleman, and his wife, Miss Sallie, was the best mistress anybody ever had. She was a Christian. I can hear her praying yet! She wouldn't let one of her slaves hit a tap on Sunday. They must rest and go to church. They had preaching at the cabin of some one of the slaves, and in the summertime sometimes they had it out in the shade under the trees. Yes, and the slaves on each plantation had their own church. They didn't go gallivanting over the neighborhood or country like niggers do now. Colonel Chaney had lots and lots of slaves, and all their houses were in a row, all one-room cabins. Everything happened in that one room—birth, sickness, death, and everything, but in them days niggers kept their houses clean and their door yards too. These houses where they lived was called "the quarters." I used to love to walk down by that row of houses. It looked like a town, and late of an evening as you'd go by the doors you could smell meat a-frying, coffee making, and good things cooking. We were fed good and had plenty clothes to keep us dry and warm. . . .

If all slaves had belonged to white folks like ours, there wouldn't been any freedom wanted.

We wore drawers made out of domestic that come down longer than our dresses, and we wore seven petticoats with sleeves in them petticoats in the winter, and the boys wore big old long shirts. They didn't know nothing 'bout no britches till they was great big, just went round in they shirttails. And we all wore shoes 'cause my pa made shoes.

Master taught Pa to make shoes, and the way he done, they killed a cow and took the hide and tanned it. The way they tanned it was to take red oak bark and put in vats made something like troughs that held water. First he would put in a layer of leather and a layer of oak ashes and a layer of leather and a layer of oak ashes till he got it all in and cover with water. After that he let it soak till the hair come off the hide. Then he would take the hide out, and it was ready for tanning. Then the hide was put to soak in with the red oak bark. It stayed in the water till the hide turned tan, then Pa took the hide out of the red oak dye, and it was a pretty tan. It didn't have to soak long. Then he would get his pattern and cut and make tan shoes outen the tanned hides. We called 'em brogans.

Other Crops

They planted indigo, and it growed just like wheat. When it got ripe, they gathered it, and we would put it in a barrel and let it soak 'bout a week, then we would take the indigo stems out and squeeze all the juice out of 'em and put the juice back in the barrel and let it stand 'bout 'nother week, then we just stirred and stirred one whole day. We let it set three or four days, then drained the water off and left the settlings, and the settlings was blueing just like we have these days. We cut ours in little blocks, and we dyed clothes with it too.

We made vinegar out of apples. Took overripe apples and ground 'em up and put 'em in a sack and let drip. Didn't add no water, and when it got through dripping we let it sour and strained and let it stand for six months and had some of the best vinegar ever made.

We had homemade tubs and didn't have no washboards. We had a block and battling stick. We put our clothes in soak, then took 'em out of soak and lay them on the block and take the battling stick and battle the dirt out of 'em. We mostly used rattan vines for clotheslines, and they made the best clotheslines they was.

Old Master raised big patches of t'baccy, and when they gather it they let it dry and then put it in 'lasses. After the 'lasses dripped off, then they roll it up and twisted it and let it dry in the sun ten or twelve days. It sure was ready for some grand chewing and it was sweet and stuck together so you could chew and spit and 'joy it.

The way we got our perfume we took rose leaves, Cape jasmines, and sweet basil and laid 'em with our clothes and let 'em stay three or four days, then we had good-smelling clothes that would last too.

When there was distressful news Master would ring the bell. When the niggers in the field would hear the bell, everyone would listen and wonder what the trouble was. You'd see 'em stirring too. They would always ring the bell at twelve 'clock.

Sometime then they would think it was something serious and they would stand up straight, but if they could see they shadow right under 'em they would know it was time for dinner.

The reason so many white folks was rich was they made money and didn't have nothing to do but save it. They made money and raised everything they used, and just didn't have no use for money. Didn't have no banks in them days, and Master buried his money.

Cleaning the Floors

The floors in the big house was so pretty and white. We always kept them scoured good. We didn't know what it was to use soap. We just took oak ashes out of the fireplace and sprinkled them on the floor and scoured with a corn-shuck mop. Then we would sweep the ashes off and rinse two times and let it dry. When it dried it was the cleanest floor they was. To make it white, clean sand was sprinkled on the floor, and we let it stay a couple of days, then the floor would be too clean to walk on. The way we dried the floor was with a sack and a rag. We would get down on our knees and dry it so dry.

I 'member one night one of Old Master's girls was going to get married. That was after I was big 'nough to cook, and we was sure doing some cooking. Some of the niggers of the place just naturally would steal, so we cook a big cake of corn bread and iced it all pretty and put it out to cool, and some of 'em stole it. This way Old Master found out who was doing the stealing 'cause it was such a joke on 'em they had to tell.

All Old Master's niggers was married by the white preacher, but he had a neighbor who would marry his niggers hisself. He would say to the man: "Do you want this woman?" and to the girl, "Do you want this boy?" Then he would call the Old Mistress to fetch the broom, and Old Master would hold one end and Old Mistress the other and tell the boy and girl to jump this broom, and he would say: "That's your wife." They called marrying like that jumping the broom.

Being Free

Now, child, I can't 'member everything I done in them days, but we didn't have to worry 'bout nothing. Old Mistress was the one to worry. Twasn't then like it is now, no 'twasn't. We had such a good time, and everybody cried when the Yankees cried out: "Free." T'other niggers say they had a hard time 'fore they was free, but 'twas then like 'tis now. If you had a hard time, we done it ourselves.

Old Master didn't want to part with his niggers, and the niggers didn't want to part with Old Master, so they thought by coming to Arkansas they would have a chance to keep 'em. So they got on their way. We loaded up our wagons and put up our wagon sheet, and we had plenty to eat and plenty of horse feed. We traveled 'bout fifteen or twenty miles a day and would stop and camp at night. We would cook enough in the morning to last all day. The cows was drove together. Some was gentle and some was not, and did they have a time. I mean, they *had* a time. While we was on our way, Old Master died, and three of the slaves died too. We buried the slaves there, but we camped while Old Master was carried back to North Carolina. When Old Mistress come back, we started on to Arkansas and reached here safe, but when we got here we found freedom here too. Old Mistress begged us to stay with her, and we stayed till she died, then they took her back to Carolina. There wasn't nobody left but Miss Nancy, and she soon married and left, and I lost track of her and Mr. Tom.

VIEWPOINT 6

"Slavery was the worst days was ever seed in the world."

A Negative Reminiscence of Slavery

Mary Reynolds (1837?–?)

Mary Reynolds was born a slave in Louisiana around 1837. She was interviewed at the age of 100 as part of the 1930s Federal Writers' Project. This interview and others were published as a collection called *Lay My Burden Down* in 1989. In the following viewpoint, she describes her life under slavery, including her relationship with her masters, working in the cotton fields, slave runaways, and other aspects of the slave life.

My paw's name was Tom Vaughn, and he was from the North, born free man and lived and died free to the end of his days. He wasn't no educated man, but he was what he calls himself a piano man. He told me once he lived in New York and Chicago and he built the insides of pianos and knew how to make them play in tune. He said some white folks from the South told he if he'd come with them to the South he'd find a lot of work to do with pianos in them parts, and he come off with them.

He saw my maw on the place and her man was dead. He told my massa he'd buy my maw and her three children with all the money he had, iffen he'd sell her. But Massa was never one to sell any but the old niggers who was past working in the fields and past their breeding times. So my paw married my maw and works the fields, same as any other nigger. They had six gals: Martha and Panela and Josephine and Ellen and Katherine and me.

I was born same time as Miss Dora. Massa's first wife and my

108

maw come to their time right together. Miss Dora's maw died, and they brung Miss Dora to suck with me. It's a thing we ain't never forgot. My maw's name was Sallie and Miss Dora always looked with kindness on my maw. We sucked till we was a fair size and played together, which wasn't no common thing. None the other little niggers played with the white children. But Miss Dora loved me so good.

I was just 'bout big 'nough to start playing with a broom to go 'bout sweeping up and not even half doing it when Massa sold me. They was a old white man in Trinity, and his wife died and he didn't have chick or child or slave or nothing. Massa sold me cheap, 'cause he didn't want Miss Dora to play with no nigger young-un. That old man bought me a big doll and went off and left me all day, with the door open. I just sot on the floor and played with that doll. I used to cry. He'd come home and give me something to eat and then go to bed, and I slept on the foot of the bed with him. I was scared all the time in the dark. He never did close the door.

Miss Dora pined and sickened. Massa done what he could, but they wasn't no pertness in her. She got sicker and sicker, and Massa brung 'nother doctor. He say, "You little gal is grieving the life out her body, and she sure gwine die iffen you don't do something 'bout it." Miss Dora says over and over, "I wants Mary." Massa say to the doctor, "That a little nigger young-un I done sold." The doctor tells him he better git me back iffen he wants to save the life of his child. Massa has to give a big plenty more to git me back than what he sold me for, but Miss Dora plumps up right off and grows into fine health.

Then Massa marries a rich lady from Mississippi, and they had children for company to Miss Dora and seem like for a time she forgits me.

A Big Plantation

Massa wasn't no piddling man. He was a man of plenty. He had a big house with no more style to it than a crib, but it could room plenty people. He was a medicine doctor, and they was rooms in the second story for sick folks what come to lay in. It would take two days to go all over the land he owned. He had cattle and stock and sheep and more'n a hundred slaves and more besides. He bought the best of niggers near every time the speculators come that way. He'd make a swap of the old ones and give money for young ones what could work.

He raised corn and cotton and cane and 'taters and goobers, 'sides the peas and other feeding for the niggers. I 'member I held a hoe handle mighty unsteady when they put a old woman to larn me and some other children to scrape the fields. That old woman would be in a frantic. She'd show me and then turn 'bout to show some other little nigger, and I'd have the young corn cut clean as the grass. She say, "For the love of God, you better larn it right, or Solomon will beat the breath out you body." Old Man Solomon was the nigger driver.

My Master Used to Whip Me

Ella Wilson was one of the ex-slaves interviewed in the 1930s as part of the Federal Writers' Project on slave narratives. Wilson's interview was published in the book To Be a Slave, *edited by Julius Lester and published in 1968.*

My master used to throw me in a buck and whip me. He would put my hands together and tie them. Then he would strip me naked. Then would make me squat down. Then he would run a stick through behind my knees and in front of my elbows. My knee was up against my chest. My hands was tied together just in front of my shins. The stick between my arms and my knees held me in a squat. That's what they call a buck. You couldn't stand up and you couldn't get your feet out. You couldn't do nothing but just squat there and take what he put on. You couldn't move no way at all. Just try to. You just fall over on one side and have to stay there till you were turned over by him. He would whip me on one side till that was sore and full of blood and then he would whip me on the other side till that was all tore up. I got a scar big as the place my ol' mistress hit me. She took a bull whip once. The bull whip had a piece of iron in the handle of it—and she got mad. She was so mad she took the whip and hit me over the head with the butt end of it and the blood flew. It ran all down my back and dripped off my heels.

Slavery was the worst days was ever seed in the world. They was things past telling, but I got the scars on my old body to show to this day. I seed worse than what happened to me. I seed them put the men and women in the stock with they hands screwed down through holes in the board and they feets tied together and they naked behinds to the world. Solomon the overseer beat them with a big whip and Massa look on. The niggers better not stop in the fields when they hear them yelling. They cut the flesh 'most to the bones, and some they was when they taken them out of stock and put them on the beds, they never got up again.

When a nigger died, they let his folks come out the fields to see him afore he died. They buried him the same day, take a big plank and bust it with a ax in the middle 'nough to bend it back, and put the dead nigger in betwixt it. They'd cart them down to the graveyard on the place and not bury them deep 'nough that buzzards wouldn't come circling round. Niggers mourns now, but in them days they wasn't no time for mourning.

The conch shell blowed afore daylight, and all hands better git out for roll call, or Solomon bust the door down and git them out. It was work hard, git beatings, and half-fed. They brung the victuals and water to the fields on a slide pulled by a old mule. Plenty times they was only a half barrel water and it stale and hot, for all us niggers on the hottest days. Mostly we ate pickled pork and corn bread and peas and beans and 'taters. They never was as much as we needed.

The times I hated most was picking cotton when the frost was on the bolls. My hands git sore and crack open and bleed. We'd have a little fire in the fields, and iffen the ones with tender hands couldn't stand it no longer, we'd run and warm our hands a little bit. When I could steal a 'tater, I used to slip it in the ashes, and when I'd run to the fire I'd take it out and eat it on the sly.

In the cabins it was nice and warm. They was built of pine boarding, and they was one long row of them up the hill back of the big house. Near one side of the cabins was a fireplace. They'd bring in two-three big logs and put on the fire, and they'd last near a week. The beds was made out of puncheons fitted in holes bored in the wall, and planks laid 'cross them poles. We had ticking mattresses filled with corn shucks. Sometimes the men build chairs at night. We didn't know much 'bout having nothing, though.

Sometimes Massa let niggers have a little patch. They'd raise 'taters or goobers. They liked to have them to help fill out on the victuals. 'Taters roasted in the ashes was the best-tasting eating I ever had. I could die better satisfied to have just one more 'tater roasted in hot ashes. The niggers had to work the patches at night and dig the 'taters and goobers at night. Then if they wanted to sell any in town, they'd have to git a pass to go. They had to go at night, 'cause they couldn't ever spare a hand from the fields.

Once in a while they'd give us a little piece of Saturday evening to wash out clothes in the branch. We hanged them on the ground in the woods to dry. They was a place to wash clothes from the well, but they was so many niggers all couldn't git round to it on Sundays. When they'd git through with the clothes on Saturday evenings, the niggers which sold they goobers and 'taters brung fiddles and guitars and come out and play. The others clap they hands and stomp they feet and we young-uns cut a step round. I was plenty biggity and liked to cut a step.

Prayer Meetings

We was scared of Solomon and his whip, though, and he didn't like frolicking. He didn't like for us niggers to pray, either. We never heared of no church, but us have praying in the cabins.

We'd set on the floor and pray with our heads down low and sing low, but if Solomon heared he'd come and beat on the wall with the stock of his whip. He'd say, "I'll come in there and tear the hide off you backs." But some the old niggers tell us we got to pray to God that He don't think different of the blacks and the whites. I know that Solomon is burning in hell today, and it pleasures me to know it.

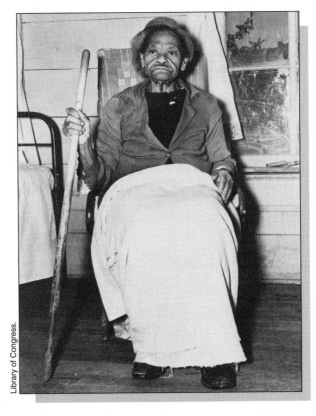

Library of Congress.

Mary Reynolds, photographed in 1937 in Dallas, Texas.

Once my maw and paw taken me and Katherine after night to slip to 'nother place to a praying and singing. A nigger man with white beard told us a day am coming when niggers only be slaves of God. We prays for the end of tribulation and the end of beatings and for shoes that fit our feet. We prayed that us niggers could have all we wanted to eat and special for fresh meat. Some the old ones say we have to bear all, 'cause that all we can do. Some say they was glad to the time they's dead, 'cause they'd rather rot in the ground than have the beatings. What I hated most was when they'd beat me and I didn't know what they beat me for, and I hated them stripping me naked as the day I was born.

When we's coming back from that praying, I thunk I heared the nigger dogs and somebody on horseback. I say, "Maw, it's them nigger hounds and they'll eat us up." You could hear them old hounds and sluts a-baying. Maw listens and say, "Sure 'nough, them dogs am running and God help us!" Then she and Paw talk and they take us to a fence corner and stands us up 'gainst the rails and say don't move and if anyone comes near, don't breathe loud. They went to the woods, so the hounds chase them and not git us. Me and Katherine stand there, holding hands, shaking so we can hardly stand. We hears the hounds come nearer, but we don't move. They goes after Paw and Maw, but they circles round to the cabins and gits in. Maw say it the power of God.

In them days I weared shirts, like all the young-uns. They had collars and come below the knees and was split up the sides. That's all we weared in hot weather. The men weared jeans and the women gingham. Shoes was the worstest trouble. We weared rough russets when it got cold, and it seem powerful strange they'd never git them to fit. Once when I was a young gal, they got me a new pair and all brass studs in the toes. They was too little for me, but I had to wear them. The brass trimmings cut into my ankles and them places got miserable bad. I rubs tallow in them sore places and wrops rags round them and my sores got worser and worser. The scars are there to this day.

I wasn't sick much, though. Some the niggers had chills and fever a lot, but they hadn't discovered so many diseases then as now. Massa give sick niggers ipecac and asafetida and oil and turpentine and black fever pills.

The Master's Children

They was a cabin called the spinning-house and two looms and two spinning wheels going all the time, and two nigger women sewing all the time. It took plenty sewing to make all the things for a place so big. Once Massa goes to Baton Rouge and brung back a yaller gal dressed in fine style. She was a seamster nigger. He builds her a house 'way from the quarters, and she done fine sewing for the whites. Us niggers knowed the doctor took a black woman quick as he did a white and took any on his place he wanted, and he took them often. But mostly the children born on the place looked like niggers. Aunt Cheyney always say four of hers was Massa's, but he didn't give them no mind. But this yaller gal breeds so fast and gits a mess of white young-uns. She larnt them fine manners and combs out they hair.

Oncet two of them goes down the hill to the dollhouse, where the Missy's children am playing. They wants to go in the doll-house and one the Missy's boys say, "That's for white children." They say, "We ain't no niggers, 'cause we got the same daddy you has, and he comes to see us near every day and fotches us clothes and things from town." They is fussing, and Missy is listening out her chamber window. She heard them white niggers say, "He is our daddy and we call him daddy when he comes to our house to see our mama."

No Good Times

Jenny Proctor was born a slave in Alabama in 1850. She was interviewed in Texas in the 1930s as part of the Federal Writers' Project slave narrative program. This narrative was published in the collection Lay My Burden Down *in 1989.*

I's hear tell of them good slave days, but I ain't never see no good times then. My mother's name was Lisa, and when I was a very small child I hear that driver going from cabin to cabin as early as 3 o'clock in the morning, and when he comes to our cabin he say, "Lisa, Lisa, git up from there and git that breakfast." My mother, she was cook, and I don't recollect nothing 'bout my father. If I had any brothers and sisters I didn't know it. We had old ragged huts made out of poles and some of the cracks chinked up with mud and moss and some of them wasn't. We didn't have no good beds, just scaffolds nailed up to the wall out of poles and the old ragged bedding throwed on them. That sure was hard sleeping, but even that feel good to our weary bones after them long hard days' work in the field. I 'tended to the children when I was a little gal and tried to clean the house just like Old Miss tells me to. Then soon as I was ten years old, Old Master, he say, "Git this here nigger to that cotton patch."

When Massa come home that evening, his wife hardly say nothing to him, and he ask her what the matter, and she tells him, "Since you asks me, I'm studying in my mind 'bout them white young-uns of that yaller nigger wench from Baton Rouge." He say, "Now, honey, I fotches that gal just for you, 'cause she a fine seamster." She say, "It look kind of funny they got the same kind of hair and eyes as my children, they got a nose look like yours." He say, "Honey, you just paying 'tention to talk of little children that ain't got no mind to what they say." She say, "Over in Mississippi I got a home and plenty with my daddy, and I got that in my mind."

Well, she didn't never leave, and Massa bought her a fine, new span of surrey hosses. But she don't never have no more children, and she ain't so cordial with the Massa. That yaller gal has more white young-uns, but they don't never go down the hill no more to the big house.

Aunt Cheyney was just out of bed with a suckling baby one time, and she run away. Some say that was 'nother baby of

Massa's breeding. She don't come to the house to nurse her baby, so they misses her and Old Solomon gits the nigger hounds and takes her trail. They gits near her and she grabs a limb and tries to hist herself in a tree, but them dogs grab her and pull her down. The men hollers them onto her, and the dogs tore her naked and et the breasts plumb off her body. She got well and lived to be a old woman, but 'nother woman has to suck her baby, and she ain't got no sign of breasts no more.

They give all the niggers fresh meat on Christmas and a plug tobacco all round. The highest cotton-picker gits a suit of clothes, and all the women what had twins that year gits a outfitting of clothes for the twins and a double, warm blanket.

Seems like after I got bigger, I 'member more and more niggers run away. They's 'most always cotched. Massa used to hire out his niggers for wage hands. One time he hired me and a nigger boy, Turner, to work for some ornery white trash, name of Kidd. One day Turner goes off and don't come back. Old Man Kidd say I knowed 'bout it, and he tied my wrists together and stripped me. He hanged me by the wrists from a limb on a tree and spraddled my legs round the trunk and tied my feet together. Then he beat me. He beat me worser then I ever been beat before, and I faints dead away. When I come to I'm in bed. I didn't care so much iffen I died.

I didn't know 'bout the passing of time, but Miss Dora come to me. Some white folks done git word to her. Mr. Kidd tries to talk hisself out of it, but Miss Dora fotches me home when I'm well 'nough to move. She took me in a cart and my maw takes care of me. Massa looks me over good and says I'll git well, but I'm ruint for breeding children.

After while I taken a notion to marry and Massa and Missy marries us same as all the niggers. They stands inside the house with a broom held crosswise of the door and we stands outside. Missy puts a little wreath on my head they kept there, and we steps over the broom into the house. Now, that's all they was to the marrying. After freedom I gits married and has it put in the book by a preacher.

The Yankees Arrive

One day we was working in the fields and hears the conch shell blow, so we all goes to the back gate of the big house. Massa am there. He say, "Call the roll for every nigger big 'nough to walk, and I wants them to go to the river and wait there. They's gwine be a show and I wants you to see it." They was a big boat down there, done built up on the sides with boards and holes in the boards and a big gun barrel sticking through every hole. We ain't never seed nothing like that. Massa goes up the plank onto the

115

boat and comes out on the boat porch. He say, "This am a Yankee boat." He goes inside and the water wheels starts moving and that boat goes moving up the river, and they says it goes to Natchez.

The boat wasn't more'n out of sight when a big drove of soldiers comes into town. They say they's Federals. More'n half the niggers goes off with them soldiers, but I goes on back home 'cause of my old mammy.

Next day them Yankees is swarming the place. Some the niggers wants to show them something. I follows to the woods. The niggers shows them soldiers a big pit in the ground, bigger'n a big house. It is got wooden doors that lifts up, but the top am sodded and grass growing on it, so you couldn't tell it. In that pit is stock, hosses and cows and mules and money and chinaware and silver and a mess of stuff them soldiers takes.

We just sot on the place doing nothing till the white folks comes home. Miss Dora come out to the cabin and say she wants to read a letter to my mammy. It come from Louis, which is brother to my mammy, and he done follow the Federals to Galveston. A white man down there write the letter for him. It am tored in half and Massa done that. The letter say Louis am working in Galveston and wants Mammy to come with us, and he'll pay our way. Miss Dora say Massa swear, "Damn Louis. I ain't gwine tell Sallie nothing," and he starts to tear the letter up. But she won't let him, and she reads it to Mammy.

After a time Massa takes all his niggers what wants to Texas with him and Mammy gits to Galveston and dies there. I goes with Massa to the Tennessee Colony and then to Navasota. Miss Dora marries and goes to El Paso. She wrote and told me to come to her, and I always meant to go.

Life After Slavery

My husband and me farmed round for times, and then I done housework and cooking for many years. I come to Dallas and cooked for seven year for one white family. My husband died years ago. I guess Miss Dora been dead these long years. I always kept my years by Miss Dora's years, 'count we is born so close.

I been blind and 'most helpless for five year. I'm gitting mighty enfeebling, and I ain't walked outside the door for a long time back. I sets and 'members the times in the world. I 'members now clear as yesterday things I forgot for a long time. I 'members 'bout the days of slavery, and I don't 'lieve they ever gwine have slaves no more on this earth. I think God done took that burden offen his black children, and I'm aiming to praise Him for it to His face in the days of glory what ain't so far off.

CHAPTER 3

Slave Resistance, Slave Rebellion

Chapter Preface

The history of slavery in the United States includes slave revolts and rebellions. Although the country never experienced any large-scale slave revolt that was not defeated and suppressed, the prospect of such an event was taken very seriously by both proponents and opponents of slavery.

The lack of successful rebellions does not mean that American slaves docilely accepted their condition. Many rebelled or resisted slavery in a variety of other ways. Historians Winthrop D. Jordan and Leon F. Litwack write: "Throughout two centuries of slavery, slaves malingered, broke tools, abused farm animals, feigned illness, and otherwise struck out at the principal requirements of the system: hard work and productivity."

Other slaves rebelled against their situation by running away from their masters. Still others used more violent means. Jordan and Litwack write:

> Slavery rested on a base of violence, and slaves sometimes responded in kind. There were just enough instances to keep the white population thoroughly on edge. Two of the most effective and drastic means at the slaves' disposal were arson and poisoning. Probably more common were the many instances when a slave suddenly and simply decided that he would rather fight and die than be whipped.

A former slave interviewed in the 1930s offered this reminiscence:

> One day when an old woman was plowing in the field, an overseer came by and reprimanded her for being so slow—she gave him some back talk, he took out a long closely woven whip and lashed her severely. The woman became sore and took her hoe and chopped him right across his head, and, child, you should have seen how she chopped this man to a bloody death.

What was of more concern to slaveholders than such individual acts, however, was the prospect of organized rebellion. Attempted insurrections were not unknown. New York had slave rebellions as early as 1712 and 1741. Virginia had scares as early as 1663, 1687, and 1709. Historians disagree even today, however, about how common organized slave rebellions were. Most rebellions were spontaneous, relatively small uprisings involving fewer than twenty-five people, and they were easily suppressed. Often, a slave would betray knowledge of a conspiracy or plot. Many accounts of coming revolts were confessed by slaves suspected of plotting rebellion and hoping for leniency. Other potential slave rebellions may have existed only in the minds of panicked whites.

Perhaps the most significant slave rebellion for the United States took place outside its borders. The 1791 slave revolt in the French colony of Haiti, which was ultimately successful in overthrowing the government and freeing the slaves, both inspired blacks and scared whites in the United States. Fear of such rebellions was greatest in the South where slaves outnumbered whites, sometimes as much as ten to one.

One of the people inspired by the Haiti rebellion was Gabriel Prosser, a slave on a large Virginia plantation. In 1800, he planned a seizure of the federal arsenal in Richmond, Virginia, as the start of a general armed rebellion. He had eleven hundred slaves under his leadership, but another slave exposed the plot, and Virginia governor and future president James Monroe successfully suppressed the rebellion before it started. More than thirty blacks, including Prosser, were hanged. Slave-patrol laws were made more stringent, and troops were frequently called in to suppress rumored uprisings.

The most drastic slave rebellion within the United States was the uprising led by Nat Turner in Southampton, Virginia, in August 1831. A slave and lay preacher, Turner led about sixty followers in an attack that killed fifty-seven whites, including Turner's owner and the owner's family. The revolt was soon crushed by local whites with the help of Virginia and North Carolina militia, and Turner was eventually caught and hanged. Historians estimate that more than one hundred local blacks were killed by white vigilante groups in response to the rebellion. Their actions are described by Harriet Jacobs in this chapter.

The Nat Turner rebellion, like the Prosser rebellion before it, had a great impact on Virginia and the South. The Virginia legislature debated, for the last time, whether to abolish slavery but instead voted to enact restrictive laws against free blacks. In addition, they suppressed slaves' access both to religious worship and to education in an attempt to prevent slave rebellions. Similar proposals were enacted throughout the South.

While the Nat Turner rebellion effectively hardened attitudes about slavery in the South, it created controversy in the North. Black leaders debated whether armed rebellion was necessary and justifiable in ending slavery. Black activists such as David Walker and Henry Highland Garnet wrote and spoke in favor of violent rebellion as the only effective means of ending slavery. Ultimately, it was the extreme violence of the Civil War, a conflict in which many black soldiers participated, that ended slavery in the United States.

VIEWPOINT 1

"I am certain that while we are slaves, it is our duty to obey our masters, in all their lawful commands."

Resistance to Slavery Is Not Justified

Jupiter Hammon (1720?-1800?)

Jupiter Hammon was born a slave to a wealthy New York merchant family. He spent his lifetime in slavery as a valued and trusted house servant. A convert to Christianity, Hammon also preached and wrote religious poetry. He was the first black to be published in America.

The following viewpoint is excerpted from *An Address to the Negroes of the State of New York*, a speech delivered before the African society in New York City in 1786, and published in 1787. The address was reprinted in *The Mind of the Negro* (Washington, DC: The Association for the Study of Negro Life and History, Inc.: 1926). Hammon counsels slaves to be obedient to their masters and to concentrate on gaining freedom through religion rather than rebellion.

When I am writing to you with a design to say something to you for your good, and with a view to promote your happiness, I can with truth and sincerity join with the apostle Paul, when speaking of his own nation the Jews, and say: *"That I have great heaviness and continual sorrow in my heart for my brethren, my kinsmen according to the flesh."* Yes my dear brethren, when I think of you, which is very often, and of the poor, despised and miserable state you are in, as to the things of this world, and when I think of your ignorance and stupidity, and the great wickedness of the most of you, I am pained to the heart. It is at times, almost too much for human nature to bear, and I am obliged to turn my thoughts from the subject or endeavour to still my mind, by considering that it is permitted thus to be, by that God who governs all things, who setteth up one and pulleth down another. While I have been thinking on this subject, I have frequently had great struggles in my own mind, and have been at a loss to know what to do. I have wanted exceedingly to say something to you, to call upon you with the tenderness of a father and friend, and to give you the last, and I may say dying advice, of an old man, who wishes your best good in this world, and in the world to come. But while I have had such desires, a sense of my own ignorance, and unfitness to teach others, has frequently discouraged me from attempting to say any thing to you; yet when I thought of your situation, I could not rest easy.

When I was at Hartford in Connecticut, where I lived during the war, I published several pieces which were well received, not only by those of my own colour, but by a number of the white people, who thought they might do good among their servants. This is one consideration, among others, that emboldens me now to publish what I have written to you. Another is, I think you will be more likely to listen to what is said, when you know it comes from a negro, one of your own nation and colour, and therefore can have no interest in deceiving you, or in saying any thing to you, but what he really thinks is your interest, and duty to comply with. My age, I think, gives me some right to speak to you, and reason to expect you will hearken to my advice. I am now upwards of seventy years old, and cannot expect, though I am well, and able to do almost any kind of business, to live much longer. I have passed the common bounds set for man, and must soon go the way of all the earth. I have had more experience in the world than the most of you, and I have seen a great deal of the vanity and wickedness of it, I have great reason to be thankful that my lot has been so much better than most slaves have had. I suppose I have had more advantages and privileges than most of you, who are slaves, have ever known, and I believe more than many white people have enjoyed, for which I desire to bless God, and pray that he may bless those who have given them to me. I do not, my dear friends, say these things about myself, to make you think that I am wiser or better than others; but that you might hearken, without prejudice, to what I have to say to you on the following particulars.

Obedience

1st. Respecting obedience to masters.—Now whether it is right, and lawful, in the sight of God, for them to make slaves of us or not. I am certain that while we are slaves, it is our duty to obey our masters, in all their lawful commands, and mind them unless we are bid to do that which we know to be sin, or forbidden in God's word. The apostle Paul says: "Servants be obedient to them that are your masters according to the flesh, with fear and trembling in singleness in your heart as unto Christ: Not with eye service, as men pleasers, but as the servants of Christ doing the will of God from the heart: With good will doing service to the Lord, and not to men: Knowing that whatever thing a man doeth the same shall he receive of the Lord, whether he be bond or free."—Here is a plain command of God for us to obey our masters. It may seem hard for us, if we think our masters wrong in holding us slaves, to obey in all things, but who of us dare dispute with God! He has commanded us to obey, and we ought to do it cheerfully, and freely. This should be done by us, not only because God commands, but because our own peace and comfort depend upon it. As we depend upon our masters, for what we eat and drink and wear, and for all our comfortable things in this world, we cannot be happy, unless we please them. This we cannot do without obeying them freely, without muttering or finding fault. If a servant strives to please his master and studies and takes pains to do it, I believe there are but few masters who would use such a servant cruelly. Good servants frequently make good masters. If your master is really hard, unreasonable and cruel, there is no way so likely for you to convince him of it, as always to obey his commands, and try to serve him, and take care of his interest, and try to promote it all in your power. If you are proud and stubborn and always finding fault, your master will think the fault lies wholly on your side; but if you are humble, and meek, and bear all things patiently, your master may think he is wrong; if he does not, his neighbours will be apt to see it, and will befriend you, and try to alter his conduct. If this does not do, you must cry to him, who has the hearts of all men in his hands, and turneth them as the rivers of waters are turned.

Honesty

2d. The particular I would mention, is honesty and faithfulness.

You must suffer me now to deal plainly with you, my dear brethren, for I do not mean to flatter, or omit speaking the truth, whether it is for you, or against you. How many of you are there who allow yourselves in stealing from your masters. It is very wicked for you not to take care of your masters goods, but how much worse is it to pilfer and steal from them, whenever you think you shall not be found out. This you must know is very wicked and provoking to God. There are none of you so ignorant, but that you must know that this is wrong. Though you may try to excuse yourselves, by saying that your masters are unjust to you, and though you may try to quiet your consciences in this way, yet if you are honest in owning the truth, you must think it is as wicked, and on some accounts more wicked, to steal from your masters, than from others.

The Law of Humanity

William Ellery Channing was a Unitarian minister and abolitionist. His stance against slavery outlined in this excerpt from The Duty of the Free States, *published in 1842, was founded on a belief in the natural rights of humanity.*

The slave has a right to liberty; but a right does not imply that it may be asserted by any and every means. There is a great law of humanity to which all are subject, the bond as well as the free, and which we must never lose sight of in redressing wrongs, or in claiming and insisting on our due. The slave cannot innocently adopt any and every expedient for vindicating his liberty. He is bound to waive his right, if in maintaining it he is to violate the law of humanity, and to spread general ruin. Were I confined unjustly to a house, I should have no right to free myself by setting it on fire, if thereby a family should be destroyed. An impressed seaman cannot innocently withhold his service in a storm, and would be bound to work even in ordinary weather, if this were needed to save the ship from foundering. We owe a debt of humanity even to him who wrongs us, and especially to those who are linked with him, and who must suffer, perhaps perish with him, if we seek to redress our wrong.

We cannot certainly, have any excuse either for taking any thing that belongs to our masters, without their leave, or for being unfaithful in their business. It is our duty to be faithful, *not with eye service as men pleasers.* We have no right to stay when we are sent on errands, any longer than to do the business we were sent upon. All the time spent idly, is spent wickedly, and is unfaithfulness to our masters. In these things I must say, that I think many of you are guilty. I know that many of you endeavour to excuse yourselves, and say, that you have nothing that you can call your own, and that you are under great temptations to be unfaithful and take from your masters. But this will not do, God will certainly punish you for stealing and for being unfaithful. All that we have to mind is our own duty. If God has put us in bad circumstances, that is not our fault, and he will not punish us for it. If any are wicked in keeping us so, we cannot help it, they must answer to God for it. Nothing will serve as an excuse to us for not doing our duty. The same God will judge both them and us. Pray then my dear friends, fear to offend in this way, but be faithful to

God, to your masters, and to your own souls.

The next thing I would mention, and warn you against, is profaneness. This you know is forbidden by God. Christ tells us: "swear not at all," and again it is said, "thou shalt not take the name of the Lord thy God in vain, for the Lord will not hold him guiltless, that taketh his name in vain." Now, though the great God has forbidden it, yet how dreadfully profane are many, and I don't know but I may say the most of you? How common is it to hear you take the terrible and awful name of the great God in vain?—To swear by it, and by Jesus Christ, his Son—How common is it to hear you wish damnation to your companions, and to your own souls—and to sport with the name of Heaven and Hell, as if there were no such places for you to hope for, or to fear. Oh my friends, be warned to forsake this dreadful sin of profaneness. Pray my dear friends, believe and realize, that there is a God—that he is great and terrible beyond what you can think—that he keeps you in life every moment—and that he can send you to that awful Hell, that you laugh at, in an instant, and confine you there forever, and that he will certainly do it, if you do not repent. . . .

Murder Is Wicked

Some of you excuse yourselves, may plead the example of others, and say that you hear a great many white people, who know more, than such poor ignorant negroes, as you are, and some who are rich and great gentlemen, swear, and talk profanely, and some of you may say this of your masters, and say no more than is true. But all this is not a sufficient excuse for you. You know that murder is wicked. If you saw your master kill a man, do you suppose this would be any excuse for you, if you should commit the same crime? You must know it would not; nor will your hearing him curse and swear, and take the name of God in vain, or any other man, be he ever so great or rich, excuse you. God is greater than all other beings, and him we are bound to obey. To him we must give an account for every idle word that we speak. He will bring us all, rich and poor, white and black, to his judgment seat. If we are found among those who *feared his name* and *trembled at his word*, we shall be called good and faithful servants. Our slavery will be at an end, and though ever so mean, low, and despised in this world, we shall sit with God in his kingdom as Kings and Priests, and rejoice forever, and ever. Do not then my dear friends, take God's holy name in vain, or speak profanely in any way. Let not the example of others lead you into the sin, but reverence and fear that *great and fearful name, the Lord our God*.

I might now caution you against other sins to which you are exposed, but as I meant only to mention those you were exposed to, more than others, by your being slaves, I will conclude what I have to say to you, by advising you to become religious, and to make religion the great business of your lives.

True Liberty

Now I acknowledge that liberty is a great thing, and worth seeking for, if we can get it honestly, and by our good conduct prevail on our masters to set us free. Though for my own part I do not wish to be free: yet I should be glad, if others, especially the young negroes were to be free, for many of us who are grown up slaves, and have always had masters to take care of us, should hardly know how to take care of ourselves; and it may be more for our own comfort to remain as we are. That liberty is a great thing we may know from our own feelings, and we may likewise judge so from the conduct of the white people, in the late war. How much money has been spent, and how many lives have been lost, to defend their liberty. I must say that I have hoped that God would open their eyes, when they were so much engaged for liberty, to think of the state of the poor blacks, and to pity us. He has done it in some measure, and has raised us up many friends, for which we have reason to be thankful, and to hope in his mercy. What may be done further, he only knows, for *known unto God are all his ways from the beginning*. But this my dear brethren is by no means, the greatest thing we have to be concerned about. Getting our liberty in this world, is nothing to having the liberty of the children of God. Now the Bible tells us that we are all by nature, sinners, that we are slaves to sin and satan, and that unless we are converted, or born again, we must be miserable forever. Christ says, except a man be born again, he cannot see the kingdom of God, and all that do not see the kingdom of God, must be in the kingdom of darkness. There are but two places where all go after death, white and black, rich and poor; those places are heaven and hell. . . .

Now my dear friends seeing the Bible is the word of God, and every thing in it is true, and it reveals such awful and glorious things, what can be more important than that you should learn to read it; and when you have learned to read, that you should study it day and night. There are some things very encouraging in God's word, for such ignorant creatures as we are: for God hath not chosen the rich of this world. Not many rich, not many noble are called, but God hath chosen the weak things of this world, and things which are not, to confound the things that are: And when the great and the rich refused coming to the gospel feast, the servant was told to go into the highways, and hedges, and compel those poor creatures that he found there, to come in. Now my brethren, it seems to me that there are no people that ought to attend to the hope of happiness in another world, so much as we. Most of us are cut off from comfort and happiness here in this world, and can expect nothing from it. Now seeing this is the case, why should we not take care to be happy after death. Why should we spend our whole lives in sinning against God: And be miserable in this world, and in the world to come. If we do thus, we shall certainly be the greatest fools. We shall be slaves here, and slaves forever. We cannot plead so great temptations to neglect religion as others. Riches and honours which drown the greater part of mankind, (who have the gospel,) in perdition, can be little or no temptation to us.

We live so little time in this world, that it is no matter how wretched and miserable we are, if it prepares us for heaven. What is forty, fifty, or sixty years, when compared to eternity. When thousands and millions of years have rolled away, this eternity will be no nigher coming to an end. Oh how glorious is an eternal life of happiness! and how dreadful, an eternity of misery. Those of us who have had religious masters, and have been taught to read the Bible, and have been brought by their example and teaching to a sense of divine things, how happy shall we be to meet them in heaven, where we shall join them in praising God forever. But if any of us have had such masters, and have yet lived and died wicked, how will it add to our misery to think of our folly. If any of us, who have wicked and profane masters should become religious, how will our estates be changed in another world. Oh my friends, let me intreat of you to think on these things, and to live as if you believed them true. If you become christians, you will have reason to bless God forever, that you have been brought into a land where you have heard the gospel, though you have been slaves. If we should ever get to heaven, we shall find nobody to reproach us for being black, or for being slaves. Let me beg of you my dear African brethren, to think very little of your bondage in this life, for your thinking of it will do you no good. If God designs to set us free, he will do it, in his own time, and way; but think of your bondage to sin and satan, and do not rest, until you are delivered from it.

VIEWPOINT 2

"No oppressed people have ever secured their liberty without resistance."

Resistance to Slavery Is Justified

Henry Highland Garnet (1815-1881)

Henry Highland Garnet was born a slave in Maryland, the son of a captured and enslaved African chief. At the age of nine he escaped with his parents and settled in New York City. Garnet served for more than forty years as pastor of Shiloh Presbyterian Church in New York.

Garnet was active in the abolitionist movement and often spoke and preached against slavery. The following viewpoint is taken from a speech he made in 1843 at the National Convention of Negro Citizens in Buffalo, New York. The speech was eventually published in a book by Garnet, *A Memorial Discourse by Rev. Henry Highland Garnet* (Philadelphia: James McCune Smith, 1865). Garnet called for slave rebellions as the surest way to end slavery. Using the Bible to support his arguments, Garnet asserted that slaves were justified in using violence to end their oppression. He praised such leaders of slave revolts as Denmark Vesey (Veazie) and Nathaniel Turner. Garnet's ideas failed by one vote of being officially adopted by the convention. John Brown, who later led a violent rebellion in 1859, had the speech published at his own expense.

BRETHREN AND FELLOW CITIZENS: Your brethren of the North, East and West have been accustomed to meet together in national conventions, to sympathize with each other, and to weep over your unhappy condition. In these meetings we have addressed all classes of the free, but we have never, until this time, sent a word of consolation and advice to you. We have been contented in sitting still and mourning over your sorrows, earnestly hoping that before this day your sacred liberties would have been restored. But we have hoped in vain. Years have rolled on, and tens of thousands have been borne on streams of blood and tears to the shores of eternity. While you have been oppressed, we have also been partakers with you; nor can we be free while you are enslaved. We, therefore, write to you as being bound with you.

Many of you are bound to us, not only by the ties of a common humanity, but we are connected by the more tender relations of parents, wives, husbands and sisters and friends. As such we most affectionately address you.

A Deep Gulf

Slavery has fixed a deep gulf between you and us, and while it shuts out from you the relief and consolation which your friends would willingly render, it afflicts and persecutes you with a fierceness which we might not expect to see in the fiends of hell. But still the Almighty Father of mercies has left to us a glimmering ray of hope, which shines out like a lone star in a cloudy sky. Mankind is becoming wiser, and better, the oppressor's power is fading, and you every day are becoming better informed and more numerous. Your grievances, brethren, are many. We shall not attempt in this short address to present to the world all the dark catalogue of the nation's sins which have been committed upon an innocent people. Nor is it indeed necessary, for you feel them from day to day, and all the civilized world looks upon them with amazement.

Two hundred and twenty-seven years ago the first of our injured race were brought to the shores of America. They came not with glad spirits to select their homes in the New World. They came not with their own consent, to find an unmolested enjoyment of the blessings of this fruitful soil. The first dealings they had with men calling themselves Christians exhibited to them the worst features of corrupt and sordid hearts, and convinced them that no cruelty is too great, no villainy and no robbery too abhorrent for even enlightened men to perform, when influenced by avarice and lust. Neither did they come flying upon the wings of Liberty to a land of freedom. But they came with broken hearts from their beloved native land and were doomed to unrequited toil and deep degradation. Nor did the evil of their bondage end at their emancipation by death. Succeeding generations inherited their chains, and millions have come from eternity into time, and have returned again to the world of spirits, cursed and ruined by American slavery.

The propagators of the system, or their immediate successors,

Slaves Are Too Servile

David Walker was a free black who in 1829 published a pamphlet called Appeal, in Four Articles *which decried slavery and exhorted slaves to resist their masters. He died under mysterious circumstances a year later. The pamphlet, the first extended political tract written by an African-American, was attacked by Southerners who attempted to limit its distribution. It was blamed for causing the 1831 Nat Turner insurrection.*

I do not think that we were natural enemies to each other. But the whites having made us so wretched, by subjecting us to slavery, and having murdered so many millions of us in order to make us work for them, and out of devilishness—and they taking our wives, whom we love as we do ourselves—our mothers who bore the pains of death to give us birth—our fathers & dear little children, and ourselves, and strip and beat us one before the other—chain, handcuff and drag us about like rattlesnakes—shoot us down like wild bears, before each other's faces, to make us submissive to and work to support them and their families. They (the whites) know well if we are *men*—and there is a secret monitor in their hearts which tells them we are—they know, I say, if we *are* men, and see them treating us in the manner they do, that there can be nothing in our hearts but death alone, for them; notwithstanding we may appear cheerful, when we see them murdering our dear mothers and wives, because we cannot help ourselves. . . . (viz. we cannot help the whites murdering our mothers and our wives) but this statement is incorrect—for we can help ourselves; for, if we lay aside abject servility, and be determined to act like men, and not brutes—the murderers among the whites would be afraid to show their cruel heads. But O, my God!—in sorrow I must say it, that my colour, all over the world, have a mean, servile spirit. They yield in a moment to the whites, let them be right or wrong—the reason the whites are able to keep their feet on our throats. Oh! my coloured brethren, all over the world, when shall we arise from this death-like apathy?—And be men!! You will notice, if ever we become men (I mean *respectable* men, such as other people are,) we must exert ourselves to the full. For remember, that it is the greatest desire and object of the greater part of the whites, to keep us ignorant, and make us work to support them and their families.—Here now, in the Southern and Western Sections of this country, there are at least three coloured persons for one white, why is it, that those few weak, good-for-nothing whites, are able to keep so many able men, one of whom, can put to flight a dozen whites, in wretchedness and misery? It shows at once, what the blacks are, we are ignorant, abject, servile, and mean—and the whites know it—they know that we are too servile to assert our rights as men—or they would not fool with us as they do. Would they fool with any other people as they do with us? No, they know too well that they would get themselves ruined.

very soon discovered its growing evil and its tremendous wickedness, and secret promises were made to destroy it. The gross inconsistency of a people holding slaves, who had themselves "ferried o'er the wave" for freedom's sake, was too apparent to be entirely overlooked. The voice of Freedom cried, "Emancipate your slaves." Humanity supplicated with tears for the deliverance of the children of Africa. Wisdom urged her solemn plea. The bleeding captive pleaded his innocence and pointed to Christianity who stood weeping at the cross. Jehovah frowned upon the nefarious institution, and thunderbolts, red with vengeance, struggled to leap forth to blast the guilty wretches who maintained it. But all was vain. Slavery had stretched its dark wings of death over the land, the Church stood silently by, the priests prophesied falsely, and the people loved to have it so. Its throne is established, and now it reigns triumphant.

Nearly three millions of your fellow citizens are prohibited by law and public opinion (which in this country is stronger than law) from reading the Book of Life. Your intellect has been destroyed as much as possible, and every ray of light they have attempted to shut out from your minds. The oppressors themselves have become involved in the ruin. They have become weak, sensual and rapacious; they have cursed you; they have cursed themselves; they have cursed the earth which they have trod.

The American Revolution

The colonies threw the blame upon England. They said that the mother country entailed the evil upon them, and they would rid themselves of it if they could. The world thought they were sincere, and the philanthropic pitied them. But time soon tested their sincerity. In a few years the colonists grew strong and severed themselves from the British government. Their independence was declared, and they took their station among the sovereign powers of the earth. The declaration was a glorious document. Sages admired it, and the patriotic of every nation reverenced the Godlike sentiments which it contained. When the power of government returned to their hands, did they emancipate the slaves? No; they rather added new links to our chains. Were they ignorant of the principles of Liberty? Certainly they were not. The sentiments of their revolutionary orators fell in burning eloquence upon their hearts, and with one voice they cried, "Liberty or death." Oh, what a sentence was that! It ran from soul to soul like electric fire and nerved the arms of thousands to fight in the holy cause of Freedom. Among the diversity of opinions that are entertained in regard to physical resistance, there are but a few found to gainsay the stern declaration. We are among those who do not.

Slavery! How much misery is comprehended in that single

word. What mind is there that does not shrink from its direful effects? Unless the image of God be obliterated from the soul, all men cherish the love of liberty. The nice discerning political economist does not regard the sacred right more than the untutored African who roams in the wilds of Congo. Nor has the one more right to the full enjoyment of his freedom than the other. In every man's mind the good seeds of liberty are planted, and he who brings his fellow down so low as to make him contented with a condition of slavery commits the highest crime against God and man. Brethren, your oppressors aim to do this. They endeavor to make you as much like brutes as possible. When they have blinded the eyes of your mind; when they have embittered the sweet waters of life; when they have shut out the light which shines from the word of God—then, and not till then, has American slavery done its perfect work.

Do Not Submit to Degradation

To such degradation it is sinful in the extreme for you to make voluntary submission. The divine commandments you are in duty bound to reverence and obey. If you do not obey them, you will surely meet with the displeasure of the Almighty. He requires you to love Him supremely, and your neighbor as yourself, to keep the Sabbath day holy, to search the Scriptures, and bring up your children with respect for His laws, and to worship no other God but Him. But slavery sets all these at nought and hurls defiance in the face of Jehovah. The forlorn condition in which you are placed does not destroy your obligation to God. You are not certain of heaven, because you allow yourselves to remain in a state of slavery, where you cannot obey the commandments of the Sovereign of the universe. If the ignorance of slavery is a passport to heaven, then it is a blessing, and no curse, and you should rather desire its perpetuity than its abolition. God will not receive slavery, nor ignorance, nor any other state of mind, for love and obedience to Him. Your condition does not absolve you from your moral obligation. The diabolical injustice by which your liberties are cloven down, neither God nor angels, nor just men command you to suffer for a single moment. Therefore it is your solemn and imperative duty to use every means, both moral, intellectual and physical, that promises success. If a band of heathen men should attempt to enslave a race of Christians, and to place their children under the influence of some false religion, surely Heaven would frown upon the men who would not resist such aggression, even to death. If, on the other hand, a band of Christians should attempt to enslave a race of heathen men, and to entail slavery upon them, and to keep them in heathenism in the midst of Christianity, the God of heaven would smile upon every effort which the injured might make to disenthral themselves.

Brethren, it is as wrong for your lordly oppressors to keep you in slavery as it was for the man thief to steal our ancestors from the coast of Africa. You should therefore now use the same manner of resistance as would have been just in our ancestors when the bloody footprints of the first remorseless soul thief was placed upon the shores of our fatherland. The humblest peasant is as free in the sight of God as the proudest monarch that ever swayed a scepter. Liberty is a spirit sent out from God and, like its great Author, is no respector of persons.

"A Call to Rebellion"

This 1849 editorial entitled "A Call to Rebellion" was originally published in a New York newspaper by and for blacks called The Liberator. *It calls for slaves to rise up against slavery.*

Slaves of the South, Now Is Your Time!

Strike for your freedom *now*, at the suggestion of your enslavers. . . . What have you to gain by procrastination in a manly struggle for liberty? You have nothing to lose, but every thing to gain. God is with you for liberty. Good men will sympathize for your success, and even slaveholders are ready . . . to cheer you on in the holy cause of freedom. Men will respect you in proportion to the physical efforts you put forth in resisting tyranny and slavery.

We do not tell you to murder the slaveholders; but we do advise you to refuse longer to work without pay. Make up your minds to die, rather than bequeath a state of slavery to your posterity.

Brethren, the time has come when you must act for yourselves. It is an old and true saying that, "if hereditary bondmen would be free, they must themselves strike the blow." You can plead your own cause and do the work of emancipation better than any others. The nations of the Old World are moving in the great cause of universal freedom, and some of them at least will, ere long, do you justice. The combined powers of Europe have placed their broad seal of disapprobation upon the African slave trade. But in the slaveholding parts of the United States the trade is as brisk as ever. They buy and sell you as though you were brute beasts. The North has done much; her opinion of slavery in the abstract is known. But in regard to the South, we adopt the opinion of the *New York Evangelist*—"We have advanced so far, that the cause apparently waits for a more effectual door to be thrown open than has been yet." We are about to point you to that more effectual door. Look around you and behold the bosoms of your loving wives heaving with untold agonies! Hear the cries of your poor children! Remember the stripes your fathers bore. Think of the torture and disgrace of your noble mothers. Think of your wretched sisters, loving virtue and purity, as they are driven into concubinage and are exposed to the unbridled lusts of incarnate devils. Think of the undying glory that hangs around the ancient name of Africa—and forget not that you are native-born American citizens, and as such you are justly entitled to all the rights that are granted to the freest. Think how many tears you have poured out upon the soil which you have cultivated with unrequited toil and enriched with your blood; and then go to your lordly enslavers and tell them plainly that you *are determined to be free.* Appeal to their sense of justice and tell them that they have no more right to oppress you than you have to enslave them. Entreat them to remove the grievous burdens which they have imposed upon you, and to remunerate you for your labor. Promise them renewed diligence in the cultivation of the soil, if they will render to you an equivalent for your services. Point them to the increase of happiness and prosperity in the British West Indies since the Act of Emancipation. [Slavery was abolished in the British West Indies by an act of Parliament in 1833.] Tell them, in language which they cannot misunderstand, of the exceeding sinfulness of slavery and of a future judgment and of the righteous retributions of an indignant God. Inform them that all you desire is freedom, and that nothing else will suffice. Do this, and forever after cease to toil for the heartless tyrants, who give you no other reward but stripes and abuse. If they then commence work of death, they, and not you, will be responsible for the consequences. You had far better all die—*die immediately*—than live slaves and entail your wretchedness upon your posterity. If you would be free in this generation, here is your only hope. However much you and all of us may desire it, there is not much hope of redemption without the shedding of blood. If you must bleed, let it all come at once—rather *die freemen than live to be the slaves.* It is impossible, like the children of Israel, to make a grand exodus from the land of bondage. The Pharaohs are on both sides of the blood-red waters! You cannot move *en masse* to the dominions of the British Queen, nor can you pass through Florida and overrun Texas and at last find peace in Mexico. The propagators of American Slavery are spending their blood and treasure that they may plant the black flag in the heart of Mexico and riot in the halls of the Montezumas. In the language of the Reverend Robert Hall, when addressing the volunteers of Bristol who were rushing forth to repel the invasion of Napoleon, who threatened to lay waste the fair homes of England, "Religion is too much interested in your behalf not to shed over you her most gracious influences."

You will not be compelled to spend much time in order to become inured to hardships. From the first moment that you breathed the air of heaven, you have been accustomed to nothing else but hardships. The heroes of the American Revolution were never put upon harder fare than a peck of corn and few herrings per week. You have not become enervated by the luxuries of life. Your sternest energies have been beaten out upon the anvil of severe trial. Slavery has done this to make you subservient to its own purposes. But it has done more than this; it has prepared you for any emergency. If you receive good treatment, it is what you can hardly expect; if you meet with pain, sorrow, and even death, these are the common lot of the slaves.

Fellow men, patient sufferers, behold your dearest rights crushed to the earth! See your sons murdered, and your wives, mothers and sisters doomed to prostitution. In the name of the merciful God, and by all that life is worth, let it no longer be a debatable question, whether it is better to choose liberty or death.

In 1822, Denmark Veazie [Vesey], of South Carolina, formed a plan for the liberation of his fellow men. In the whole history of human efforts to overthrow slavery, a more complicated and tremendous plan was never formed. He was betrayed by the treachery of his own people, and died a martyr to freedom. Many a brave hero fell, but history, faithful to her high trust, will transcribe his name on the same monument with Moses, Hampden, Tell, Bruce and Wallace, Toussaint L'Ouverture, Lafayette and Washington. That tremendous movement shook the whole empire of slavery. The guilty soul thieves were overwhelmed with fear. It is a matter of fact that at this time, and in consequence of the threatened revolution, the slave states talked strongly of emancipation. But they blew but one blast of the trumpet of freedom, and then laid it aside. As these men became quiet, the slaveholders ceased to talk about emancipation; and now behold your condition to-day! Angels sigh over it, and humanity has long since exhausted her tears in weeping on your account!

Heroes

The patriotic Nathaniel Turner followed Denmark Veazie. He was goaded to desperation by wrong and injustice. By despotism, his name has been recorded on the list of infamy, and future generations will remember him among the noble and brave.

Next arose the immortal Joseph Cinque, the hero of the *Amistad*. He was a native African, and by the help of God he emancipated a whole shipload of his fellow men on the high seas. And he now sings of liberty on the sunny hills of Africa and beneath his native palm trees, where he hears the lion roar and feels himself as free as the king of the forest.

Next arose Madison Washington, that bright star of freedom, and took his station in the constellation of true heroism. He was a slave on board the brig *Creole*, of Richmond, bound to New Orleans, that great slave mart, with a hundred and four others. Nineteen struck for liberty or death. But one life was taken, and the whole were emancipated, and the vessel was carried into Nassau, New Providence.

Noble men! Those who have fallen in freedom's conflict, their memories will be cherished by the true-hearted and the God-fearing in all future generations; those who are living, their names are surrounded by a halo of glory.

Brethren, arise, arise! Strike for your lives and liberties. Now is the day and the hour. Let every slave throughout the land do this, and the days of slavery are numbered. You cannot be more oppressed than you have been; you cannot suffer greater cruelties than you have already. *Rather die freemen than live to be slaves.* Remember that you are *four millions!*

It is in your power so to torment the God-cursed slaveholders that they will be glad to let you go free. If the scale was turned, and black men were the masters and white men the slaves, every destructive agent and element would be employed to lay the oppressor low. Danger and death would hang over their heads day and night. Yes, the tyrants would meet with plagues more terrible than those of Pharaoh. But you are a patient people. You act as though you were made for the special use of these devils. You act as though your daughters were born to pamper the lusts of your masters and overseers. And worse than all, you tamely submit while your lords tear your wives from your embraces and defile them before your eyes. In the name of God, we ask, are you men? Where is the blood of your fathers? Has it all run out of your veins? Awake, awake; millions of voices are calling you! Your dead fathers speak to you from their graves. Heaven, as with a voice of thunder, calls on you to arise from the dust.

Resistance

Let your motto be Resistance! *Resistance!* RESISTANCE! No oppressed people have ever secured their liberty without resistance. What kind of resistance you had better make you must decide by the circumstances that surround you, and according to the suggestion of expediency. Brethren, adieu! Trust in the living God. Labor for the peace of the human race, and remember that you are *four millions!*

"The murder of this family, five in number, was the work of a moment."

The Southampton Slave Insurrection Was Necessary

Nat Turner (1800-1831)

Nat Turner was the slave leader of the 1831 Southampton insurrection, the best known and most violent slave rebellion in the United States. On August 21, 1831, Turner and five other slaves killed Turner's master and his family. They then proceeded to other white households and killed a total of about sixty whites. Turner's followers grew to around seventy and caused a panic throughout the South, but within a few days local white militias had crushed the revolt. Turner went into hiding until he was captured on October 30. He was tried, was found guilty of murder, and on November 11 was executed. The event had great influence on the South, leading to a tightening of slave codes and laws and dampening what was left of abolitionist feeling in the South.

The following viewpoint is taken from *The Confessions of Nat Turner* originally published in 1831 and reprinted in the December 1859 issue of *Anglo-African Magazine*. Turner explains his reasons for leading the insurrection and vividly describes his actions during the event. The confessions were edited, published, and sold by Thomas R. Gray, a lawyer identified by some historians as Turner's attorney. Some historians question the authenticity of the confession, suggesting that much of the language and wording was by Gray, but the general consensus is that Gray did spend time with Turner at the Southampton County Jail, and did obtain a confession.

Sir, you have asked me to give a history of the motives which induced me to undertake the late insurrection, as you call it. To do so I must go back to the days of my infancy, and even before I was born. I was thirty-one years of age the 2nd of October last and born the property of Benj. Turner, of this county. In my childhood a circumstance occurred which made an indelible impression on my mind and laid the groundwork of that enthusiasm which has terminated so fatally to many both white and black, and for which I am about to atone at the gallows. It is here necessary to relate this circumstance, trifling as it may seem; it was the commencement of that belief which has grown with time, and even now, sir, in this dungeon, helpless and forsaken as I am, I cannot divest myself of. Being at play with other children, when three or four years old, I was telling them something, which my mother overhearing, said it had happened before I was born; I stuck to my story, however, and related some things which went in the opinion to confirm it; others being called on were greatly astonished, knowing that these things had happened, and caused them to say in my hearing, I surely would be a prophet, as the Lord had shown me things that had happened before my birth. And my father and mother strengthened me in this my first impression, saying in my presence, I was intended for some great purpose. . . .

Spiritual Revelations

Several years rolled round, in which many events occurred to strengthen me in this belief. . . . Now finding I had arrived to man's estate and was a slave, and these revelations being made known to me, I began to direct my attention to this great object, to fulfill the purpose for which, by this time, I felt assured I was intended. Knowing the influence I had obtained over the minds of my fellow servants, (not by the means of conjuring and such like tricks, for to them I always spoke of such things with contempt) but by the communion of the Spirit whose revelations I often communicated to them, and they believed and said my wisdom came from God. I now began to prepare them for my purpose, by telling them something was about to happen that would terminate in fulfilling the great promise that had been made to me.

About this time I was placed under an overseer, from whom I ran away; and after remaining in the woods thirty days, I returned, to the astonishment of the Negroes on the plantation, who thought I had made my escape to some other part of the country, as my father had done before. But the reason of my return was, that the Spirit appeared to me and said I had my wishes directed to the things of this world, and not to the kingdom of Heaven, and that I should return to the service of my earthly master, "For he who knoweth his Master's will, and doeth it not, shall be beaten with many stripes, and thus have I chastened you." And the Negroes found fault, and murmured against me, saying that if they had my sense they would not serve any master in the world. And about this time I had a vision, and I saw white spirits and black spirits engaged in battle, and the sun was darkened, the thunder rolled in the heavens, and blood flowed in streams, and I heard a voice saying, "Such is your luck, such you are called to see, and let it come rough or smooth, you must surely bear it." ...

Nat Turner and his followers plot their rebellion. The insurrection prompted Southern communities to increase police patrols and redouble efforts to suppress revolts.

I sought more than ever to obtain true holiness before the great day of judgment should appear, and then I began to receive the true knowledge of faith. ...

And by signs in the heavens that it would make known to me when I should commence the great work, and until the first sign appeared, I should conceal it from the knowledge of men. And on the appearance of the sign, (the eclipse of the sun last February) I should arise and prepare myself and slay my enemies with their own weapons. And immediately on the sign appearing in the heavens, the seal was removed from my lips, and I communicated the great work laid out for me to do, to four in whom I had the greatest confidence (Henry, Hark, Nelson, and Sam). It was intended by us to have begun the work of death on the 4th of July last. Many were the plans formed and rejected by us, and it af-

Historical Pictures/Stock Montage.

fected my mind to such a degree that I fell sick, and the time passed without our coming to any determination how to commence; still forming new schemes and rejecting them, when the sign appeared again, which determined me not to wait longer.

Since the commencement of 1830, I had been living with Mr. Joseph Travis, who was to me a kind master and placed the greatest confidence in me; in fact, I had no cause to complain of his treatment to me. On Saturday evening, the 20th of August, it was agreed between Henry, Hark and myself, to prepare a dinner the next day for the men we expected, and then to concert a plan, as we had not yet determined on any. Hark on the following morning brought a pig, and Henry brandy, and being joined by Sam, Nelson, Will, and Jack, they prepared in the woods a dinner, where, about three o'clock, I joined them. . . .

First Blood

I saluted them on coming up and asked Will how came he there; he answered, his life was worth no more than others, and his liberty as dear to him. I asked him if he thought to obtain it? He said he would, or lose his life. This was enough to put him in full confidence. Jack, I knew, was only a tool in the hands of Hark, it was quickly agreed we should commence at home (Mr. J. Travis') on that night, and until we had armed and equipped ourselves and gathered sufficient force, neither age nor sex was to be spared (which was invariably adhered to).

We remained at the feast until about two hours in the night, when we went to the house and found Austin; they all went to the cider press and drank, except myself. On returning to the house, Hark went to the door with an axe, for the purpose of breaking it open, as we knew we were strong enough to murder the family, if they were awaked by the noise; but, reflecting that it might create an alarm in the neighborhood, we determined to enter the house secretly and murder them while sleeping. Hark got a ladder and set it against the chimney on which I ascended and, hoisting a window, entered and came down stairs, unbarred the door, and removed the guns from their places. It was then observed that I must spill the first blood. On which, armed with a hatchet and accompanied by Will, I entered my master's chamber. It being dark, I could not give a death blow; the hatchet glanced from his head; he sprang from the bed and called his wife. It was his last word. Will laid him dead with a blow of his axe, and Mrs. Travis shared the same fate, as she lay in bed.

The murder of this family, five in number, was the work of a moment, not one of them awoke; there was a little infant, sleeping in a cradle, that was forgotten until we had left the house and gone some distance, when Henry and Will returned and killed it;

we got here four guns that would shoot and several old muskets, with a pound or two of powder. We remained some time at the barn, where we paraded; I formed them in a line as soldiers and, after carrying them through all the maneuvers I was master of, marched them off to Mr. Salathul Francis', about 600 yards distant. Sam and Will went to the door and knocked. Mr. Francis asked who was there; Sam replied it was him and he had a letter for him, on which he got up and came to the door; they immediately seized him, and dragging him out a little from the door, he was dispatched by repeated blows on the head; there was no other white person in the family.

We started from there for Mrs. Reese's, maintaining the most perfect silence on our march, where finding the door unlocked, we entered and murdered Mrs. Reese in her bed, while sleeping; her son awoke, but it was only to sleep the sleep of death. He had only time to say who is that, and he was no more. From Mrs. Reese's we went to Mrs. Turner's, a mile distant, which we reached about sunrise on Monday morning. Henry, Austin, and Sam went to the still, where, finding Mr. Peebles, Austin shot him, and the rest of us went to the house; as we approached, the family discovered us and shut the door. Vain hope! Will, with one stroke of his axe, opened it, and we entered and found Mrs. Turner and Mrs. Newsome in the middle of a room almost frightened to death. Will immediately killed Mrs. Turner with one blow of his axe. I took Mrs. Newsome by the hand, and with the sword I had when I was apprehended, I struck her several blows over the head, but not being able to kill her, as the sword was dull. Will turning around and discovering it, dispatched her also.

Destruction of Property

A general destruction of property and search for money and ammunition always succeeded the murders. By this time my company amounted to fifteen, and nine men mounted, who started for Mrs. Whitehead's (the other six were to go through a by way to Mr. Bryant's and rejoin us at Mrs. Whitehead's). As we approached the house we discovered Mr. Richard Whitehead standing in the cotton patch, near the lane fence; we called him over into the lane, and Will, the executioner, was near at hand, with his fatal axe, to send him to an untimely grave. As we pushed on to the house, I discovered some one run round the garden, and, thinking it was some of the white family, I pursued them, but finding it was a servant girl belonging to the house, I returned to commence the work of death, but they whom I left had not been idle; all the family were already murdered but Mrs. Whitehead and her daughter Margaret. As I came round to the door I saw Will pulling Mrs. Whitehead out of the house, and at

Impressions of Nat Turner

Thomas R. Gray, a lawyer who according to some historians served as Nat Turner's defense attorney, obtained and published The Confessions of Nat Turner *in 1831. In this excerpt Gray describes his personal impression of Nat Turner.*

It has been said he was ignorant and cowardly, and that his object was to murder and rob for the purpose of obtaining money to make his escape. It is notorious, that he was never known to have a dollar in his life, to swear an oath, or drink a drop of spirits. As to his ignorance, he certainly never had the advantages of education, but he can read and write (it was taught him by his parents) and for natural intelligence and quickness of apprehension is surpassed by few men I have ever seen. As to his being a coward, his reason as given for not resisting Mr. Phipps shows the decision of his character. When he saw Mr. Phipps present his gun, he said he knew it was impossible for him to escape, as the woods were full of men; he therefore thought it was better to surrender and trust to fortune for his escape. He is a complete fanatic, or plays his part most admirably.

On other subjects he possesses an uncommon share of intelligence, with a mind capable of attaining anything; but warped and perverted by the influence of early impressions. He is below the ordinary stature, though strong and active, having the true Negro face, every feature of which is strongly marked. I shall not attempt to describe the effect of his narrative, as told and commented on by himself, in the condemned hole of the prison. The calm, deliberate composure with which he spoke of his late deeds and intentions, the expression of his fiendlike face when excited by enthusiasm, still bearing the stains of the blood of helpless innocence about him; clothed with rags and covered with chains; yet daring to raise his manacled hands to heaven, with a spirit soaring above the attributes of man; I looked on him and my blood curdled in my veins.

---

the step he nearly severed her head from her body with his broad axe. Miss Margaret, when I discovered her, had concealed herself in the corner formed by the projection of the cellar cap from the house; on my approach she fled, but was soon overtaken, and after repeated blows with a sword, I killed her by a blow on the head with a fence rail. By this time, the six who had gone by Mr. Bryant's rejoined us and informed me they had done the work of death assigned them.

We again divided, part going to Mr. Porter's, and from thence to Nathaniel Francis', the others to Mr. Howell Harris' and Mr. T. Doyle's. On my reaching Mr. Porter's, he had escaped with his family. I understood there, that the alarm had already spread, and I immediately returned to bring up those sent to Mr. Doyle's and

Mr. Howell Harris'; the party I left going on to Mr. Francis', having told them I would join them in that neighborhood. I met these sent to Mr. Doyle's and Mr. Harris' returning, having met Mr. Doyle on the road and killed him; and learning from some who joined them that Mr. Harris was from home, I immediately pursued the course taken by the party gone on before; but knowing they would complete the work of death and pillage at Mr. Francis' before I could get there, I went to Mr. Peter Edwards', expecting to find them there, but they had been here also. I then went to Mr. John T. Barrow's; they had been here and murdered him. I pursued on their track to Capt. Newit Harris', where I found the greater part mounted and ready to start; the men, now amounting to about forty, shouted and hurrahed as I rode up; some were in the yard, loading their guns, others drinking. They said Captain Harris and his family had escaped, the property in the house they destroyed, robbing him of money and other valuables. I ordered them to mount and march instantly, this was about nine or ten o'clock Monday morning.

I proceeded to Mr. Levi Waller's, two or three miles distant. I took my station in the rear, and as it was my object to carry terror and devastation wherever we went, I placed fifteen or twenty of the best mounted and most to be relied on in front who generally approached the houses as fast as their horses could run; this was for two purposes, to prevent their escape and strike terror to the inhabitants; on this account I never got to the houses, after leaving Mrs. Whitehead's until the murders were committed, except in one case. I sometimes got in sight in time to see the work of death completed, viewed the mangled bodies as they lay, in silent satisfaction, and immediately started in quest of other victims.

Having murdered Mrs. Waller and ten children, we started for Mr. William Williams'; having killed him and two little boys that were there; while engaged in this, Mrs. Williams fled and got some distance from the house, but she was pursued, overtaken, and compelled to get up behind one of the company, who brought her back, and after showing her the mangled body of her lifeless husband, she was told to get down and lay by his side, where she was shot dead. I then started for Mr. Jacob Williams', where the family were murdered. Here we found a young man named Drury, who had come on business with Mr. Williams; he was pursued, overtaken and shot. Mrs. Vaughan's was the next place we visited, and, after murdering the family here, I determined on starting for Jerusalem. Our number amounted now to fifty or sixty, all mounted and armed with guns, axes, swords, and clubs.

On reaching Mr. James W. Parker's gate, immediately on the road leading to Jerusalem and about three miles distant, it was proposed to me to call there, but I objected, as I knew he was gone to Jerusalem, and my object was to reach there as soon as possible; but some of the men having relations at Mr. Parker's, it was agreed that they might call and get his people. I remained at the gate on the road with seven or eight; the others going across the field to the house about half a mile off. After waiting some time for them, I became impatient and started to the house for them, and on our return we were met by a party of white men, who had pursued our blood-stained track, and who had fired on those at the gate and dispersed them, which I knew nothing of, not having been at that time rejoined by any of them.

Confrontation

Immediately on discovering the whites, I ordered my men to halt and form, as they appeared to be alarmed. The white men, eighteen in number, approached us in about one hundred yards, when one of them fired (this was against the positive orders of Captain Alexander P. Peete, who commanded, and who had directed the men to reserve their fire until within thirty paces). And I discovered about half of them retreating. I then ordered my men to fire and rush on them; the few remaining stood their ground until we approached within fifty yards, when they fired and retreated. We pursued and overtook some of them who we thought we left dead (they were not killed); after pursuing them about two hundred yards and rising a little hill, I discovered they were met by another party, and had halted and were reloading their guns. (This was a small party from Jerusalem who knew the Negroes were in the field and had just tied their horses to await their return to the road knowing that Mr. Parker and family were in Jerusalem, but knew nothing of the party that had gone in with Captain Peete. On hearing the firing they immediately rushed to the spot and arrived just in time to arrest the progress of these barbarous villains and save the lives of their friends and fellow citizens.)

Thinking that those who retreated first, and the party who fired on us at fifty or sixty yards distant, had all only fallen back to meet others with ammunition. As I saw them reloading their guns, and more coming up than I saw at first, and several of my bravest men being wounded, the others became panic struck and scattered over the field; the white men pursued and fired on us several times. Hark had his horse shot under him, and I caught another for him as it was running by me; five or six of my men were wounded, but none left on the field; finding myself defeated here I instantly determined to go through a private way and cross the Nottoway River at the Cypress Bridge, three miles below Jerusalem, and attack that place in the rear, as I expected they would look for me on the other road, and I had a great desire to get there to procure arms and ammunition. After going a short distance in this private way, accompanied by about twenty men, I overtook two or three who told me the others were dispersed in every direction. After trying in vain to collect a sufficient force to proceed to Jerusalem, I determined to return, as I was sure they would make back to their old neighborhood, where they would rejoin me, make new recruits, and come down again. On my way back, I called at Mrs. Thomas', Mrs. Spencer's, and several other places, the white families having fled; we found no more victims to gratify our thirst for blood. We stopped at Maj. Ridley's quarter for the night, and being joined by four of his men, with the recruits made since my defeat, we mustered now about forty strong.

After placing out sentinels, I laid down to sleep, but was quickly roused by a great racket; starting up, I found some mounted and others in great confusion; one of the sentinels having given the alarm that we were about to be attacked, I ordered some to ride around and reconnoiter, and on their return the others being more alarmed, not knowing who they were, fled in different ways, so that I was reduced to about twenty again, with this I determined to attempt to recruit, and proceed on to rally in the neighborhood I had left. Dr. Blunt's was the nearest house, which we reached just before day; on riding up the yard, Hark fired a gun. We expected Dr. Blunt and his family were at Maj. Ridley's, as I knew there was a company of men there; the gun was fired to ascertain if any of the family were at home; we were immediately fired upon and retreated leaving several of my men. I do not know what became of them, as I never saw them afterwards.

Pursuing our course back and coming in sight of Captain Harris', where we had been the day before, we discovered a party of white men at the house, on which all deserted me but two (Jacob and Nat). We concealed ourselves in the woods until near night, when I sent them in search of Henry, Sam, Nelson, and Hark, and directed them to rally all they could at the place we had had our dinner the Sunday before, where they would find me, and I accordingly returned there as soon as it was dark and remained until Wednesday evening, when discovering white men riding around the place as though they were looking for some one, and none of my men joining me, I concluded Jacob and Nat had been taken and compelled to betray me.

In Hiding

On this I gave up all hope for the present; and on Thursday night, after having supplied myself with provisions from Mr. Travis', I scratched a hole under a pile of fence rails in a field, where I concealed myself for six weeks, never leaving my hiding place but for a few minutes in the dead of night to get water, which was very near. Thinking by this time I could venture out, I began to go about in the night and eavesdrop the houses in the neighborhood; pursuing this course for about a fortnight and gathering little or no intelligence, afraid of speaking to any human being, and returning every morning to my cave before the dawn of day. I know not how long I might have led this life, if accident had not betrayed me. A dog in the neighborhood, passing by my hiding place one night while I was out, was attracted by some meat I had in my cave, and crawled in and stole it, and was coming out just as I returned. A few nights after, two Negroes having started to go hunting with the same dog, and passed that way, the dog came again to the place, and having just gone out to walk about, discovered me and barked, on which thinking myself discovered, I spoke to them to beg concealment. On making myself known, they fled from me. Knowing then they would betray me, I immediately left my hiding place and was pursued almost incessantly until I was taken a fortnight afterwards by Mr. Benjamin Phipps, in a little hole I had dug out with my sword, for the purpose of concealment, under the top of a fallen tree. On Mr. Phipps discovering the place of my concealment, he cocked his gun and aimed at me. I requested him not to shoot, and I would give up, upon which he demanded my sword. I delivered it to him, and he brought me to prison. During the time I was pursued, I had many hairbreadth escapes, which your time will not permit you to relate. I am here loaded with chains, and willing to suffer the fate that awaits me.

VIEWPOINT 4

"It was a grand opportunity for the low whites, who had no negroes of their own to scourge."

The Southampton Rebellion Resulted in White Violence

Harriet A. Jacobs (1813-1897)

Harriet A. Jacobs was born a slave in North Carolina in 1813. In 1835 she became a fugitive; she remained in hiding for seven years before moving to the North in 1842. She became involved in the abolitionist movement and in 1861 published *Incidents in the Life of a Slave Girl*. The book is an autobiographical novel in which Jacobs changed the names of people and places but essentially described her own experiences—her mistreatment as a slave and the sexual harassment she suffered from her master.

The following viewpoint is a chapter from her book in which she describes how whites responded to the 1831 Nat Turner slave rebellion. Jacobs portrays many whites reacting with indiscriminate violence and looting against blacks, both slave and free.

Not far from this time Nat Turner's insurrection broke out; and the news threw our town into great commotion. Strange that they should be alarmed, when their slaves were so "contented and happy"! But so it was.

It was always the custom to have a muster every year. On that occasion every white man shouldered his musket. The citizens and the so-called country gentlemen wore military uniforms. The poor whites took their places in the ranks in every-day dress, some without shoes, some without hats. This grand occasion had already passed; and when the slaves were told there was to be another muster, they were surprised and rejoiced. Poor creatures! They thought it was going to be a holiday. I was informed of the true state of affairs, and imparted it to the few I could trust. Most gladly would I have proclaimed it to every slave; but I dared not. All could not be relied on. Mighty is the power of the torturing lash.

Country Bullies

By sunrise, people were pouring in from every quarter within twenty miles of the town. I knew the houses were to be searched; and I expected it would be done by country bullies and the poor whites. I knew nothing annoyed them so much as to see colored people living in comfort and respectability; so I made arrangements for them with especial care. I arranged every thing in my grandmother's house as neatly as possible. I put white quilts on the beds, and decorated some of the rooms with flowers. When all was arranged, I sat down at the window to watch. Far as my eye could reach, it rested on a motley crowd of soldiers. Drums and fifes were discoursing martial music. The men were divided into companies of sixteen, each headed by a captain. Orders were given, and the wild scouts rushed in every direction, wherever a colored face was to be found.

It was a grand opportunity for the low whites, who had no negroes of their own to scourge. They exulted in such a chance to exercise a little brief authority, and show their subserviency to the slaveholders; not reflecting that the power which trampled on the colored people also kept themselves in poverty, ignorance, and moral degradation. Those who never witnessed such scenes can hardly believe what I know was inflicted at this time on innocent men, women, and children, against whom there was not the slightest ground for suspicion. Colored people and slaves who lived in remote parts of the town suffered in an especial manner. In some cases the searchers scattered powder and shot among their clothes, and then sent other parties to find them, and bring them forward as proof that they were plotting insurrection. Every where men, women, and children were whipped till the blood stood in puddles at their feet. Some received five hundred lashes; others were tied hands and feet, and tortured with a bucking paddle, which blisters the skin terribly. The dwellings of the colored people, unless they happened to be protected by some influential white person, who was nigh at hand, were robbed of clothing and every thing else the marauders thought worth carrying away. All day long these unfeeling wretches went round, like a troop of demons, terrifying and tormenting the helpless. At night, they formed themselves into patrol bands, and went wherever they chose among the colored people, acting out their brutal will. Many women hid themselves in woods and swamps, to keep out of their way. If any of the husbands or fathers told of these outrages, they were tied up to the public whipping post, and cruelly scourged for telling lies about white men. The consternation was universal. No two people that had the slightest tinge of color in their faces dared to be seen talking together.

The Slaughter of Blacks

John Hampden Pleasants, the son of a former Virginia governor, was a lawyer, newspaper editor, and a member of the local militia that helped suppress the 1831 Southampton slave revolt led by Nat Turner. In this excerpt from his newspaper account of the event called "Southampton Affair," he expresses regret at the lynchings and other white-on-black violence that resulted.

It is with pain we speak of another feature of the Southampton Rebellion; for we have been most unwilling to have our sympathies for the sufferers diminished or affected by their misconduct. We allude to the slaughter of many blacks, without trial, and under circumstances of great barbarity. How many have thus been put into death (generally by decapitation or shooting) reports vary; probably however some five and twenty and from that to 40; possibly a yet larger number. To the great honor of General Eppes, he used every precaution in his power, and we hope and believe with success, to put a stop to the disgraceful procedure.

I entertained no positive fears about our household, because we were in the midst of white families who would protect us. We were ready to receive the soldiers whenever they came. It was not long before we heard the tramp of feet and the sound of voices. The door was rudely pushed open; and in they tumbled, like a pack of hungry wolves. They snatched at every thing within their reach. Every box, trunk, closet, and corner underwent a thorough examination. A box in one of the drawers containing some silver change was eagerly pounced upon. When I stepped forward to take it from them, one of the soldiers turned and said angrily, "What d'ye foller us fur? D'ye s'pose white folks is come to steal?"

Searches

I replied, "You have come to search; but you have searched that box, and I will take it, if you please."

At that moment I saw a white gentleman who was friendly to us; and I called to him, and asked him to have the goodness to come in and stay till the search was over. He readily complied. His entrance into the house brought in the captain of the company, whose business it was to guard the outside of the house, and see that none of the inmates left it. This officer was Mr. Litch, the wealthy slaveholder whom I mentioned, in the account of neighboring planters, as being notorious for his cruelty. He felt above soiling his hands with the search. He merely gave orders; and if a bit of writing was discovered, it was carried to him by his ignorant followers, who were unable to read.

My grandmother had a large trunk of bedding and table cloths. When that was opened, there was a great shout of surprise; and one exclaimed, "Where'd the damned niggers git all dis sheet an' table clarf?"

My grandmother, emboldened by the presence of our white protector, said, "You may be sure we didn't pilfer 'em from *your* houses."

"Look here, mammy," said a grim-looking fellow without any coat, "you seem to feel mighty gran' 'cause you got all them 'ere fixens. White folks oughter have 'em all."

His remarks were interrupted by a chorus of voices shouting, "We's got 'em! We's got 'em! Dis 'ere yaller gal's got letters!"

There was a general rush for the supposed letter, which, upon examination, proved to be some verses written to me by a friend. In packing away my things, I had overlooked them. When their captain informed them of their contents, they seemed much disappointed. He inquired of me who wrote them. I told him it was one of my friends. "Can you read them?" he asked. When I told him I could, he swore, and raved, and tore the paper into bits. "Bring me all your letters!" said he, in a commanding tone. I told him I had none. "Don't be afraid," he continued, in an insinuating way. "Bring them all to me. Nobody shall do you any harm." Seeing I did not move to obey him, his pleasant tone changed to oaths and threats. "Who writes to you? half free niggers?" inquired he. I replied, "O, no; most of my letters are from white people. Some request me to burn them after they are read, and some I destroy without reading."

An exclamation of surprise from some of the company put a stop to our conversation. Some silver spoons which ornamented an old-fashioned buffet had just been discovered. My grandmother was in the habit of preserving fruit for many ladies in the town, and of preparing suppers for parties; consequently she had many jars of preserves. The closet that contained these was next invaded, and the contents tasted. One of them, who was helping himself freely, tapped his neighbor on the shoulder, and said, "Wal done! Don't wonder de niggers want to kill all de white folks, when dey live on 'sarves" [meaning preserves]. I stretched out my hand to take the jar, saying, "You were not sent here to search for sweetmeats."

"And what *were* we sent for?" said the captain, bristling up to me. I evaded the question.

The search of the house was completed, and nothing found to condemn us. They next proceeded to the garden, and knocked about every bush and vine, with no better success. The captain called his men together, and, after a short consulation, the order to march was given. As they passed out of the gate, the captain turned back, and pronounced a malediction on the house. He said it ought to be burned to the ground, and each of its inmates receive thirty-nine lashes. We came out of this affair very fortunately; not losing any thing except some wearing apparel.

Cruelties Committed

Towards evening the turbulence increased. The soldiers, stimulated by drink, committed still greater cruelties. Shrieks and shouts continually rent the air. Not daring to go to the door, I peeped under the window curtain. I saw a mob dragging along a number of colored people, each white man, with his musket upraised, threatening instant death if they did not stop their shrieks. Among the prisoners was a respectable old colored minister. They had found a few parcels of shot in his house, which his wife had for years used to balance her scales. For this they were going to shoot him on Court House Green. What a spectacle was that for a civilized country! A rabble, staggering under intoxication, assuming to be the administrators of justice!

The better class of the community exerted their influence to save the innocent, persecuted people; and in several instances they succeeded, by keeping them shut up in jail till the excitement abated. At last the white citizens found that their own property was not safe from the lawless rabble they had summoned to protect them. They rallied the drunken swarm, drove them back into the country, and set a guard over the town.

The next day, the town patrols were commissioned to search colored people that lived out of the city; and the most shocking outrages were committed with perfect impunity. Every day for a fortnight, if I looked out, I saw horsemen with some poor panting negro tied to their saddles, and compelled by the lash to keep up with their speed, till they arrived at the jail yard. Those who had been whipped too unmercifully to walk were washed with brine, tossed into a cart, and carried to jail. One black man, who had not fortitude to endure scourging, promised to give information about the conspiracy. But it turned out that he knew nothing at all. He had not even heard the name of Nat Turner. The poor fellow had, however, made up a story, which augmented his own sufferings and those of the colored people.

The day patrol continued for some weeks, and at sundown a night guard was substituted. Nothing at all was proved against the colored people, bond or free. The wrath of the slaveholders was somewhat appeased by the capture of Nat Turner. The imprisoned were released. The slaves were sent to their masters, and the free were permitted to return to their ravaged homes. Visiting was strictly forbidden on the plantations. The slaves begged the privilege of again meeting at their little church in the woods, with their burying ground around it. It was built by the colored people, and they had no higher happiness than to meet there and sing hymns together, and pour out their hearts in spontaneous prayer. Their request was denied, and the church was demolished. They were permitted to attend the white churches, a certain portion of the galleries being appropriated to their use. There, when every body else had partaken of the communion, and the benediction had been pronounced, the minister said, "Come down, now, my colored friends." They obeyed the summons, and partook of the bread and wine, in commemoration of the meek and lowly Jesus, who said, "God is your Father, and all ye are brethren."

VIEWPOINT 5

"As the means of guarding against the possible repetition of these sanguinary scenes, I cannot fail to recommend to your early attention, the revision of all the laws intended to preserve, in due subordination, the slave population of our State."

Stricter Laws Can Prevent Slave Revolts

John Floyd (1783-1837)

John Floyd served as governor of Virginia from 1830 to 1834. Prior to that he had been a medical doctor and an influential Virginia representative in the U.S. Congress.

The following viewpoint is taken from Floyd's annual address to the Virginia legislature, given on December 6, 1831. Much of that address was focused on the Southampton slave revolt led by Nat Turner. It describes the events of that time and presents Floyd's recommendations on how the Virginia government should respond.

Floyd, in his diary and personal letters, had expressed a desire for the gradual emancipation of slaves and the banishment of all blacks from Virginia. A strong supporter of economic modernization and development of Virginia, his opposition to slavery, in the view of historian Henry Irving Tragle, was "not because of humanitarian considerations, but because, to him, it represented a barrier to the kind of development that he sought." Floyd, however, did not strongly promote emancipation while he was governor and he does not mention emancipation in his address. He instead calls for stricter laws regulating the behavior of slaves and of free blacks in Virginia and for strengthening the local militia.

Fellow-Citizens of the Senate and of the House of Delegates:

You are again assembled, under circumstances calculated to inspire the community with a just expectation, that your deliberations will be followed by measures equal in energy and decision, to the crisis in which your country is placed: an expectation, which I am sure will not be disappointed. The deep interest which the citizens in every part of this Commonwealth have felt and manifested, in relation to occurrences of a grave and distressing character, which have taken place since your adjournment, new, unexpected and heretofore unknown to the State; together with the anxiety felt in the future fate of some of the great subjects which were agitated at your last session, and the unpleasant aspect of our Federal Relations, all conspire to cause the people to turn their eyes upon you at this time, with profound and fixed attention. You alone possess the power of accomplishing all the great objects which the public desire, and much of the future welfare of this Republic depends upon your present deliberations; deliberations, which doubtless will be first turned to the melancholy subject which has filled the country with affliction, and one of the fairest counties in the Commonwealth with mourning.

Bloody Deeds

Whilst we were enjoying the abundance of the last season, reposing in the peace and quiet of domestic comfort and safety, we were suddenly aroused from that security, by receiving information that a portion of our fellow-citizens had fallen victims to the relentless fury of assassins and murderers, even whilst wrapped in profound sleep, and that those bloody deeds had been perpetrated in a spirit of wantonness and cruelty, unknown to savage warfare, even in their most revolting form.

In August last, a banditti of slaves, consisting of but a few at first, and not at any time exceeding a greater number than seventy, rose upon some of the unsuspecting and defenceless inhabitants of Southampton, and under circumstances of the most shocking and horrid barbarity, put to death sixty-one persons, of whom the greater number were women and helpless children. Much of this bloody work was done on Monday morning; and on the day following, about ten o'clock, the last murder was committed. The citizens of that and the adjacent counties promptly assembled, and all real danger was speedily terminated.

The conspiracy was at first believed to be general; wherefore I was induced to call into service a force sufficient to crush at a single blow all opposing power, whatever might be its strength. To this end, detachments of Light Infantry from the seventh and fifty-fourth Regiments, and from the fourth Regiment of Cavalry and fourth Light Artillery, under Captains Harrison and Richardson, were ordered to repair to the scene of action with all possible speed. . . .

It gives me great pleasure to communicate to the General Assembly, the high satisfaction I feel in bearing testimony to the zeal, promptitude and dispatch with which every officer discharged his duty, and the cheerful alacrity with which every citizen obeyed the call of the law.

Though the call upon the Light Troops was so promptly obeyed, yet before their arrival the revolt was subdued, and many of these deluded fanatics were either captured, or were placed beyond the possibility of escape; some had already been immolated by an excited people. . . .

All of those who participated in the bloody tragedy, have expiated their crimes by undergoing public execution, whilst some, who had been condemned, have been reprieved for reasons which were deemed satisfactory. There is much reason to believe, that the spirit of insurrection was not confined to Southampton; many convictions have taken place elsewhere, and some few in distant counties. From the documents, which I herewith lay before you, there is too much reason to believe those plans of treason, insurrection and murder, have been designed, planned and matured by unrestrained fanatics in some of the neighbouring States, who find facilities in distributing their views and plans amongst our population, either through the post office, or by agents sent for that purpose throughout our territory.

Upon inspecting these documents, and contemplating that state of things which they are intended to produce, I felt it my duty to open a correspondence with the Governors of some of the neighbouring powers of this Confederacy, to preserve, as far as possible, the good understanding which exists, and which ought to be cherished between the different members of this Union. The result of this correspondence will be made known to you, so soon as it is ascertained.

Negro Preachers

The most active among ourselves, in stirring up the spirit of revolt, have been the negro preachers. They had acquired great ascendancy over the minds of their fellows, and infused all their opinions, which had prepared them for the development of the final design: there is also, some reason to believe, those preachers have a perfect understanding in relation to these plans throughout the eastern counties; and have been the channels through which the inflammatory papers and pamphlets, brought here by the agents and emissaries from other States, have been circulated amongst our slaves. The facilities, thus afforded for plotting treason and conspiracy to rebel and make insurrection, have been great. Through the indulgence of the magistracy and the laws, large collections of slaves have been permitted to take place, at any time through the week for the ostensible purpose of indulging in religious worship, but in many instances the real purpose with the preacher was of a different character. The sentiments and sometimes words of these inflammatory pamphlets, which the meek and charitable of other States have seen cause to distribute as fire-brands in the bosom of our society, have been read. What shall be thought of those fiends, who, having no interest in our community, nevertheless, seek to excite a servile war; a war, which exhausts itself in the massacre of unoffending women and children on the one side, and on the other, in the sacrifice of all who have borne part in the savage undertaking? Not only should the severest punishment be inflicted upon those disturbers of our peace, whenever they or their emissaries are found within our reach, but decisive measures should be adopted to make all their measures abortive. The public good requires the negro preachers to be silenced, who, full of ignorance, are incapable of inculcating any thing but notions of the wildest superstition, thus preparing fit instruments, in the hands of the crafty agitators, to destroy the public tranquility.

As the means of guarding against the possible repetition of these sanguinary scenes, I cannot fail to recommend to your early attention, the revision of all the laws intended to preserve, in due subordination, the slave population of our State. In urging these considerations upon you, let me not be understood, as expressing the slightest doubt or apprehension of general results. All communities are liable to suffer from the dagger of the murderer and midnight assassin, and it behoves them to guard against them. With us, the first returning light dispels the danger, and soon witnesses the murderer in chains.

Free People of Color

Though means have been taken by those of other States to agitate our community, and discontent our slaves and incite them to attempt an unattainable object, some proof is also furnished, that for the class of free people of color, they have opened more enlarged views, and urge the achievement of a higher destiny, by means for the present less violent, but not differing in the end from those presented to the slaves. That class of the community, our laws have heretofore treated with indulgent kindness, and many instances of solicitude for their welfare have marked the progress of legislation. If the slave is confined by law to the estate of his master, as it is advisable he should be, the free people of colour may nevertheless convey all the incendiary pamphlets and papers with which we are sought to be inundated.

This class, too, has been the first to place itself in hostile array against every measure designed to remove them from amongst us. Though it will be indispensably necessary for them to withdraw from this community, yet in the spirit of kindness which has ever characterized the Legislature of Virginia, it is submitted whether, as the last benefit which we can confer upon them, it may not be wise to appropriate annually a sum of money to aid in their removal from this Commonwealth.

Whilst recent events had created apprehension in the minds of a few, some agitation was also more extensively felt: wherefore it was deemed prudent, to arm the militia in a manner calculated to quiet all apprehensions, and arms were accordingly furnished to nearly all the regiments on the eastern frontier. The want of them, upon this sudden emergency, was so sensibly felt by those in the vicinity of Norfolk, as to induce Commodore Warrington, in command of the navy yard in Gosport, to distribute a portion of the public arms under his care. That gallant and patriotic officer did not hesitate to assume the responsibility of this step, and it is gratifying to perceive that his conduct has met the approbation of the public functionaries. The policy of disarming the militia, it is believed, was pursued as a measure of economy, as the men and officers had been culpably negligent in their attention to their preservation, so that many were lost, or by neglect became unfit for service. Now, however, the necessity for preserving them is distinctly felt, and a doubt cannot be entertained, that more care will be taken of them in future. I could not weigh the expense incurred by this measure, against the possible sacrifice of life, much less the possible repetition of the scenes of Southampton.

VIEWPOINT 6

"Cast no reproach upon the conduct of the slaves, but let your lips and cheeks wear the blisters of condemnation!"

Only the Abolition of Slavery Can Prevent Slave Revolts

William Lloyd Garrison (1805-1879)

William Lloyd Garrison was one of the most prominent leaders of the abolitionist movement. From 1831 to 1865 he edited and published *The Liberator*, a newspaper noted for its uncompromising abolitionist stance. He helped found the American Anti-Slavery Society in 1833 and was its president from 1843 to 1865. Garrison's writings were blamed by some people as a cause of slave uprisings. Following the 1831 Nat Turner revolt, southern states outlawed the circulation of the *Liberator*, and some sought to prosecute Garrison.

The following viewpoint was published in the September 3, 1831, issue of the *Liberator* shortly after the Nat Turner revolt. In it, Garrison denies charges that he supports violence or inspired the incident. But, he argues, as long as slavery remains, the threat of slave insurrections will persist in the South. He calls for immediate emancipation of the slaves.

The Insurrection

What we have long predicted,—at the peril of being stigmatized as an alarmist and declaimer,—has commenced its fulfillment. The first step of the earthquake, which is ultimately to shake down the fabric of oppression, leaving not one stone upon the other, has been made. The first drops of blood, which are but the prelude to a deluge from the gathering clouds, have fallen. The first flash of lightning, which is to ignite and consume, has been felt. The first wailings of a bereavement, which is to clothe the earth in sackcloth, have broken upon our ears.

In the first number of the Liberator, we alluded to the hour of vengeance in the following lines:

> Wo if it come with storm, and blood, and fire,
>> When midnight darkness veils the earth and sky!
>> *Wo to the innocent babe*—the guilty sire—
>> *Mother and daughter*—friends of kindred tie!
>> *Stranger and citizen alike shall die!*
> Red-handed Slaughter his revenge shall feed,
>> And Havoc yell his ominous death-cry,
> And wild Despair in vain for mercy plead—
>> While hell itself shall shrink and sicken at the deed!

Read the account of the insurrection in Virginia, and say whether our prophecy be not fulfilled. What was poetry—imagination—in January, is now a bloody reality. 'Wo to the innocent babe—to mother and daughter!' Is it not true? Turn again to the record of slaughter! Whole families have been cut off—not a mother, not a daughter, not a babe left. Dreadful retaliation! 'The dead bodies of white and black lying just as they were slain, unburied'—the oppressor and the oppressed equal at last in death—what a spectacle!

Only the Beginning

True, the rebellion is quelled. Those of the slaves who were not killed in combat, have been secured, and the prison is crowded with victims destined for the gallows!

> 'Yet laugh not in your carnival of crime
> Too proudly, ye oppressors!'

You have seen, it is to be feared, but the beginning of sorrows. All the blood which has been shed will be required at your hands. At your hands alone? No—but at the hands of the people of New-England and of all the free states. The crime of oppression is national. The south is only the agent in this guilty traffic. But, remember! the same causes are at work which must inevitably produce the same effects; and when the contest shall have again begun, it must be again a war of extermination. In the present instance, no quarters have been asked or given.

But we have killed and routed them now—we can do it again and again—we are invincible! A dastardly triumph, well becoming a nation of oppressors. Detestable complacency, that can think, without emotion, of the extermination of the blacks! We have the power to kill *all*—let us, therefore, continue to apply the whip and forge new fetters!

In his fury against the revolters, who will remember their wrongs? What will it avail them, though the catalogue of their sufferings, dripping with warm blood fresh from their lacerated bodies, be held up to extenuate their conduct? It is enough that the victims were black—that circumstance makes them less precious than the dogs which have been slain in our streets! They were black—brutes, pretending to be men—legions of curses on their memories! They were black—God made them to serve us!

Ye patriotic hypocrites! ye panegyrists of Frenchmen, Greeks, and Poles! ye fustian declaimers for liberty! ye valiant sticklers for equal rights among yourselves! ye haters of aristocracy! ye assailants of monarchies! ye republican nullifiers! ye treasonable disunionists! be dumb! Cast no reproach upon the conduct of the slaves, but let your lips and cheeks wear the blisters of condemnation!

Ye accuse the pacific friends of emancipation of instigating the slaves to revolt. Take back the charge as a foul slander. The slaves need no incentives at our hands. They will find them in their stripes—in their emaciated bodies—in their ceaseless toil—in their ignorant minds—in every field, in every valley, on every hill-top and mountain, wherever you and your fathers have fought for liberty—in your speeches, your conversations, your celebrations, your pamphlets, your newspapers—voices in the air, sounds from across the ocean, invitations to resistance above, below, around them! What more do they need? Surrounded by such influences, and smarting under their newly made wounds, is it wonderful that they should rise to contend—as other 'heroes' have contended—for their lost rights? It is *not* wonderful.

Not Justifying Violence

In all that we have written, is there aught to justify the excesses of the slaves? No. Nevertheless, they deserve no more censure than the Greeks in destroying the Turks, or the Poles in exterminating the Russians, or our fathers in slaughtering the British. Dreadful, indeed, is the standard erected by worldly patriotism!

For ourselves, we are horror-struck at the late tidings. We have exerted our utmost efforts to avert the calamity. We have warned our countrymen of the danger of persisting in their unrighteous conduct. We have preached to the slaves the pacific precepts of Jesus Christ. We have appealed to christians, philanthropists and patriots, for their assistance to accomplish the great work of national redemption through the agency of moral power—of public opinion—of individual duty. How have we been received? We have been threatened, proscribed, vilified and imprisoned—a laughing-stock and a reproach. Do we falter, in view of these things? Let time answer. If we have been hitherto urgent, and bold, and denunciatory in our efforts,—hereafter we shall grow vehement and active with the increase of danger. We shall cry, in trumpet tones, night and day,—Wo to this guilty land, unless she speedily repents of her evil doings! The blood of millions of her sons cries aloud for redress! IMMEDIATE EMANCIPATION can alone save her from the vengeance of Heaven, and cancel the debt of ages!

CHAPTER 4

Abolitionism and Its Opponents

Chapter Preface

The debate in the United States over slavery was not merely between those who sought to abolish the institution and those who sought to preserve it. Many within the antislavery movement itself disagreed over just how the abolition of slavery was to be achieved and the best strategies and methods to use.

In the early days of the antislavery movement in the eighteenth and early nineteenth centuries, opponents of slavery concentrated their efforts on persuading slaveholders to voluntarily free their slaves and on developing plans for gradual emancipation. A proposal made by Virginia lawyer St. George Tucker, for example, would have freed slaves over a period of many years, while compensating the owners and trying to prevent too much social disruption. Many Northern states freed their slaves using similar plans of gradual emancipation.

But by the 1820s and 1830s, a variety of factors had combined to cause people to question the concept of gradual emancipation. The 1793 invention of the cotton gin and the subsequent cotton boom made slaves vital to the Southern economy. Many of the Southern states passed laws making it more difficult for slaveholders to free their slaves. The hopes of those who predicted that slavery might gradually fade away in the South were dashed.

In the North, religious revivalism was sweeping through the states. Its influence caused people to view slavery as a serious national sin. A growing number of blacks and whites denounced the discrepancy between America's ideals of freedom and the existence of slavery.

Finally, Great Britain set an example for the United States by abolishing slavery throughout its empire in 1833. Abolitionists in Britain had set the immediate end of slavery as their goal a few years before, and their success inspired their U.S. counterparts to set a similar goal. These factors led many abolitionists to call for the immediate emancipation of all American slaves. That goal became the focus of the antislavery movement for the next thirty years.

The term *abolitionist* came into use around 1835, and it was used to describe those people who crusaded for the ending of slavery in all states of the Union. Noted abolitionists included William Lloyd Garrison, Frederick Douglass, Theodore Dwight Weld, Lydia Maria Child, Arthur and Lewis Tappan, and Abby Kelley. They spread the message of the evils of slavery through lectures, pamphlets, and newspapers. Among the most influential of abolitionist publications were the autobiographical *Narrative of the Life of Frederick Douglass* and Harriet Beecher Stowe's novel *Uncle Tom's Cabin.*

Abolitionists faced numerous obstacles, including public criticism and resistance that was sometimes violent. Critics in both the South and North denounced abolitionists as dangerous meddlers who disrupted society. A New York State antislavery convention in 1835 was delayed and had to be moved because of riots. Elijah P. Lovejoy, the editor of an abolitionist newspaper in Illinois, was killed and his press destroyed by a mob in 1837. Ironically, such violence and the abolitionists' courageous defense of their rights of free speech and press attracted many people to their cause.

A more significant impediment to the abolitionist movement was its internal divisions. Abolitionists never fully agreed on a plan to free the slaves. Some, such as Frederick Douglass, a former slave, and James Birney, a former slaveholder and 1840 and 1844 presidential candidate for the antislavery Liberty Party, believed in working within America's political system to achieve their goals. These people became known as political abolitionists. They were opposed by more idealistic abolitionists, led by Garrison and Wendell Phillips. They believed the U.S. government had been hopelessly corrupted by slavery supporters and that abolitionists should not even vote or hold public office. They argued that abolitionists should instead focus on "moral suasion" to persuade Americans to end slavery. Some advocated secession from the United States, and a few even urged violent rebellion.

In a tumultuous meeting of the American Anti-Slavery Society in 1840, the abolitionist movement officially split into rival factions over these and other issues, and abolitionism was never again a united movement. However, abolitionists continued to play an important role in the debate over slavery. Abolitionist pressure helped push President Abraham Lincoln to issue the Emancipation Proclamation in 1863.

VIEWPOINT 1

"Human prudence forbids that we should precipitately engage in a work of such hazard as a general and simultaneous emancipation."

Emancipation Should Be Gradual

St. George Tucker (1752-1827)

St. George Tucker was a judge of the Virginia Supreme Court of Appeals and a professor of law at the College of William and Mary in Williamsburg, Virginia. In 1796 he published a long pamphlet called *A Dissertion on Slavery* in which he proposed a plan for the gradual abolition of slavery in Virginia.

Tucker's thinking on slavery was greatly affected by slave insurrections in the French colony of St. Domingue (later Haiti), which began in 1791 and ultimately led to the independence of Haiti and the abolition of slavery there. Tucker believed Virginia, with its increasing black population, could suffer insurrections and conflict if slavery was not ended in some fashion. One feature of Tucker's plan was the denial of all political rights to freed slaves.

Tucker did not envision the peaceful coexistence of blacks and whites once slavery was abolished. Consequently, he believed blacks should be induced to settle somewhere outside of Virginia.

Although gradual plans of emancipation were enacted in some northern colonies, where the slave population was low, Tucker's proposals generated little response in the North or South, and were never enacted in Virginia.

In the preceding enquiry into the absolute rights of the citizens of united America, we must not be understood as if those rights were equally and universally the privilege of all the inhabitants of the United States, or even of all those, who may challenge this land of freedom as their native country. Among the blessings which the Almighty hath showered down on these states, there is a large portion of the bitterest draught that ever flowed from the cup of affliction. Whilst America hath been the land of promise to Europeans, and their descendants, it hath been the vale of death to millions of the wretched sons of Africa. The genial light of liberty, which hath here shone with unrivalled lustre on the former, hath yielded no comfort to the latter, but to them hath proved a pillar of darkness, whilst it hath conducted the former to the most enviable state of human existence. Whilst we were offering up vows at the shrine of Liberty, and sacrificing hecatombs upon her altars; whilst we swore irreconcilable hostility to her enemies, and hurled defiance in their faces; whilst we adjured the God of Hosts to witness our resolution to live free, or die, and imprecated curses on their heads who refused to unite with us in establishing the empire of freedom; we were imposing upon our fellow men, who differ in complexion from us, a slavery, ten thousand times more cruel than the utmost extremity of those grievances and oppressions, of which we complained.

An Arduous Task

The extirpation of slavery from the United States, is a task equally arduous and momentous. To restore the blessings of liberty to near a million of oppressed individuals, who have groaned under the yoke of bondage, and to their descendants, is an object, which those who trust in Providence, will be convinced would not be unaided by the divine Author of our being, should we invoke his blessings upon our endeavours. Yet human prudence forbids that we should precipitately engage in a work of such hazard as a general and simultaneous emancipation. The mind of man must in some measure be formed for his future condition. The early impressions of obedience and submission, which slaves have received amongst us, and the no less habitual arrogance and assumption of superiority, among the whites, contribute, equally, to unfit the former for *freedom*, and the latter for *equality*. To expel them all at once, from the United States, would in fact be to devote them only to a lingering death by famine, by disease, and other accumulated miseries. . . . To retain them among us, would be nothing more than to throw so many of the human race upon the earth without the means of subsistence: they would soon become idle, profligate, and miserable. Unfit for their new condition, and unwilling to return to their former laborious course, they would become the caterpillars of the earth, and the tigers of the human race. The recent history of the French

Emancipation Must Be Gradual

Ferdinando Fairfax, a wealthy Virginia planter, slaveowner, and associate of George Washington, published his Plan for Liberating the Negroes Within the United States *in 1790. It was the first detailed plan in the United States for emancipating the slaves. Fairfax tied his gradual emancipation plan with the insistence that freed blacks must move to Africa.*

It seems to be the general opinion, that emancipation must be gradual; since, to deprive a man, at once, of all his right in the property of his negroes, would be the height of injustice, and such as, in this country, would never be submitted to: and the resources of government are by no means adequate to making at once a full compensation. It must therefore be by voluntary consent—consequently in a gradual manner.

West Indies exhibits a melancholy picture of the probable consequences of a general, and momentary emancipation in any of the states, where slavery has made considerable progress. In Massachusetts the abolition of it was effected by a single stroke; a clause in their constitution: but the whites at that time, were as sixty-five to one, in proportion to the blacks. The whole number of free persons in the United States, south of Delaware state, are 1,233,829, and there are 648,439 slaves; the proportion being less than two to one. Of the cultivators of the earth in the same district, it is probable that there are four slaves for one free white man.—To discharge the former from their present condition, would be attended with an immediate general famine, in those parts of the United States, from which not all the productions of the other states, could deliver them; similar evils might reasonably be apprehended from the adoption of the measure by any one of the southern states; for in all of them the proportion of slaves is too great, not to be attended with calamitous effects, if they were immediately set free. These are serious, I had almost said unsurmountable obstacles, to a general, simultaneous emancipation.—There are other considerations not to be disregarded. A great part of the *property* of individuals consists in *slaves*. The laws have sanctioned this species of property. Can the laws take away the property of an individual without his own consent, or without a *just compensation*? Will those who do not hold slaves agree to be taxed to make this compensation? Creditors also, who have trusted their debtors upon the faith of this visible property will be defrauded. If justice demands the emancipation of the slave, she, also, *under these circumstances*, seems to plead for the owner, and for his creditor. The claims of nature, it will be said are stronger than those which arise from social institutions, only. I admit it, but nature also dictates to us to provide for our *own* safety, and authorizes all *necessary* measures for that purpose. And we have shewn that our own security, nay, our very existence, might be endangered by the hasty adoption of any measure for the *immediate* relief of the *whole* of this unhappy race. Must we then quit the subject, in despair of the success of any project for the amendment of their, as well as our own, condition! I think not.—Strenuously as I feel my mind opposed to a simultaneous emancipation, for the reasons already mentioned, the abolition of slavery in the United States, and especially in that state, to which I am attached by every tie that nature and society form, is *now* my *first*, and will probably be my last, expiring wish. But here let me avoid the imputation of inconsistency, by observing, that the abolition of slavery may be effected without the *emancipation* of a single slave; without depriving any man of the *property* which he *possesses*, and without defrauding a creditor who has trusted him on the faith of that property. The experiment in that mode has already been begun in some of our sister states. Pennsylvania, under the auspices of the immortal Franklin, begun the work of gradual abolition of slavery in the year 1780, by enlisting nature herself, on the side of humanity. Connecticut followed the example four years after. New-York very lately made an essay which miscarried, by a very inconsiderable majority. Mr. Jefferson informs us, that the committee of revisors, of which he was a member, had prepared a bill for the emancipation of all slaves born after passing that act. This is conformable to the Pennsylvania and Connecticut laws.—Why the measure was not brought forward in the general assembly I have never heard. Possibly because objections were foreseen to that part of the bill which relates to the disposal of the blacks, after they had attained a certain age. It certainly seems liable to many, both as to the policy and the practicability of it. To establish such a colony in the territory of the United States, would probably lay the foundation of intestine wars, which would terminate only in their extirpation, or final expulsion. To attempt it in any other quarter of the globe would be attended with the utmost cruelty to the colonists, themselves, and the destruction of their whole race. If the plan were at this moment in operation, it would require the annual exportation of 12,000 persons. This requisite number must, for a series of years be considerably increased, in order to keep pace with the increasing population of those people. In twenty years it would amount to upwards of twenty thousand persons; which is half the number which are now supposed to be annually exported from Africa.—Where would a fund to support this expence be found? Five times the present revenue of the state would barely defray the charge of their passage. Where provisions for their support after their arrival? Where those necessaries which must preserve them from perishing?—Where a territory sufficient to support them?—Or where could they be received as friends, and not as invaders? To colonize them in the United States might seem less difficult. If the territory to be assigned them were beyond the settlements of the whites, would they not be put upon a forlorn hope against the Indians? Would not the expence of transporting them thither, and supporting them, at least for the first and second year, be also far beyond the revenues and abilities of the state? The expence attending a small army in that country hath been found enormous. To transport as many colonists, annually, as we have shewn were necessary to eradicate the evil, would probably require five times as much money as the support of such an army. But the expence would not stop there: they must be assisted and supported at least for another year after their arrival in their new settlements. Suppose them arrived. Illiterate and ignorant as they are, is it probable that they would be capable of instituting such a government, in their new colony, as would be necessary for their own internal happiness, or to secure them from destruction from without? European emigrants, from whatever country they arrive, have been accustomed to the restraint of laws, and the respect for government. These people, accustomed to be ruled with a rod of iron, will not easily submit to milder restraints. They would become hordes of vagabonds, robbers and murderers. Without the aids of an enlightened policy, morality, or religion, what else could be expected from their still savage state, and debased condition?—"But why not retain and *incorporate the blacks into the state*?" This question has been well answered by Mr. Jefferson, and who is there so free from prejudices among us, as candidly to declare that he has none against such a measure? The recent scenes transacted in the French colonies in the West Indies are enough to make one shudder with the apprehension of realizing similar calamities in this country. Such probably would be the event of an attempt to smother those prejudices which have been cherished for a period of almost two centuries. Those who secretly favour, whilst they affect to regret, domestic slavery, contend that in abolishing it, we must also abolish that scion from it which I have denominated *civil* slavery. That there must be no distinction of rights; that the descendants of Africans, as men, have an equal claim to all civil rights, as the descendants of Europeans; and upon being delivered from the yoke of bondage have a right to be admitted to all the privileges of a citizen.—But have not men when they enter into a state of society, a right to admit, or exclude any description of persons, as they think proper? If it be true, as Mr. Jefferson seems to suppose, that the Africans are really an inferior race of mankind, will not sound policy advise their exclusion from a society in which they have not yet been admitted to participate in civil rights; and even to guard against such admission, at any future period, since it may eventually depreciate the whole national character? And if prejudices have taken such deep root in our minds, as to render it impossible to eradicate this opinion, ought not so general an error, if it be one, to be respected? Shall we not relieve the necessities of the naked diseased beggar, unless we will invite him to a seat at our table; nor afford him shelter from the inclemencies of the night air, unless we admit him also to share our bed? To deny that we ought to abolish slavery, without incorporating the Negroes into the state, and admitting them to a full participation of all our civil and social rights, appears to me to rest upon a similar foundation. The experiment so far as it has been already made amongst us, proves that the emancipated blacks are not ambitious of civil rights. To prevent the generation of such an ambition, appears to comport with sound policy; for if it should ever rear its head, its partizans, as well as its opponents, will be enlisted by nature herself, and always ranged in formidable array against each other. We must therefore endeavour to find some middle course, between the tyrannical and iniquitous policy which holds so many human creatures in a state of grievous bondage; and that which would turn loose a numerous, starving, and enraged banditti, upon the innocent descendants of their former oppressors. *Nature, time,* and *sound policy* must co-operate with each other to produce such a change: if either be neglected, the work will be incomplete, dangerous, and not improbably destructive.

A Plan of Gradual Abolition

The plan therefore which I would presume to propose for the consideration of my countrymen is such, as the number of slaves, the difference of their nature, and habits, and the state of agriculture, among us, might render it *expedient,* rather than *desirable* to adopt: and it would partake partly of that proposed by Mr. Jefferson, and adopted in other states; and partly of such cautionary restrictions, as a due regard to situation and circumstances, and even to *general* prejudices, might recommend to those, who engage in so arduous, and perhaps unprecedented an undertaking.

1. Let every female born after the adoption of the plan be free, and transmit freedom to all her descendants, both male and female.

2. As a compensation to those persons, in whose families such females, or their descendants may be born, for the expence and trouble of their maintenance during infancy, let them serve such persons until the age of twenty-eight years: let them then receive twenty dollars in money, two suits of clothes, suited to the sea-

son, a hat, a pair of shoes, and two blankets. If these things be not voluntarily done, let the county courts enforce the performance, upon complaint.

3. Let all Negroe children be registered with the clerk of the county or corporation court, where born, within one month after their birth: let the person in whose family they are born take a copy of the register, and deliver it to the mother, or if she die to the child, before it is of the age of twenty-one years. Let any Negroe claiming to be free, and above the age of puberty, be considered as of the age of twenty-eight years, if he or she be not registered, as required.

Emancipation Must Accommodate Slaveowners

Frances Wright was a feminist and reformer. In A PLAN *for the* Gradual Abolition of Slavery in the United States, *published in 1825, she proposed establishing a community in Tennessee for freed slaves. The community, called Nashoba, failed after five years.*

It appears superfluous, in proposing a plan for the general abolition of slavery from the United States, to observe upon the immensity of the evil, and the gloomy prospect of dangers it presents to the American people—disunion, bloodshed, servile wars of extermination, horrible in their nature and consequences, and disgraceful in the eyes of the civilized world.

It is conceived that any plan of emancipation, to be effectual, must consult at once the pecuniary interests and prevailing opinions of the southern planters, and bend itself to the existing laws of the southern states. In consequence, it appears indispensable, that emancipation be connected with colonization, and that it demand no pecuniary sacrifice from existing slaveholders, and entail no loss of property on their children.

---

4. Let all such Negroe servants be put on the same footing as white servants and apprentices now are, in respect to food, raiment, correction, and the assignment of their service from one to another.

5. Let the children of Negroes and mulattoes, born in the families of their parents, be bound to service by the overseers of the poor, until they shall attain the age of twenty-one years. Let all above that age, who are not housekeepers, nor have voluntarily bound themselves to service for a year before the first day of February annually, be then bound for the remainder of the year by the overseers of the poor. Let the overseers of the poor receive fifteen per cent. of their wages, from the person hiring them, as a compensation for their trouble, and ten per cent. per annum out of the wages of such as they may bind apprentices.

6. If at the age of twenty-seven years, the master of a Negroe or mulattoe servant be unwilling to pay his freedom dues, above mentioned, at the expiration of the succeeding year, let him bring him into the county court, clad and furnished with necessaries as before directed, and pay into court five dollars, for the use of the servant, and thereupon let the court direct him to be hired by the overseers of the poor for the succeeding year, in the manner before directed.

7. Let no Negroe or mulattoe be capable of taking, holding, or exercising, any public office, freehold, franchise or privilege, or any estate in lands or tenements, other than a lease not exceeding twenty-one years.—Nor of keeping, or bearing arms, unless authorized so to do by some act of the general assembly, whose duration shall be limited to three years. Nor of contracting matrimony with any other than a Negroe or mulattoe; nor be an attorney; nor be a juror; nor a witness in any court of judicature, except against, or between Negroes and mulattoes. Nor be an executor or administrator; nor capable of making any will or testament; nor maintain any real action; nor be a trustee of lands or tenements himself, nor any other person to be a trustee to him or to his use.

8. Let all persons born after the passing of the act, be considered as entitled to the same mode of trial in criminal cases, as free Negroes and mulattoes are now entitled to.

Encouraging Freed Slaves to Deport

The restrictions in this place may appear to favour strongly of prejudice: whoever proposes any plan for the abolition of slavery, will find that he must either encounter, or accommodate himself to prejudice.—I have preferred the latter; not that I pretend to be wholly exempt from it, but that I might avoid as many obstacles as possible to the completion of so desirable a work, as the abolition of slavery. Though I am opposed to the banishment of the Negroes, I wish not to encourage their future residence among us. By denying them the most valuable privileges which civil government affords, I wished to render it their inclination and their interest to seek those privileges in some other climate. There is an immense unsettled territory on this continent [the Louisiana Purchase] more congenial to their natural constitutions than ours, where they may perhaps be received upon more favourable terms than we can permit them to remain with us. Emigrating in small numbers, they will be able to effect settlements more easily than in large numbers; and without the expence or danger of numerous colonies. By releasing them from the yoke of bondage, and enabling them to seek happiness wherever they can hope to find it, we surely confer a benefit, which no one can sufficiently appreciate, who has not tasted of the bitter curse of compulsory servitude.

By excluding them from offices, the seeds of ambition would be buried too deep, ever to germinate: by disarming them, we may calm our apprehensions of their resentments arising from past sufferings; by incapacitating them from holding lands, we should add one inducement more to emigration, and effectually remove the foundation of ambition, and party-struggles. Their personal rights, and their property, though limited, would whilst they remain among us be under the protection of the laws; and their condition not at all inferior to that of the *labouring* poor in most other countries. Under such an arrangement we might reasonably hope, that time would either remove from us a race of men, whom we wish not to incorporate with us, or obliterate those prejudices, which now form an obstacle to such incorporation.

But it is not from the want of liberality to the emancipated race of blacks that I apprehend the most serious objections to the plan I have ventured to suggest. Those slave holders (whose numbers I trust are few) who have been in the habit of considering their fellow creatures as no more than cattle, and the rest of the brute creation, will exclaim that they are to be deprived of their *property*, without compensation. Men who will shut their ears against this moral truth, that all men are by nature *free*, and *equal*, will not even be convinced that they do not possess a *property* in an *unborn* child: they will not distinguish between allowing to *unborn* generations the absolute and unalienable rights of human nature, and taking away that which they *now possess*; they will shut their ears against truth, should you tell them, the loss of the mother's labour for nine months, and the maintenance of a child for a dozen or fourteen years, is amply compensated by the services of that child for as many years more, as he has been an expence to them. But if the voice of reason, justice and humanity be not stifled by sordid avarice, or unfeeling tyranny, it would be easy to convince even those who have entertained such erroneous notions, that the right of one man over another is neither founded in nature, nor in sound policy. That it cannot extend to those *not in being*; that no man can in reality be *deprived* of what he doth not possess: that fourteen years labour by a young person in the prime of life, is an ample compensation for a few months of labour lost by the mother, and for the maintenance of a child, in that coarse homely manner that Negroes are brought up: And lastly, that a state of slavery is not only perfectly incompatible with the principles of government, but with the safety and security of their masters. History evinces this.

172

VIEWPOINT 2

"I utterly reject, as delusive and dangerous in the extreme, every plea which justifies a procrastinated and an indefinite emancipation."

Emancipation Should Be Immediate

William Lloyd Garrison (1805-1879)

William Lloyd Garrison was one of the most prominent leaders of the abolitionist movement. From 1831 to 1865 he edited and published *The Liberator*, a newspaper noted for its uncompromising abolitionist stance. In 1833 he helped found the American Anti-Slavery Society and was its president from 1843 to 1865. Garrison's writings were blamed by some people as a cause of slave uprisings. Following the 1831 Nat Turner revolt, southern states outlawed the circulation of the *Liberator*, and some sought to prosecute Garrison.

Originally a supporter of gradual abolition and of returning freed slaves to Africa, by 1830 Garrison had revised his views and was a strong critic of both gradualism and African colonization. The following viewpoint is taken from his 1832 book *Thoughts on African Colonization*. Garrison attacks the whole concept of gradual abolition of slavery. He argues that slavery is a clear evil that can only be cured by an immediate emancipation of the slaves.

Since the deception practised upon our first parents by the old serpent, there has not been a more fatal delusion in the minds of men than that of the gradual abolition of slavery. *Gradual* abolition! do its supporters really know what they talk about? Gradually abstaining from what? From sins the most flagrant, from conduct the most cruel, from acts the most oppressive! Do colonizationists mean, that slave-dealers shall purchase or sell a few victims less this year than they did the last? that slave-owners shall liberate one, two or three out of every hundred slaves during the same period? that slave-drivers shall apply the lash to the scarred and bleeding backs of their victims somewhat less frequently? Surely not—I respect their intelligence too much to believe that they mean any such thing. But if any of the slaves should be exempted from sale or purchase, why not all? if justice require the liberation of the few, why not of the many? if it be right for a driver to inflict a number of lashes, how many shall be given? Do colonizationists mean that the practice of separating the husband from the wife, the wife from the husband, or children from their parents, shall come to an end by an almost imperceptible process? or that the slaves shall be defrauded of their just remuneration, less and less every month or every year? or that they shall be under the absolute, irresponsible control of their masters? Oh no! I place a higher value upon their good sense, humanity and morality than this! Well, then, they would immediately break up the slave traffic—they would put aside the whip—they would have the marriage relations preserved inviolate—they would not separate families—they would not steal the wages of the slaves, nor deprive them of personal liberty! This is abolition—*immediate abolition*. It is simply declaring that slave owners are bound to fulfill—now, without any reluctance or delay—the golden rule, namely, to do as they would be done by; and that, as the right to be free is inherent and inalienable in the slaves, there ought now to be a disposition on the part of the people to break their fetters. All the horrid spectres which are conjured up, on this subject, arise from a confusion of the brain, as much as from a corruption of the heart.

I utterly reject, as delusive and dangerous in the extreme, every plea which justifies a procrastinated and an indefinite emancipation, or which concedes to a slave owner the right to hold his slaves as *property* for any limited period, or which contends for the gradual preparation of the slaves for freedom; believing all such pretexts to be a fatal departure from the high road of justice into the bogs of expediency, a surrender of the great principles of equity, an indefensible prolongation of the curse of slavery, a concession which places the guilt upon any but those who incur it, and directly calculated to perpetuate the thraldom of our species.

What Immediate Abolition Means

Immediate abolition does not mean that the slaves shall immediately exercise the right of suffrage, or be eligible to any office, or be emancipated from law, or be free from the benevolent restraints of guardianship. We contend for the immediate personal

The Benefits of Immediate Abolition

The New England Anti-Slavery Society was founded in December 1831 by William Lloyd Garrison and other Bostonians. Its aim was the immediate emancipation of all slaves. This excerpt is taken from the society's annual report, published in 1833.

Immediate abolition would save the lives of the planters, enhance the value of their lands, promote their temporal and eternal interests, and secure for them the benignant smiles of Heaven. It would destroy the market for slaves, and, consequently, to a certain extent, destroy the foreign slave trade; for when the Africans cannot be sold, they will not be stolen.

freedom of the slaves, for their exemption from punishment except where law has been violated, for their employment and reward as free laborers, for their exclusive right to their own bodies and those of their own children, for their instruction and subsequent admission to all the trusts, offices, honors and emoluments of intelligent freemen. Emancipation will increase and not destroy the value of their labor; it will also increase the demand for it. Holding out the stimulus of good treatment and an adequate reward, it will induce the slaves to toil with a hundred fold more assiduity and faithfulness. Who is so blind as not to perceive the peaceful and beneficial results of such a change? The slaves, if freed, will come under the watchful cognizance of law; they will not be idle, but *avariciously* industrious; they will not rush through the country, firing dwellings and murdering the inhabitants; for freedom is all they ask—all they desire—the obtainment of which will transform them from enemies into friends, from nuisances into blessings, from a corrupt, suffering and degraded, into a comparatively virtuous, happy and elevated population.

Nor does immediate abolition mean that any compulsory power, other than moral, should be used in breaking the fetters of slavery. It calls for no bloodshed, or physical interference; it jealously regards the welfare of the planters; it simply demands an entire revolution in public sentiment, which will lead to better conduct, to contrition for past crimes, to a love instead of a fear of justice, to a reparation of wrongs, to a healing of breaches, to a suppression of revengeful feelings, to a quiet, improving, prosperous state of society! . . .

[Friends of the Colonization Society say] 'To say that immediate emancipation will only increase the wretchedness of the slaves, and that we must pursue a system of *gradual* abolition, is to present to us the double paradox, that we must continue to do evil, in order to cure the evil which we are doing; and that we must continue to be unjust, and to do evil, that good may come.' The fatal error of *gradualists* lies here: They talk as if the friends of abolition contended only for the emancipation of the slaves, without specifying or caring what should be done with or for them! as if the planters were invoked to cease from one kind of villany, only to practise another! as if the manumitted slaves must necessarily be driven out from society into the wilderness, like wild beasts! This is talking nonsense: it is a gross perversion of reason and common sense. Abolitionists have never said, that mere manumission would be doing justice to the slaves: they insist upon a remuneration for years of unrequited toil, upon their employment as free laborers, upon their immediate and coefficient instruction, and upon the exercise of a benevolent supervision over them on the part of their employers. They declare, in the first place, that to break the fetters of the slaves, and turn them loose upon the country, without the preservative restraints of law, and destitute of occupation, would leave the work of justice only half done; and, secondly, that it is absurd to suppose that the planters would be wholly independent of the labor of the blacks—for they could no more dispense with it next week, were emancipation to take place, than they can to-day. The very ground which they assume for their opposition to slavery,—that it necessarily prevents the improvement of its victims,—shows that they contemplate the establishment of schools for the education of the slaves, and the furnishing of productive employment, immediately upon their liberation. If this were done, none of the horrors which are now so feelingly depicted, as the attendants of a sudden abolition, would ensue.

Emancipation and Education

But we are gravely told that education must *precede* emancipation. The logic of this plea is, that intellectual superiority justly gives one man an oppressive control over another! Where would such a detestable principle lead but to practices the most atrocious, and results the most disastrous, if carried out among ourselves? Tell us, ye hair-splitting sophists, the exact quantum of knowledge which is necessary to constitute a freeman. If every dunce should be a slave, your servitude is inevitable; and richly do you deserve the lash for your obtuseness. Our white population, too, would furnish blockheads enough to satisfy all the classical kidnappers in the land.

The reason why the slaves are so ignorant, is because they are held in bondage; and the reason why they are held in bondage, is because they are so ignorant! They ought not to be freed until they are educated; and they ought not be educated, because on the acquisition of knowledge they would burst their fetters! Fine logic, indeed! How men, who make any pretensions to honesty or common sense, can advance a paradox like this, is truly inexplicable. . . .

National Portrait Gallery, Washington, D.C./Art Resource, New York.

Over a period of three decades, abolitionist William Lloyd Garrison wrote hundreds of editorials and articles attacking slavery.

It is said, by way of extenuation, that the present owners of slaves are not responsible for the origin of this system. I do not arraign them for the crimes *of their ancestors,* but for the constant perpetration and extension of similar crimes. The plea that the evil of slavery was entailed upon them, shall avail them nothing: in its length and breadth it means that the robberies of one generation justify the robberies of another! that the inheritance of stolen property converts it into an honest acquisition! that the atrocious conduct of their fathers exonerates them from all accountability, thus presenting the strange anomaly of a race of men incapable of incurring guilt, though daily practising the vilest deeds! Scarcely any one denies that blame attaches somewhere: the present generation throws it upon the past—the past, upon its predecessor—and thus it is cast, like a ball, from one to another, down to the first importers of the Africans! 'Can that be *innocence* in the temperate zone, which is the *acme of all guilt* near the equator? Can that be *honesty* in one meridian of longitude, which, at one hundred degrees east, is the *climax of injustice?'* Sixty thousand infants, the offspring of slave-parents, are annually born in this country, and doomed to remediless bondage. Is it not as atrocious a crime to kidnap these, as to kidnap a similar number on the coast of Africa?

Faulty Emancipation Plans

It is said, moreover, that we ought to legislate prospectively, on this subject; that the fetters of the present generation of slaves cannot be broken; and that our single aim should be, to obtain the freedom of their offspring, by fixing a definite period after which none shall be born slaves. But this is inconsistent, inhuman and unjust. The following extracts from the speech of the Rev. Dr. Thomson are conclusive on this point:

'It amounts to an indirect sanction of the continued slavery of all who are now alive, and of all who may be born before the period fixed upon. This is a renunciation of the great moral principles upon which the demand for abolition proceeds. It consigns more than 800,000 human beings to bondage and oppression, while their title to freedom is both indisputable and acknowledged. And it is not merely an inconsistency on the part of the petitioners, and a violation of the duty which they owe to such a multitude of their fellow-men, but it weakens or surrenders the great argument by which they enforce their application for the extinction of colonial slavery. . . .

'Supposing all children born after January 1, 1831, were declared free, how are they to be educated? That they may be prepared for the enjoyment of that liberty with which you have invested them, they must undergo a particular and appropriate training. So say the *gradualists*. Very well; under whom are they to get this training? Are they to be separated from their parents? Is that dearest of natural ties to be broken asunder? Is this necessary for your plan? And are not you thus endeavoring to cure one species of wickedness by the instrumentality of another? But if they are to be left with their parents and brought up under their care, then either they will be imbued with the faults and degeneracies that are characteristic of slavery, and consequently be as unfit for freedom as those who have not been disenthralled: or they will be well nurtured and well instructed by their parents, and this implies a confession that their parents themselves are sufficiently prepared for liberty, and that there is no good reason for withholding from them, the boon that is bestowed upon their children.

'Whatever view, in short, we take of the question, the prospective plan is full of difficulty or contradictions, and we are made more sensible than ever that there is nothing left for us, but to take the consistent, honest, uncompromising course of demanding the abolition of slavery with respect to the present, as well as to every future generation of the negroes in our colonies.'

We are told that 'it is not right that men should be free, when their freedom will prove injurious to themselves and others.' This has been the plea of tyrants in all ages. If the immediate emancipation of the slaves would prove a curse, it follows that slavery is a blessing; and that it cannot be unjust, but benevolent, to defraud the laborer of his hire, to rank him as a beast, and to deprive him of his liberty. But this, every one must see, is at war with common sense, and avowedly doing evil that good may come. This plea must mean, either that a state of slavery is more favorable to the growth of virtue and the dispensation of knowledge than a state of freedom—(a glaring absurdity)—or that an immediate compliance with the demands of justice would be most unjust—(a gross contradiction.)

What Immediate Emancipation Means

A Boston clergyman, Amos A. Phelps was one of the early leaders of the American Anti-Slavery Society. He traveled throughout the United States lecturing on the need for immediate emancipation of the slaves. This excerpt is taken from his book Lectures on Slavery and Its Remedy, *published in 1834.*

Immediate emancipation means,
1. That the slaveholder, so far as he is concerned, should cease at once to hold or employ human beings as property.
2. That he should put them at once, in his regard and treatment of them, on the footing of men, possessing the inalienable rights of man.
3. That instead of turning them adrift on society, uncared for, he should offer to employ them as free hired laborers, giving them, however, liberty of choice whether to remain in his service or not.
4. That from this *starting point—this emancipation from slavery itself,* he should at once *begin* to make amends for the past, by entering heartily on the work of qualifying them for, and elevating them to all the privileges and blessings of freedom and religion;—thus doing what he can to emancipate them from their ignorance, degradation, &c.—in other words, from the *consequences* of slavery, as well as from the thing itself.

It is boldly asserted by some colonizationists, that '*the negroes are happier when kept in bondage,*' and that 'the condition of the great mass of emancipated Africans is one in comparison with which the condition of the slaves is *enviable.*' What is the inference? Why, either that slavery is not oppression—(another paradox)—or that real benevolence demands the return of the free people of color to their former state of servitude. Every kidnapper, therefore, is a true philanthropist! Our legislature should immediately offer a bounty for the body of every free colored person! The colored population of Massachusetts, at $200 per each man, woman and child, would bring at least *one million three hundred thousand dollars*. This sum would seasonably replenish our exhausted treasury. The whole free colored population of the United States, at the same price, (which is a low estimate,) would be worth *sixty-five millions of dollars!!* Think how many churches this would build, schools and colleges establish, beneficiaries educate, missionaries support, bibles and tracts circulate, railroads and canals complete, &c. &c. &c. !!! . . .

The Need for Immediate Abolition

Those who prophesy evil, and only evil, concerning immediate abolition, absolutely disregard the nature and constitution of man, as also his inalienable rights, and annihilate or reverse the causes and effects of human action. They are continually fearful lest the slaves, in consequence of their grievous wrongs and intolerable sufferings, should attempt to gain their freedom by revolution; and yet they affect to be equally fearful lest a general emancipation should produce the same disastrous consequences. How absurd! They *know* that oppression must cause rebellion; and yet they pretend that a removal of the cause will produce a bloody effect! This is to suppose an effect without a cause, and, of course, is a contradiction in terms. Bestow upon the slaves personal freedom, and all motives for insurrection are destroyed. Treat them like rational beings, and you may surely expect rational treatment in return: treat them like beasts, and they will behave in a beastly manner.

Besides, precedent and experience make the ground of abolitionists invulnerable. In no single instance where their principles have been adopted, has the result been disastrous or violent, but beneficial and peaceful even beyond their most sanguine expectations. The immediate abolition of slavery in Mexico, in Colombia, and in St. Domingo, was eminently preservative and useful in its effects. . . . According to the Anti-Slavery Reporter for January, 1832, three thousand prize negroes at the Cape of Good Hope had received their freedom—four hundred in one day; 'but not the least difficulty or disorder occurred: servants found masters, masters hired servants—all gained homes, and at night scarcely an idler was to be seen.'

These and many other similar facts show conclusively the safety of immediate abolition. Gradualists can present, in abatement of them, nothing but groundless apprehensions and criminal distrust. The argument is irresistible.

VIEWPOINT 3

"[Colonization] tends . . . to rid us, gradually and entirely, in the United States, of slaves and slavery: a great moral and political evil."

Returning Blacks to Africa Will Help End Slavery

Robert Goodloe Harper (1765-1825)

Many Americans who supported the abandonment of slavery believed that freed slaves should not remain in the United States. They promoted the return of blacks to Africa as the only long-term solution to slavery. Conversely, others supported African colonization as a way of ridding the United States of troublesome free blacks and strengthening the institution of slavery in the United States.

The American Colonization Society was formed in 1816 to promote the resettlement of blacks in Africa. It quickly gained the support of many prominent leaders, including Henry Clay, Daniel Webster, and Andrew Jackson. The society purchased land on the West Coast of Africa in 1821 and over the next forty years sent more than eleven thousand blacks there.

The following viewpoint is taken from a letter by Robert Goodloe Harper, a senator and lawyer from Baltimore, Maryland, to the American Colonization Society of Baltimore. The letter was published on August 20, 1817, in the society's first annual report, and the arguments expressed here were used by the society to gain public support. Harper expounds on what he sees as the major advantages of colonization.

In reflecting on the utility of a plan for colonizing the free people of color, with whom our country abounds, it is natural that we should be first struck by its tendency to confer a benefit on ourselves, by ridding us of a population for the most part idle and useless, and too often vicious and mischievous. These persons are condemned to a state of hopeless inferiority and degradation by their color, which is an indelible mark of their origin and former condition, and establishes an impassable barrier between them and the whites. This barrier is closed forever by our habits and our feelings, which perhaps it would be more correct to call our prejudices, and which, whether feelings or prejudices, or a mixture of both, make us recoil with horror from the idea of an intimate union with the free blacks, and preclude the possibility of such a state of equality, between them and us, as alone could make us one people. Whatever justice, humanity, and kindness, we may feel towards them, we cannot help considering them, and treating them, as our inferiors; nor can they help viewing themselves in the same light, however hard and unjust they may be inclined to consider such a state of things. We cannot help associating them in our feelings and conduct, nor can they help associating themselves, with the slaves, who have the same color, the same origin, and the same manners, and with whom they or their parents have been recently in the same condition. Be their industry ever so great, and their conduct ever so correct, whatever property they may acquire, or whatever respect we may feel for their characters, we never could consent, and they never could hope, to see the two races placed on a footing of perfect equality with each other; to see the free blacks, or their descendants, visit in our houses, form part of our circle of acquaintance, marry into our families, or participate in public honors and employments. This is strictly true of every part of our country, even those parts where slavery has long ceased to exist, and is held in abhorrence. There is no State in the Union where a negro or mulatto can ever hope to be a member of Congress, a judge, a militia officer, or even a justice of the peace; to sit down at the same table with the respectable whites, or to mix freely in their society. I may safely assert that Paul Cuffee, [a part Indian, part Negro sea captain who was active in promoting African colonization] respectable, intelligent, and wealthy as he is, has no expectation or chance of ever being invited to dine with any gentleman in Boston; of marrying his daughter, whatever may be her fortune or education, to one of their sons; or of seeing his son obtain a wife among their daughters.

This circumstance, arising from the difference of color and origin between the slaves and the free class, distinguishes the slavery of America from that of every other country, ancient or modern. Slavery existed among almost all the ancient nations; it now exists throughout Asia, Africa, and America, and in every part of the Russian and Turkish dominions in Europe; that is, in more than three-fourths of the world. But the great body of the slaves every where, except in North and South America, are of the same race, origin, color, and general character, with the free people. So it was among the ancients. Manumission therefore, by removing the slave from the condition of slavery, exempted him from its consequences, and opened his way to a full participation in all the benefits of freedom. He was raised to an equality with the free class, became incorporated into it with his family, and might, by good fortune or good conduct, soon wash out the stain, and obliterate the remembrance, of his former degraded condition.

A Freed Slave Is Still Black

But in the United States this is impossible. You may manumit the slave, but you cannot make him a white man; he still remains a negro or a mulatto. The mark and the recollection of his origin and former state still adhere to him; the feelings produced by that condition in his own mind, and in the minds of the whites, still exist; he is associated, by his color and by these recollections and feelings, with the class of slaves; and a barrier is thus raised between him and the whites, that is, between him and the free class, which he can never hope to transcend. With the hope he gradually loses the desire. The debasement, which was at first compulsory, has now become habitual and voluntary. The incitement to good conduct and exertion, which arises from the hope of raising himself or his family in the world, is a stranger to his breast. He looks forward to no distinction, aims at no excellence, and makes no effort beyond the supply of his daily wants; and the restraints of character being lost to him, he seeks, regardless of the future, to obtain that supply by the means which cost him the least present trouble. The authority of the master being removed, and its place not being supplied by moral restraints or incitements, he lives in idleness, and probably in vice, and obtains a precarious support by begging or theft. If he should avoid those extremes, and follow some regular course of industry, still the habits of thoughtless improvidence, which he contracted while a slave himself, or has caught from the slaves among whom he is forced to live, who of necessity are his companions and associates, prevent him from making any permanent provision for his support by prudent foresight and economy, and, in case of sickness, or of bodily disability from any other cause, send him to live as a pauper at the expense of the community. . . .

It is not in themselves merely that the free people of color are a nuisance and burden. They contribute greatly to the corruption of the slaves, and to aggravate the evils of their condition, by rendering them idle, discontented, and disobedient. This also arises from the necessity, under which the free blacks are, of remaining incorporated with the slaves, of associating habitually with them, and forming part of the same class in society. The slave, seeing his free companion live in idleness, or subsist, however scantily or precariously, by occasional and desultory employment, is apt to grow discontented with his own condition, and to regard as tyranny and injustice the authority which compels him to labor. Hence, he is strongly incited to elude this authority, by neglecting his work as much as possible, to withdraw himself from it altogether by flight, and sometimes to attempt direct resistance. This provokes or impels the master to severity, which would not otherwise be thought necessary; and that severity, by rendering the slave still more discontented with his condition, and more hostile towards his master, by adding the sentiments of resentment and revenge to his original dissatisfaction, often renders him more idle and more worthless, and thus induces the real or supposed necessity of still greater harshness on the part of the master. Such is the tendency of that comparison which the slave cannot easily avoid making between his own situation and that of the free people of his own color, who are his companions, and in every thing, except exemption from the authority of a master, his equals, whose condition, though often much worse than his own, naturally appears better to him; and, being continually under his observation, and in close contact with his feelings, is apt to chafe, goad, and irritate him incessantly. This effect, indeed, is not always produced; but such is the tendency of this state of things, and it operates more extensively, and with greater force, than is commonly supposed. . . .

Ending Slavery

Great, however, as the benefits are which we may thus promise ourselves from the colonization of the free people of color, by its tendency to prevent the discontent and corruption of our slaves, and to secure to them a better treatment, by rendering them more worthy of it, there is another advantage, infinitely greater in every point of view, to which it may lead the way. It tends, and may powerfully tend, to rid us, gradually and entirely, in the United States, of slaves and slavery: a great moral and political evil, of increasing virulence and extent, from which much mischief is now felt, and very great calamity in future is justly apprehended. It is in this point of view, I confess, that your scheme of colonization most strongly recommends itself, in my opinion, to attention and support. The alarming danger of cherishing in our bosom a

The Benefits of Colonization

One of the foremost U.S. senators of the first half of the nineteenth century, Henry Clay was an early supporter of African colonization and one of the founders of the American Colonization Society. His prejudices against blacks are expressed in this speech, originally given on January 20, 1827, before the American Colonization Society. Clay's opinions were not uncommon in the United States at this time.

There is a moral fitness in the idea of returning to Africa her children, whose ancestors have been torn from her by the ruthless hand of fraud and violence. Transplanted in a foreign land, they will carry back to their native soil the rich fruits of religion, civilization, law, and liberty. May it not be one of the great designs of the Ruler of the universe, (whose ways are often inscrutable by shortsighted mortals,) thus to transform an original crime into a signal blessing, to that most unfortunate portion of the globe. Of all classes of our population, the most vicious is that of the free colored. It is the inevitable result of their moral, political, and civil degradation. Contaminated themselves, they extend their vices to all around them, to the slaves and to the whites. If the principle of colonization should be confined to them; if a colony can be firmly established, and successfully continued in Africa which should draw off annually an amount of that portion of our population equal to its annual increase, much good will be done. If the principle be adopted and applied by the States, whose laws sanction the existence of slavery to an extent equal to the annual increase of slaves, still greater good will be done. This good will be felt by the Africans who go, by the Africans who remain, by the white population of our country, by Africa, and by America. It is a project which recommends itself to favor in all the aspects in which it can be contemplated.

distinct nation, which can never become incorporated with us, while it rapidly increases in numbers and improves in intelligence; learning from us the arts of peace and war, the secret of its own strength, and the talent of combining and directing its force—a nation which must ever be hostile to us, from feeling and interest, because it can never incorporate with us, nor participate in the advantages which we enjoy; the danger of such a nation in our bosom need not be pointed out to any reflecting mind. It speaks not only to our understandings, but to our very senses; and however it may be derided by some, or overlooked by others, who have not the ability or the time, or do not give themselves the trouble to reflect on and estimate properly the force and extent of those great moral and physical causes which prepare gradually, and at length bring forth, the most terrible convulsions in civil society, it will not be viewed without deep and awful apprehension by any who shall bring sound minds and some share of political knowledge and sagacity to the serious consideration of the subject. Such persons will give their most serious attention to any proposition which has for its object the eradication of this terrible mischief lurking in our vitals. I shall presently have occasion to advert a little to the manner in which your intended colony will conduce to this great end. It is therefore unnecessary to touch on it here. Indeed, it is too obvious to require much explanation.

But, independently of this view of the case, there is enough in the proposed measure to command our attention and support on the score of benefit to ourselves.

No person who has seen the slaveholding States, and those where slavery does not exist, and has compared ever so slightly their condition and situation, can have failed to be struck with the vast difference in favor of the latter. . . .

Where slavery exists, the slave labors as little as possible, because all the time that he can withdraw from labor is saved to his own enjoyments; and consumes as much as possible, because what he consumes belongs to his master; while the free white man is insensibly but irresistibly led to regard labor, the occupation of slaves, as a degradation, and to avoid it as much as he can. The effect of these combined and powerful causes, steadily and constantly operating in the same direction, may easily be conceived. It is seen in the striking difference which exists between the slaveholding sections of our country and those where slavery is not permitted.

Replacing Slaves with White Workers

It is therefore obvious that a vast benefit would be conferred on the country, and especially on the slaveholding districts, if all the slave laborers could be gradually and imperceptibly withdrawn from cultivation, and their place supplied by free white laborers—I say gradually and imperceptibly, because, if it were possible to withdraw, suddenly and at once, so great a portion of the effective labor of the community as is now supplied by slaves, it would be productive of the most disastrous consequences. It would create an immense void, which could not be filled; it would impoverish a great part of the community, unhinge the whole frame of society in a large portion of the country, and probably end in the most destructive convulsions. But it is clearly impossible, and therefore we need not enlarge on the evils which it would produce.

But to accomplish this great and beneficial change gradually and imperceptibly, to substitute a free white class of cultivators for the slaves, with the consent of the owners, by a slow but steady and certain operation, I hold to be as practicable as it would be beneficial; and I regard this scheme of colonization as the first step in that great enterprise.

The considerations stated in the first part of this letter have long since produced a thorough conviction in my mind that the existence of a class of free people of color in this country is highly injurious to the whites, the slaves, and the free people of color themselves. Consequently, that all emancipation, to however small an extent, which permits the persons emancipated to remain in this country, is an evil which must increase with the increase of the operation, and would become altogether intolerable, if extended to the whole, or even to a very large part, of the black population. I am therefore strongly opposed to emancipation, in every shape and degree, unless accompanied by colonization.

I may perhaps on some future occasion develop a plan, on which I have long meditated, for colonizing gradually, and with the consent of their owners, and of themselves, where free, the whole colored population, slaves and all; but this is not the proper place for such an explanation, for which indeed I have not time now. But it is an essential part of the plan, and of every such plan, to prepare the way for its adoption and execution, by commencing a colony of blacks, in a suitable situation and under proper management. This is what your society proposes to accomplish. Their project therefore, if rightly formed and well conducted, will open the way for this more extensive and beneficial plan of removing, gradually and imperceptibly, but certainly, the whole colored population from the country, and leaving its place to be imperceptibly supplied, as it would necessarily be, by a class of free white cultivators. In every part of the country this operation must necessarily be slow. In the Southern and Southwestern States it will be very long before it can be accomplished, and a very considerable time must probably elapse before it can even commence. It will begin first, and be first completed, in the Middle States, where the evils of slavery are most sensibly felt, the desire of getting rid of the slaves is already strong, and a greater facility exists of supplying their place by white cultivators. From thence it will gradually extend to the South and Southwest, till, by its steady, constant, and imperceptible operation, the evils of slavery shall be rooted out from every part of the United States, and the slaves themselves, and their posterity, shall be converted into a free, civilized, and great nation, in the country from which their progenitors were dragged, to be wretched themselves and a curse to the whites.

This great end is to be attained in no other way than by a plan of universal colonization, founded on the consent of the slaveholders and of the colonists themselves. For such a plan, that of the present colonization society opens and prepares the way, by exploring the ground, selecting a proper situation, and planting a colony, which may serve as a receptacle, a nursery, and a school, for those that are to follow. It is in this point of view that I consider its benefits as the most extensive and important, though not the most immediate.

Advantages of Colonization

The advantages of this undertaking, to which I have hitherto adverted, are confined to ourselves. They consist in ridding us of the free people of color, and preparing the way for getting rid of the slaves and of slavery. In these points of view they are undoubtedly very great. But there are advantages to the free blacks themselves, to the slaves, and to the immense population of middle and southern Africa, which no less recommend this undertaking to our cordial and zealous support.

To the free blacks themselves the benefits are the most obvious, and will be the most immediate. Here they are condemned to a state of hopeless inferiority, and consequent degradation. As they cannot emerge from this state, they lose by degrees the hope and at last the desire of emerging. With this hope and desire they lose the most powerful incitements to industry, frugality, good conduct, and honorable exertion. For want of this incitement, this noble and ennobling emulation, they sink for the most part into a state of sloth, wretchedness, and profligacy. The few honorable exceptions serve merely to show of what the race is capable in a proper situation. Transplanted to a colony composed of themselves alone, they would enjoy real equality: in other words, real freedom. They would become proprietors of land, master mechanics, shipowners, navigators, and merchants, and by degrees schoolmasters, justices of the peace, militia officers, ministers of religion, judges, and legislators. There would be no white population to remind them of and to perpetuate their original inferiority; but, enjoying all the privileges of freedom, they would soon enjoy all its advantages and all its dignity. The whites who might visit them would visit them as equals, for the purposes of a commerce mutually advantageous. They would soon feel the noble emulation to excel, which is the fruitful source of excellence in all the various departments of life; and, under the influence of this generous and powerful sentiment, united with the desire and hope of improving their condition, the most universal and active incitements to exertion among men, they would rise rapidly in the scale of existence, and soon become equal to the people of Europe, or of European origin, so long their masters and oppressors. Of all this the most intelligent among them would soon become sensible. The others would learn it from them; and the prospect and hope of such blessings would have an immediate and most beneficial effect on their condition and character; for it will be as easy to adopt such regulations as to exclude from this colony all but those who shall deserve by their conduct to be admitted: thus rendering the hope of admission a powerful incentive to industry, honesty, and religion.

To the slaves, the advantages, though not so obvious or immediate, are yet certain and great.

In the first place, they would be greatly benefited by the removal of the free blacks, who now corrupt them, and render them discontented: thus exposing them to harsher treatment and greater privations. In the next place, this measure would open the way to their more frequent and easier manumission; for many persons, who are now restrained from manumitting their slaves by the conviction that they generally become a nuisance when manumitted in the country, would gladly give them freedom, if they were to be sent to a place where they might enjoy it usefully to themselves and to society. And, lastly, as this species of manumission, attended by removal to a country where they might obtain all the advantages of freedom, would be a great blessing, and would soon be so considered by the slaves, the hope of deserving and obtaining it would be a great solace to their sufferings, and a powerful incitement to good conduct. It would thus tend to make them happier and better before it came, and to fit them better for usefulness and happiness afterwards. . . .

The greatest benefit, however, to be hoped from this enterprise, that which, in contemplation, most delights the philanthropic mind, still remains to be unfolded. It is the benefit to Africa herself, from this return of her sons to her bosom, bearing with them arts, knowledge, and civilization, to which she has hitherto been a stranger. . . . These colonies, composed of blacks already instructed in the arts of civilized life and the truths of the gospel, judiciously placed, well conducted, and constantly enlarged, will extend gradually into the interior, will form commercial and political connexions with the native tribes in their vicinity, will extend those connexions to tribes more and more remote, will incorporate many of the natives with the colonies, and in their turn make establishments and settlements among the natives, and thus diffuse all around the arts of civilization, and the benefits of literary, moral, and religious instruction.

VIEWPOINT 4

"The southern masters will colonize only those whom it may be dangerous to keep among them. The bondage of a large portion of our brothers will thus be rendered perpetual."

Returning Blacks to Africa Will Not End Slavery

Colored Citizens of Philadelphia (1817)

The idea of sending freed slaves to colonize Africa was attractive to many people who felt that blacks and whites could not live together in the United States without severe problems. Several prominent free blacks were initially supportive of African colonization, viewing it as the only alternative to the continued mistreatment and discrimination they were receiving in the United States. However, the concept sparked strong opposition among much of the free black population in the United States.

The following viewpoint is taken from a meeting of the free black citizens of Philadelphia in 1817 in response to the founding of the American Colonization Society. In their proclamation, they express their opposition to colonization, arguing that blacks have a full right to remain in the United States as citizens. They also express doubts as to whether colonization could in fact end slavery.

The resolution reprinted here is one of many that were gathered in abolitionist William Lloyd Garrison's book *Thoughts on African Colonization* published in 1832. James Forten, who closely assisted Garrison in this book, played a key role in the 1817 Philadelphia declaration. Forten, born into a free black family in Philadelphia, participated in the American Revolution as a powderboy and later rose to become a successful sailmaker and one of Philadelphia's wealthiest and most prominent citizens. He was a noted

190

advocate of abolition and of the rights of free blacks. Like several other black leaders of his time, he initially was supportive of the idea of returning to Africa but ultimately led the fight against it.

To the humane and benevolent inhabitants of the city and county of Philadelphia.

The free people of color, assembled together, under circumstances of deep interest to their happiness and welfare, humbly and respectfully lay before you this expression of their feelings and apprehensions.

Relieved from the miseries of slavery, many of us by your aid, possessing the benefits which industry and integrity in this prosperous country assure to all its inhabitants, enjoying the rich blessings of religion, by opportunities of worshipping the only true God, under the light of Christianity, each of us according to his understanding; and having afforded to us and to our children the means of education and improvement; we have no wish to separate from our present homes, for any purpose whatever. Contented with our present situation and condition, we are not desirous of increasing their prosperity but by honest efforts, and by the use of those opportunities for their improvement, which the constitution and laws allow to all. It is therefore with painful solicitude, and sorrowing regret, we have seen a plan for colonizing the free people of color of the United States on the coast of Africa, brought forward under the auspices and sanction of gentlemen whose names give value to all they recommend, and who certainly are among the wisest, the best, and the most benevolent of men, in this great nation.

We Do Not Seek Colonization

If the plan of colonizing is intended for our benefit; and those who now promote it, will never seek our injury; we humbly and respectfully urge, that it is not asked for by us; nor will it be required by any circumstances, in our present or future condition; as long as we shall be permitted to share the protection of the excellent laws and just government which we now enjoy, in common with every individual of the community.

We, therefore, a portion of those who are the objects of this plan, and among those whose happiness, with that of others of our color, it is intended to promote; with humble and grateful acknowledgments to those who have devised it, renounce and disclaim every connexion with it; and respectfully but firmly declare our determination not to participate in any part of it.

If this plan of colonization now proposed, is intended to provide a refuge and a dwelling for a portion of our brethren, who are now held in slavery in the south, we have other and stronger objections to it, and we entreat your consideration of them.

Colonization and Slavery

The ultimate and final abolition of slavery in the United States, by the operation of various causes, is, under the guidance and protection of a just God, progressing. Every year witnesses the release of numbers of the victims of oppression, and affords new and safe assurances that the freedom of all will be in the end accomplished. As they are thus by degrees relieved from bondage, our brothers have opportunities for instruction and improvement; and thus they become in some measure fitted for their liberty. Every year, many of us have restored to us by the gradual, but certain march of the cause of abolition—parents, from whom we have been long separated—wives and children whom we had left in servitude—and brothers, in blood as well as in early sufferings, from whom we had been long parted.

But if the emancipation of our kindred shall, when the plan of colonization shall go into effect, be attended with transportation to a distant land, and shall be granted on no other condition; the consolation for our past sufferings and of those of our color who are in slavery, which have hitherto been, and under the present situation of things would continue to be, afforded to us and to them, will cease for ever. The cords, which now connect them with us, will be stretched by the distance to which their ends will be carried, until they break; and all the sources of happiness, which affection and connexion and blood bestow, will be ours and theirs no more.

Nor do we view the colonization of those who may become emancipated by its operation among our southern brethren, as capable of producing their happiness. Unprepared by education, and a knowledge of the truths of our blessed religion, for their new situation, those who will thus become colonists will themselves be surrounded by every suffering which can afflict the members of the human family.

Without arts, without habits of industry, and unaccustomed to provide by their own exertions and foresight for their wants, the colony will soon become the abode of every vice, and the home of every misery. Soon will the light of Christianity, which now dawns among that portion of our species, be shut out by the clouds of ignorance, and their day of life be closed, without the illuminations of the gospel.

To those of our brothers, who shall be left behind, there will be assured perpetual slavery and augmented sufferings. Diminished

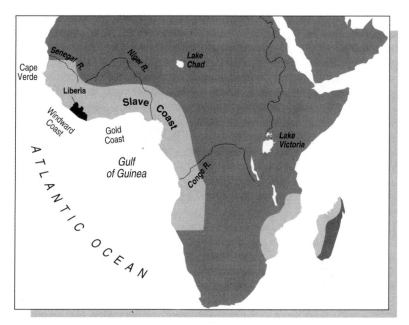

American slaves came from many parts of Africa, as the lighter-shaded areas of the map show. Many slaves from the interior of Africa were captured by African merchants and chieftains, chained and brought overland to the coast and sold to European traders. In 1821, the American Colonization Society purchased land in Africa to be colonized by freed American slaves. However, only about eleven thousand black Americans made the journey between 1821 and the Civil War. The territory became the independent country of Liberia in 1847.

in numbers, the slave population of the southern states, which by its magnitude alarms its proprietors, will be easily secured. Those among their bondmen, who feel that they should be free, by rights which all mankind have from God and from nature, and who thus may become dangerous to the quiet of their masters, will be sent to the colony; and the tame and submissive will be retained, and subjected to increased rigor. Year after year will witness these means to assure safety and submission among their slaves, and the southern masters will colonize only those whom it may be dangerous to keep among them. The bondage of a large portion of our brothers will thus be rendered perpetual.

Should the anticipations of misery and want among the colonists, which with great deference we have submitted to your better judgment, be realized; to emancipate and transport to Africa will be held forth by slaveholders as the worst and heaviest of punishments; and they will be threatened and successfully used to enforce increased submission to their wishes, and subjection to their commands.

Nor ought the sufferings and sorrows, which must be produced by an exercise of the right to transport and colonize such only of their slaves as may be selected by the slaveholders, escape the attention and consideration of those whom with all humility we now address. Parents will be torn from their children —husbands from their wives—brothers from brothers—and all the heart-rending agonies which were endured by our forefathers when they were dragged into bondage from Africa, will be again renewed, and with increased anguish. The shores of America will, like the sands of Africa, be watered by the tears of those who will be left behind. Those who shall be carried away will roam childless, widowed, and alone, over the burning plains of Guinea.

Disclaiming, as we emphatically do, a wish or desire to interpose our opinions and feelings between all plans of colonization, and the judgment of those whose wisdom as far exceeds ours as their situations are exalted above ours; *we humbly*, respectfully, and fervently intreat and beseech your disapprobation of the plan of colonization now offered by 'the American Society for colonizing the free people of color of the United States.'—Here, in the city of Philadelphia, where the voice of the suffering sons of Africa was first heard; where was first commenced the work of abolition, on which heaven has smiled, for it could have had success only from the Great Maker; let not a purpose be assisted which will stay the cause of the entire abolition of slavery in the United States, and which may defeat it altogether; which proffers to those who do not ask for them what it calls benefits, but which they consider injuries; and which must insure to the multitudes whose prayers can only reach you through us, MISERY, *sufferings, and perpetual slavery.*

JAMES FORTEN, Chairman.

Russell Parrott, Secretary.

"We consider [emancipation] ... so fraught with danger and mischief both to the whites and blacks ... that we cannot ... give it our sanction."

Emancipation Is Impractical

Thomas R. Dew (1802-1846)

After the Nat Turner slave revolt in 1831, the Virginia legislature seriously debated abandoning slavery in the 1831-32 session, but it ultimately rejected abolition. The session was the last time in the South the idea of abolishing slavery was seriously considered.

Following the session, Thomas R. Dew, a professor of political economy and law at the College of William and Mary in Williamsburg, Virginia, and later president of that institution, wrote a book called *Review of the Debate in the Virginia Legislature of 1831 and 1832* (Richmond, VA: TW White) that staunchly defended slavery as a positive good. The book became a source and inspiration for many proslavery writings in the following decades. In the excerpts presented here, Dew concentrates on the practical aspects of emancipation and what would happen to Virginia if the slaves were freed. Dew argues that the social and economic disruptions and other disadvantages of emancipation greatly outweigh whatever benefits emancipation might confer.

We shall now ... inquire seriously and fairly, whether there be any means by which we may get rid of slavery....

We will examine first, those schemes which propose abolition and deportation; and secondly, those which contemplate emancipation without deportation.

1st. *Emancipation and Deportation.*—In the late Virginia Legislature, where the subject of slavery underwent the most thorough discussion, all seemed to be perfectly agreed in the necessity of removal in case of emancipation. Several members from the lower counties, which are deeply interested in this question, seemed to be sanguine in their anticipations of the final success of some project of emancipation and deportation to Africa, the original home of the negro. "Let us translate them," said one of the most respected and able members of the Legislature, (Gen. Broadnax,) "to those realms from which, in evil times, under inauspicious influences, their fathers were unfortunately abducted. . . ."

Deportation Impractical

Fortunately for reason and common sense, all these projects of deportation may be subjected to the most rigid and accurate calculations, which are amply sufficient to dispel all doubt, even in the minds of the most sanguine, as to their practicability.

We take it for granted, that the right of the owner to his slave is to be respected, and, consequently, that he is not required to emancipate him, unless his full value is paid by the State. Let us, then, keeping this in view, proceed to the very simple calculation of the expense of emancipation and deportation in Virginia. The slaves, by the last census (1830,) amounted within a small fraction to 470,000; the average value of each one of these is, $200; consequently, the whole aggregate value of the slave population of Virginia, in 1830, was $94,000,000; and allowing for the increase since, we cannot err far in putting the present value at $100,000,000. The assessed value of all the houses and lands in the State, amounts to $206,000,000, and these constitute the material items in the wealth of the State, the whole personal property besides bearing but a very small proportion to the value of slaves, lands, and houses. Now, do not these very simple statistics speak volumes upon this subject? It is gravely recommended to the State of Virginia to give up a species of property which constitutes nearly one-third of the wealth of the whole state, and almost one-half of that of Lower Virginia, and with the remaining two-thirds to encounter the additional enormous expense of transportation and colonization on the coast of Africa. But the loss of $100,000,000 of property is scarcely the half of what Virginia would lose, if the immutable laws of nature could suffer (as fortunately they cannot) this tremendous scheme of colonization to be carried into full effect. . . .

Slaves Give Virginia Value

It is, in truth, the slave labor in Virginia which gives value to her soil and her habitations; take away this, and you pull down the Atlas that upholds the whole system; eject from the State the whole slave population, and we risk nothing in the prediction, that on the day in which it shall be accomplished, the worn soils of Virginia would not bear the paltry price of the government lands in the West, and the Old Dominion will be a "waste howling wilderness";—"the grass shall be seen growing in the streets, and the foxes peeping from their holes."

Abolition Would Create Bloodshed

John C. Calhoun, a senator and political leader of South Carolina, was a forceful and eloquent defender of slavery and states' rights. This excerpt is taken from a speech Calhoun delivered before the U.S. Senate in February 1837.

We of the South will not, cannot surrender our institutions. To maintain the existing relations between the two races inhabiting that section of the Union is indispensable to the peace and happiness of both. It cannot be subverted without drenching the country in blood and extirpating one or the other of the races. Be it good or bad, it has grown up with our society and institutions and is so interwoven with them that to destroy it would be to destroy us as a people. But let me not be understood as admitting, even by implication, that the existing relations between the two races, in the slaveholding states, is an evil. Far otherwise; I hold it to be a good, as it has thus far proved itself to be, to both, and will continue to prove so, if not disturbed by the fell spirit of Abolition.

But the favorers of this scheme say they do not contend for the sudden emancipation and deportation of the whole black population; they would send off only the increase, and thereby keep down the population to its present amount, while the whites, increasing at their usual rate, would finally become relatively so numerous as to render the presence of the blacks among us for ever afterwards entirely harmless. This scheme, which at first, to the unreflecting, seems plausible, and much less wild than the project of sending off the whole, is nevertheless impracticable and visionary, as we think a few remarks will prove. It is computed that the annual increase of the slaves and free colored population of Virginia is about six thousand. Let us first, then, make a calculation of the expense of purchase and transportation. At $200 each, the six thousand will amount in value to $1,200,000. At $30 each, for transportation, which we shall soon see is too little, we have the whole expense of purchase and transportation $1,380,000, an expense to be annually incurred by Virginia to keep down her black population to its present amount. And let us ask, is there anyone who can seriously argue that Virginia can incur such an annual expense as this for the next twenty-five or fifty years, until the whites have multiplied so greatly upon the blacks, as, in the *opinion* of the *alarmists,* for ever to quiet the fears of the community? Vain and delusive hope, if any were ever wild enough to entertain it! Poor old Virginia! . . .

It is almost useless to inquire whether this deportation of slaves to Africa would, as some seem most strangely to anticipate, invite the whites of other States into the Commonwealth. Who would be disposed to enter a State with worn out soil, and a black population mortgaged to the payment of millions *per annum,* for the purpose of emancipation and deportation, when in the West the most luxuriant soils, unincumbered with heavy exactions, could be purchased for the paltry sum of $1.25 per acre?

Where, then, is that multitude of whites to come from, which the glowing fancy of orators has sketched out as flowing into and filling up the *vacuum* created by the removal of slaves? . . .

Seeing, then, that the effort to send away the increase, on even the present increase of our slaves, must be vain and fruitless, how stupendously absurd must be the project, proposing to send off the whole increase, so as to keep down the negro population at its present amount! There are some things which man, arrayed in all his "brief authority," cannot accomplish, and this is one of them. . . .

Emancipation without Deportation.—We candidly confess, that we look upon this last mentioned scheme as much more practicable, and likely to be forced upon us, than the former. We consider it, at the same time, so fraught with danger and mischief both to the whites and blacks—so utterly subversive of the welfare of the slaveholding country, in both an economical and moral point of view, that we cannot, upon any principle of right or expediency, give it our sanction. . . .

Much was said in the Legislature of Virginia about superiority of free labor over slave, and perhaps, under certain circumstances, this might be true; but, in the present instance, the question is between *the relative amounts of labor which may be obtained from slaves before and after their emancipation.* Let us, then, first commence with our country, where, it is well known to everybody, that slave labor is vastly more efficient and productive than the labor of free blacks.

A Worthless Class

Taken as a whole class, the latter must be considered the most worthless and indolent of the citizens of the United States. It is well known that throughout the whole extent of our Union, they are looked upon as the very *drones* and *pests* of society. Nor does this character arise from the disabilities and disfranchisement by which the law attempts to guard against them. In the non-slave-holding States, where they have been more elevated by law, this kind of population is in a worse condition, and much more troublesome to society, than in the slaveholding, and especially in the planting States. Ohio, some years ago, formed a sort of land of promise for this deluded class, to which many have repaired from the slaveholding States,—and what has been the consequence? They have been most harshly expelled from that State, and forced to take refuge in a foreign land. Look through the Northern States, and mark the class upon whom the eye of the police is most steadily and constantly kept—see with what vigilance and care they are hunted down from place to place—and you cannot fail to see that idleness and improvidence are at the root of all their misfortunes. Not only does the experience of our own country illustrate this great fact, but others furnish abundant testimony. . . .

Emancipation Would Ruin the South

Albert Taylor Bledsoe was a professor of mathematics at the University of Virginia. In this excerpt from his book, Liberty and Slavery, *he attacks abolitionist arguments.*

The slaves—now worth so many hundred millions of dollars—would become worthless to themselves, and nuisances to society. No free State in the Union would be willing to receive them—or a considerable portion of them—into her dominions. They would be regarded as pests, and, if possible, everywhere expelled from the empires of freemen.

Our lands, like those of the British West Indies, would become almost valueless for the want of laborers to cultivate them. The most beautiful garden-spots of the sunny South would, in the course of a few years, be turned into a jungle, with only here and there a forlorn plantation. Poverty and distress, bankruptcy and ruin, would everywhere be seen. In one word, the condition of the Southern States would, in all material respects, be like that of the once flourishing British colonies in which the fatal experiment of emancipation has been tried.

In the free black, the principle of idleness and dissipation triumphs over that of accumulation and the desire to better our condition; the animal part of the man gains the victory over the moral, and he, consequently, prefers sinking down into the listless, inglorious repose of the brute creation, to rising to that energetic activity which can only be generated amid the multiplied, refined, and artificial wants of civilized society. The very conception which nine slaves in ten have of liberty, is that of idleness and sloth with the enjoyment of plenty; and we are not to wonder that they should hasten to practice upon their theory so soon as liberated. But the experiment has been sufficiently tried to prove most conclusively that the free black will work nowhere except by compulsion. . . .

The great evil, however, of these schemes of emancipation, remains yet to be told. They are admirably calculated to excite plots, murders and insurrections; whether gradual or rapid in their operation, this is the inevitable tendency. In the former case, you disturb the quiet and contentment of the slave who is left unemancipated; and he becomes the midnight murderer to gain that fatal freedom whose blessings he does not comprehend. In the latter case, want and invidious distinction will prompt to revenge. Two totally different races, as we have before seen, cannot easily harmonize together, and although we have no idea that any organized plan of insurrection or rebellion can ever secure for the black the superiority, even when free, yet his idleness will produce want and worthlessness, and his very worthlessness and degradation will stimulate him to deeds of rapine and vengeance; he will oftener engage in plots and massacres, and thereby draw down on his devoted head, the vengeance of the provoked whites. But one limited massacre is recorded in Virginia history; let her liberate her slaves, and every year you would hear of insurrections and plots, and every day would perhaps record a murder; the melancholy tale of Southampton would not alone blacken the page of our history, and make the tender mother shed the tear of horror over her babe as she clasped it to her bosom; others of a deeper dye would thicken upon us; those regions where the brightness of polished life has dawned and brightened into full day, would relapse into darkness, thick and full of horrors. . . .

The Evils of Slavery

Injustice and Evils of Slavery.—1st. It is said slavery is wrong, in the *abstract* at least, and contrary to the spirit of Christianity. To this we answer as before, that any question must be determined by its circumstances, and if, as really is the case, we cannot get rid of slavery without producing a greater injury to both the masters and slaves, there is no rule of conscience or revealed law of God which *can* condemn us. The physician will not order the spreading cancer to be extirpated, although it will eventually cause the death of his patient, because he would thereby hasten the fatal. issue. So, if slavery had commenced even contrary to the laws of God and man, and the sin of its introduction rested upon our heads, and it was even carrying forward the nation by slow degrees to final ruin—yet, if it were *certain* that an attempt to remove it would only hasten and heighten the final catastrophe—that it was, in fact, a "vulnus immedicabile" on the body politic which no legislation could safely remove, then we would not only not be found to attempt the extirpation, but we would stand guilty of a high offence in the sight of both God and man, if we should rashly make the effort. But the original sin of introduction rests not on our heads, and we shall soon see that all those dreadful calamities which the false prophets of our day are pointing to, will never, in all probability, occur.

But it is time to bring this long article to a close; it is upon a subject which we have most reluctantly discussed; but, as we have already said, the example was set from a higher quarter; the seal has been broken, and we therefore determined to enter fully into the discussion. If our positions be true, and it does seem to us they may be sustained by reasoning almost as conclusive as the demonstrations of the mathematician, it follows, that the time for emancipation has not yet arrived, and perhaps it never will. We hope, sincerely, that the intelligent sons of Virginia will ponder before they move—before they enter into a scheme which will destroy more than half Virginia's wealth, and drag her down from her proud and elevated station among the mean things of the earth,—and when, Samson-like, she shall, by this ruinous scheme, be shorn of all her power and all her glory, the passing stranger may at some future day exclaim,

The Niobe of nations—there she stands, "Friendless and helpless in her voiceless woe."

Once more, then, do we call upon our statesmen to pause, ere they engage in this ruinous scheme. The power of man has limits, and he should never attempt impossibilities. We do believe it is beyond the power of man to separate the elements of our population, even if it were desirable. The deep and solid foundations of society cannot be broken up by the vain *fiat* of the legislator. . . . We must recollect, in fine, that our own country has waded through two dangerous wars—that the thrilling eloquence of the Demosthenes of our land has been heard with rapture, exhorting to death, rather than slavery,—that the most liberal principles have ever been promulgated and sustained, in our deliberate bodies, and before our judicial tribunals—and the whole has passed by without breaking or tearing asunder the elements of our social fabric. Let us reflect on these things, and learn wisdom from experience; and know that the relations of society, generated by the *lapse of ages*, cannot be altered in a *day*.

VIEWPOINT 6

"In all these instances, not one case of insurrection or of bloodshed has ever been heard of, as the result of emancipation."

Emancipation Is Practical

Lydia Maria Child (1802-1880)

Lydia Maria Child produced numerous tracts and books popularizing the anti-slavery argument. She wrote articles advocating better treatment for blacks, women, and Indians, and she was also a successful novelist.

In the following viewpoint, excerpted from her 1839 book, *Anti-Slavery Catechism* (Newburyport, MA: 1839), Child attempts to put a moderate face on abolitionism. She thus emphasizes the practical benefits of the emancipation of slaves. She uses a question-and-answer format to deal with criticisms of abolitionism.

Q. But don't you think it would be dangerous to turn the slaves at once loose upon the community?

A. The abolitionists never desired to have them turned loose. They wish to have them governed by salutary laws, so regulated as effectually to protect both master and slave. They merely wish to have the power of punishment transferred from individuals to magistrates; to have the sale of human beings cease; and to have the stimulus of *wages* applied, instead of the stimulus of the *whip*. The relation of master and laborer might still continue; but under circumstances less irksome and degrading to both parties. Even that much abused animal the jackass can be made to travel more expeditiously by suspending a bunch of turnips on a pole and keeping them before his nose, than he can by the continual application of the whip; and even when human beings are brutalized to the last degree, by the soul-destroying system of slavery, they have still sense enough left to be more willing to work two hours for twelve cents than to work one hour for nothing.

Q. I should think this system, in the long run, must be an unprofitable one.

A. It is admitted to be so. Southerners often declare that it takes six slaves to do what is easily performed by half the number of free laborers. . . .

Q. But the masters say the negroes would cut their throats, if they were emancipated.

A. It is safer to judge by uniform experience than by the assertions of the masters, who, even if they have no intention to deceive, are very liable to be blinded by having been educated in the midst of a bad system. Listen to facts on this subject. On the 10th of October, 1811, the Congress of Chili decreed that every child born after that day should be free. In April, 1812, the government of Buenos Ayres ordered that every child born after the 1st of January, 1813, should be free. In 1821, the Congress of Colombia emancipated all slaves who had borne arms in favor of the Republic, and provided for the emancipation, in eighteen years, of the whole slave population of 900,000. In September, 1829, the government of Mexico granted immediate and entire emancipation to every slave. In all these instances, *not one case of insurrection or of bloodshed has ever been heard of, as the result of emancipation.*

In St. Domingo no measures were taken gradually to fit the slaves for freedom. They were suddenly emancipated during a civil war, and armed against British invaders. They at once ceased to be property, and were recognized as human beings. Col. Malefant, who resided on the island, informs us, in his Historical and Political History of the Colonies, that, "after this public act of emancipation, the negroes remained quiet both in the south and west, and they continued to work upon all the plantations. The colony was flourishing. The whites lived happily and in peace upon their estates, and the negroes continued to work for them." General Lacroix, in his Memoirs of St. Domingo, speaking of the same period says: "The colony marched as by enchantment towards its ancient splendor; cultivation prospered; every day produced perceptible proofs of its progress." This prosperous state of things lasted about eight years, and would perhaps have continued to the present day, had not Bonaparte, at the instigation of the old French planters, sent an army to deprive the blacks of the freedom they had used so well. The enemies of abolition are always talking of the horrors of St. Domingo, as an argument to prove that emancipation is dangerous; but historical facts prove that the effort to *restore slavery* occasioned all the bloodshed in that island; while *emancipation produced only the most peaceful and prosperous results. . . .*

Q. But they say the British have had difficulties in their West Indies.

A. The enemies of the cause have tried very hard to get up a "raw-head and bloody-bones" story; but even if you take their own accounts, you will find that they have not been able to adduce any instances of violence in support of their assertions. . . .

Emancipating Slaves Is Profitable

Elizur Wright Jr. was a professor of mathematics and moral philosophy before leaving academic work to write for the abolitionist cause. His pamphlets, including The Sin of Slavery and its Remedy *published in 1833, attack slavery on moral and economic grounds.*

Your fields which now lie sterile, or produce but half a crop, because the whip of the driver, although it may secure its motion, cannot give force to the negro's hoe, would then smile beneath the plough of the freeman—the genial influence of just and equitable wages. Mark, that I say nothing of the amount of human happiness which might be reared by Christian instruction on this ground of justice, mercy and equal rights applied to 2,000,000 of men. Your own estates would be worth double the cash. The capital which you have expended in slaves—scarcely less than the value of your land—is sunk; for your slave labor after all costs more than free. And, besides, the waste arising from involuntary labor is prodigious. Make all labor free, and the purchaser can afford to pay for your land what he must now pay for the land and slaves together. Even in a pecuniary point of view the change from the slave to the free labor system would be profitable.

Q. Yet people are always saying that free negroes cannot take care of themselves.

A. It is because people are either very much prejudiced or very ignorant on the subject. In the United States, colored persons have scarcely any chance to rise. They are despised, and abused, and discouraged, at every turn. In the slave States they are subject to laws nearly as oppressive as those of the slave. They are whipped or imprisoned, if they try to learn to read or write; they are not allowed to testify in court; and there is a general disposition not to encourage them by giving them employment. In addition to this, the planters are very desirous to expel them from the State, partly because they are jealous of their influence upon the slaves, and partly because those who have slaves to let out, naturally dislike the competition of the free negroes. But if colored people are well treated, and have the same inducements to industry as other people, they work as well and behave as well. A few years ago the Pennsylvanians were very much alarmed at the representations that were made of the increase of pauperism from the ingress of free negroes. A committee was appointed to examine into the subject, and it was ascertained that the colored people not only supported their own poor, but paid a considerable additional sum towards the support of white paupers.

Q. I have heard people say that the slaves would not take their freedom, if it were offered to them.

A. I sincerely wish they would offer it. I should like to see the experiment tried. If the slaves are so well satisfied with their condition, why do they make such severe laws against running away? Why are the patroles [sic] on duty all the time to shoot every negro who does not give an account of himself as soon as they call to him? Why, notwithstanding all these pains and penalties, are their newspapers full of advertisements for runaway slaves? If the free negroes are so much worse off than those in bondage, why is it that their laws bestow freedom on any slave, "who saves his master or mistress's life, or performs any meritorious service to the State?" That must be a very bad country where the law stipulates that *meritorious* actions shall be rewarded by making a man more unhappy than he was before! . . .

Q. Some say that these people are naturally inferior to us; and that the shape of their skulls proves it.

A. If I believed that the colored people were naturally inferior to the whites, I should say that was an additional reason why we ought to protect, instruct, and encourage them. No consistent republican will say that a strong-minded man has a right to oppress those less gifted than himself. Slave-holders do not seem to think the negroes are so stupid as not to acquire knowledge, and make use of it, if they could get a chance. If they do think so, why do their laws impose such heavy penalties on all who attempt to give them any education? Nobody thinks it necessary to forbid the promulgation of knowledge among monkeys. If you believe the colored race are naturally inferior, I wish you would read the history of Toussaint L'Ouverture, the Washington of St. Domingo. Though perfectly black, he was unquestionably one of the greatest and best men of his age. I wish you would hear Mr. Williams of New York, and Mr. Douglass of Philadelphia preach a few times, before you hastily decide concerning the capacity of the colored race for intellectual improvement. As for the shape of their skulls, I shall be well satisfied if our Southern brethren will emancipate all the slaves who have *not* what is called the "African conformation.". . .

Q. But would you at once give so many ignorant creatures political power, by making them voters?

A. That would be for the wisdom of legislators to decide; and they would probably decide that it would not be judicious to invest emancipated slaves with the elective franchise; for though it is not their fault that they have been kept brutally ignorant, it unfits them for voters. . . .

Q. You know that abolitionists are universally accused of wishing to promote the amalgamation of colored and white people.

A. This is a false charge, got up by the enemies of the cause, and used as a bugbear to increase the prejudices of the community. By the hue and cry that is raised on the subject, one would really suppose that in this free country a certain set of men had power to compel their neighbors to marry contrary to their own inclination. The abolitionists have never, by example, writing, or conversation, endeavored to connect amalgamation with the subject of abolition. When their enemies insist upon urging this silly and unfounded objection, they content themselves with replying, "If there be a natural antipathy between the races, the antipathy will protect itself. If such marriages are contrary to the order of Providence, we certainly may trust Providence to take care of the matter. It is a poor compliment to the white young men to be so afraid that the moment we allow the colored ones to be educated, the girls will all be running after them.". . .

Q. Is there any truth in the charge that you wish to break down all distinctions of society; and introduce the negroes into our parlors?

A. There is not the slightest truth in this charge. People have pointed to an ignorant shoe-black, and asked me whether I would invite him to visit my house. I answered, "No; I would not do so if he were a white man; and I should not be likely to do it, merely because he was black." An educated person will not naturally like to associate with one who is grossly ignorant. It may be no merit in one that he is well-informed, and no fault of the other that he is ignorant; for these things may be the result of circumstances, over which the individual had no control; but such people will not choose each other's society merely from want of sympathy. For these reasons, I would not select an ignorant man, of any complexion, for my companion; but when you ask me whether that man's children shall have as fair a chance as my own, to obtain an education, and rise in the world, I should be ashamed of myself, both as a Christian and a republican, if I did not say, yes, with all my heart.

Overcoming Prejudice

Q. But do you believe that prejudice against color ever can be overcome?

A. Yes, I do; because I have faith that all things will pass away, which are not founded in reason and justice. In France and England, this prejudice scarcely exists at all. Their noblemen would never dream of taking offence because a colored gentleman sat beside them in a stage-coach, or at the table of an hotel. Be assured, however, that the abolitionists have not the slightest wish to force you to give up this prejudice. If, after conscientious examination, you believe it to be right, cherish it; but do not adhere to it merely because your neighbors do. Look it in the face—apply the golden rule—and judge for yourself. The Mahometans really think they could not eat at the same table with a Christian, without pollution; but I have no doubt the time will come when this prejudice will be removed. The old feudal nobles of England would not have thought it possible that their descendants could live in a community, where they and their vassals were on a perfect civil equality; yet the apparent impossibility has come to pass, with advantage to many, and injury to none. When we endeavor to conform to the spirit of the gospel, there is never any danger that it will not lead us into paths of peace. . . .

Abolition in Jamaica

Lydia Maria Child wrote The Evils of Slavery and the Cure of Slavery *in 1836. She described the successful abolition of slavery in Jamaica and other places.*

The enemies of abolition predicted that the crops in Jamaica, would perish for want of being gathered; because the negroes could not possibly be induced to work an hour longer than the law of the whip compelled them. But as soon as the planters offered them *wages* for working extra hours, more work was offered than the planters were willing to pay for. Even the low price of a penny an hour, operated like magic upon them, and inspired them to diligence!

Q. But if the system works so badly in every respect, why are people so unwilling to give it up?

A. Human nature is willing to endure much, rather than relinquish unbridled licentiousness and despotic control. The emperor of Russia, and the pachas [*sic*] of Egypt would be reluctant to abridge their own power, for the sake of introducing a system of things more conducive to the freedom, virtue and happiness of their subjects. They had rather live in constant fear of the poisoned bowl and the midnight dagger, than to give up the pleasant exercise of tyranny, to which they have so long been accustomed. In addition to this feeling, so common to our nature, there are many conscientious people, who are terrified at the idea of emancipation. It has always been presented to them in the most frightful colors; and bad men are determined, if possible, to prevent the abolitionists from proving to such minds that *the dangers of insurrection all belong to slavery, and would cease when slavery was abolished.*

At the North, the apologists of slavery are numerous and virulent, because their *interests* are closely intertwined with the pernicious system. Inquire into the private history of many of the men, who have called meetings against the abolitionists—you will find that some manufacture negro cloths for the South—some have sons who sell these cloths—some have daughters married to slave-holders—some have plantations and slaves mortgaged to them—some have ships employed in Southern commerce—and some candidates for political offices would bow until their backbones were broken, to obtain or preserve Southern influence. The Southerners understand all this perfectly well, and despise our servility, even while they condescend to make use of it.

One great reason why the people of this country have not thought and felt right on this subject, is that all our books, newspapers, almanacs and periodicals, have combined to represent the colored race as an inferior and degraded class, who never could be made good and useful citizens. Ridicule and reproach have been abundantly heaped upon them; but their virtues and their sufferings have found few historians. The South has been well satisfied with such a public sentiment. It sends back no echo to disturb their consciences, and it effectually rivets the chain on the necks of their vassals. In this department of service, the Colonization Society has been a most active and zealous agent.

Abolitionists and Violence

Q. But some people say that all the mobs, and other violent proceedings, are to be attributed to the abolitionists.

A. They might as well charge the same upon St. Paul, when his fearless preaching of the gospel brought him into such imminent peril, that his friends were obliged to "let him down over the wall in a basket," to save his life. As well might St. Stephen have been blamed for the mob that stoned him to death. With the same justice might William Penn have been called the cause of all the violent persecutions against the Quakers. When principles of truth are sent out in the midst of a perverse generation, they *always* come "not to bring peace, but a sword." The abolitionists have offered violence to no man—they have never attempted to stop the discussions of their opponents; but have, on the contrary, exerted themselves to obtain a candid examination of the subject on all sides. They merely claim the privilege of delivering peaceful addresses at orderly meetings, and of publishing what they believe to be facts, with an honest desire to have them tested by the strictest ordeal of truth.

CHAPTER 5

Slavery Divides a Nation

Chapter Preface

During the decades leading up to the Civil War, the issue of slavery in the United States increasingly became intertwined in the growing sectional divide between North and South, between free and slave states. Economically and socially the two regions evolved in very different directions. In the Northern states, where slavery had never been as well established as in the South, slavery was abolished by the early 1800s. The North developed an economy closely tied to industry and commerce and responded to labor shortages by inventing labor-saving machinery instead of resorting to human labor. The Southern economy, however, remained tied to agriculture, especially to cotton, and slave labor became even more entrenched and vital to the Southern economy than previously. Proof of slavery's role in the South was the continuing growth of the slave population despite the outlawing of the slave trade in 1808. The population of slaves rose from 1.2 million in 1810 to 4 million in 1860.

As North and South increasingly diverged in their economic, social, and political philosophies, the slavery debate became not just a disagreement over the institution itself, but over the character and future of the United States of America. Leading politicians of the South viewed the United States as a limited union in which states were free to determine their own social policies. They bitterly resisted all national attempts to restrict slavery. In the North, however, increasing numbers of people looked upon slavery as inconsistent with the fundamental American value of liberty. They viewed slavery as harmful to the economy and character of the whole nation. While slavery was not the only issue that divided the two regions, it was one of the most basic.

The conflict over slavery was most visible in the debates over the developing western territories and whether these territories should be allowed to enter the Union as free or slave states. Southern partisans wanted them to be slave states. The South needed additional pro-slavery votes in the Senate, where they only narrowly maintained enough power to block national attempts to restrict slavery. Opponents of slavery also sought additional votes in Congress and decried attempts to increase the number of slave states as an attempt to create a "slave empire." Both opponents and proponents of slavery expressed the opinion that slavery, if not allowed to expand into new territories, would eventually become obsolete and perish.

A variety of legislative and judicial actions by the U.S. government failed to resolve this conflict. The Missouri Compromise of 1820 was one such attempt. It established a North/South boundary line within the territory acquired by the United States in the 1803 Louisiana Purchase. This line defined free and slave territories and determined that future states would be slave or free depending on their location in relation to this boundary. The compromise maintained an uneasy peace for three decades, until slavery advocates and opponents began to challenge it as unfair.

In 1854 the Missouri Compromise was declared "inoperative and void" by the Kansas-Nebraska Act. This legislation, championed by U.S. senator Stephen Douglas, attempted to settle the question of whether new states should be slave or free with what Douglas called popular sovereignty. Under this system, settlers of territories decided themselves whether to allow slavery. In the Kansas territory, this act led to violent clashes as both opponents and proponents of slavery sought to impose their views on the population and to influence Kansas voters to vote their way. Armed settlers from both camps traveled to Kansas in an attempt to determine that territory's future.

In 1857 the U.S. Supreme Court attempted to settle once and for all the question of slavery in the territories. On March 6, 1857, the Court issued its momentous *Dred Scott* decision. The Court decided that blacks could not be considered citizens of the United States. It also declared that neither Congress nor territorial legislatures had the power to prohibit slavery under the U.S. Constitution. Only state legislatures, the Court argued, had that power.

The decision dismayed the new Republican party, which had run on the platform of restricting slavery in western territories. It also nullified Douglas's compromise plan of popular sovereignty by denying to territorial legislatures and populations the power to outlaw slavery before entering the Union. Pro-slavery advocates were overjoyed by the decision, however, and some Southern leaders sought to pass a national slave code legalizing slavery in all future U.S. territories. Thus, far from settling the question, *Dred Scott* simply further inflamed the country's division over slavery that ultimately caused secession and war.

The question of what caused the Civil War has been long debated by historians, but most today agree that slavery was a primary reason. Historian Irwin Unger writes:

> The element that by itself comes closest to explaining the origins of the Civil War is slavery. But it was not moral outrage over the peculiar institution that set northern armies on the march to crush the Confederacy. Only a small minority of northerners saw the war at the outset as a crusade against a fundamental social evil. The actual role of slavery was far more

subtle and diffuse. Southerners had developed a deep psychological stake in the peculiar institution and feared social and economic cataclysm if it collapsed. They also regarded northern antislavery agitation as an attempt to deny them a fundamental "right." Northerners, meanwhile, had come to fear an aggressive and demanding "slaver power" that would ride roughshod over the rights of freemen. Slavery defined the South and set it off against the North. Deeply woven into the fabric of southern life, it helped to create a southern sense of apartness. This sense, in turn, produced a combination of sectional aggressiveness and defensiveness that manifested itself in many realms and charged each with divisive power. Thus the clash of sectional economic interests became far more bitter than it might have been. Slavery also converted the Mexican Cession—an acquisition that would normally have been considered a national boon—into a constant source of friction that eventually cracked open the existing political parties and destroyed the last remaining bond between North and South.

Ultimately, all attempts at compromise failed. It would take America's bloodiest and most divisive war to settle the slavery question and prevent the United States from dividing itself.

VIEWPOINT 1

"The Constitution . . . enables a South Carolina slave-holder to drag from the soil of Massachusetts a person whom the general rule of law pronounces free."

The U.S. Constitution Supports Slavery

William Ingersoll Bowditch (1819-1909)

One of the most divisive debates within the abolitionist movement starting in the 1830s was whether the United States Constitution was an obstacle or a help to the abolitionist cause. The document never mentions slavery directly. But many abolitionists, including William Lloyd Garrison, felt that it implicitly supported the hated institution. Consequently, Garrison called the Constitution "a covenant with death." Because the Constitution is the cornerstone of authority for the U.S. government, Garrison and others felt that political action against slavery within the government system was hopeless.

The following viewpoint is taken from a pamphlet entitled *Slavery and the Constitution* published in 1849 and written by William Ingersoll Bowditch, a Boston lawyer and abolitionist. He examines several clauses of the U.S. Constitution and concludes that these passages demonstrate the document's support for slavery.

At the time of the adoption of the Constitution, slavery existed in all the States except Massachusetts. How far, if at all, does this instrument support or countenance the institution?

> Art. 1, sec. 2: "Representatives and direct taxes shall be apportioned among the several States which may be included within this union, according to their respective numbers, which shall be determined by adding to the whole number of free persons,

including those bound to service for a term of years, and excluding Indians not taxed, three-fifths of all other persons."

By this section, persons are divided into those who are free and those who are slaves; for to the whole number of *free* persons are to be added three-fifths of *all other* persons, that is, persons not free, or *slaves*. If we adopt the plain, obvious, and common meaning of the words as their true meaning, this conclusion is incontrovertible.

It is sometimes urged, that by "free person" is meant "citizen." But the expression cannot be taken in any such technical sense. Under the expression "free persons" are included those bound to service for a term of years, and therefore from it are excluded those bound to service for life, or slaves.

Recognizing Slavery

This article, therefore, recognizes slavery as explicitly as if the word *slave* itself had been used, and gives to the free persons in a Slave State, solely because they are slaveholders, a large representation, and consequently greater political power, than the same number of free persons in a Free State. A BOUNTY ON SLAVEHOLDING!

> Art. 1, sec. 9: "The *migration or importation* of such persons as any of the States now existing shall think proper to admit, shall not be prohibited by the Congress prior to the year one thousand eight hundred and eight; but a tax or duty may be imposed on such *importation*, not exceeding ten dollars for each person."

It is clear that this section recognizes a difference between the meaning of *migration* and *importation*, since, if both words mean the same thing, no reason whatever can be assigned why a tax is not permitted in both cases. This difference, whatever it is, must afford a good reason why persons imported may be taxed, and persons migrating not. The true meaning of the section seems obvious. A person who migrates does so of his own accord: he cannot be said to be migrated by any other person. He is wholly a free agent. A person who is imported does not import himself, but is imported by some other person. He is passive. The importer is the free agent; the person imported is not a free agent. Thus the slave-laws of Virginia of 1748 and 1753 begin—"All *persons* who have been or shall be *imported*," &c. &c "*shall be* accounted and be *slaves*." Whenever we hear an importation spoken of, we instantly infer an importer, an *owner*, and *property* imported. This distinction between the meaning of the two words is, then, real. It affords a good reason for the restriction on the right to tax. Therefore, we say, it is the true distinction. On our construction, Congress had power to lay a tax on persons imported as property or slaves, but had no right to tax free persons migrating.

A Vicious Compromise

In this diary excerpt, John Quincy Adams, sixth president of the United States and consistent opponent of slavery, writes about his regrets over what he views as the proslavery character of the U.S. Constitution.

The bargain between freedom and slavery contained in the Constitution of the United States is morally and politically vicious, inconsistent with the principles upon which alone our Revolution can be justified; cruel and oppressive, by riveting the chains of slavery, by pledging the faith of freedom to maintain and perpetuate the tyranny of the master; and grossly unequal and impolitic, by admitting that slaves are at once enemies to be kept in subjection, property to be secured or restored to their owners, and persons not to be represented themselves, but for whom their masters are privileged with nearly a double share of representation. The consequence has been that this slave representation has governed the Union.

By this clause, therefore, Congress was prevented, during twenty years, from prohibiting the foreign slave-trade with any State that pleased to allow it. But, by Art. 1, sec. 8, Congress had the general power "to regulate commerce with foreign nations." Consequently, *the slave-trade was excepted from the operation of the general power, with a view to place the slave-trade, during twenty years, solely under the control of the Slave States.* It could not be wholly stopped, so long as one State wished to continue it. It is a clear compromise in favor of slavery. True, the compromise was a temporary one; but it will be noticed, that Congress, even after 1808, was not obliged to prohibit the trade; and, in point of fact, until 1819 the laws of Congress authorized the States to sell into slavery, for their own benefit, negroes imported contrary to the laws of the United States! . . .

Art. 4, sec. 2: "No person held to service or labor in one State, under the laws thereof, escaping into another, shall, in consequence of any law or regulation therein, be discharged from such service or labor; but shall be delivered up, on claim of the party to whom such service or labor may be due."

The time of holding not being limited, the expression here used must include not only persons held to service or labor for a term of years, but also those held to service or labor for life. Consequently, it includes those who are free persons within the meaning of Art. 1, sec. 2, and slaves of persons held to service or labor for life.

That the expression "person held to service or labor" was a correct definition of the condition of a slave, at the time the Constitution was adopted, is evident. The sixth article of the North-western ordinance reads thus: "There shall be neither slavery nor involuntary servitude in the said territory, otherwise than in the punishment of crimes, whereof the party shall have been duly convicted; provided always, that, any person escaping into the same, from whom labor or service is lawfully claimed in any one of the original States, such fugitive may be lawfully reclaimed, and conveyed to the person claiming his or her labor or service as aforesaid." In other words, the expression "a person from whom labor or service is lawfully claimed" so correctly described the condition of a slave, that Congress deemed it necessary to except such persons from the operation of an article relating only to slaves. In less than three months after the passage of this ordinance, this clause in the Constitution was drafted. It needs no argument to show, that the expression in the Constitution means the same as that in the ordinance. "A person from whom labor or service is lawfully claimed in any one of the original States" means the same as "a person held to service or labor in one State under the laws thereof." If the former correctly described the condition of a slave, the latter did also. . . .

Fugitive Slaves

By this section, therefore, it is provided that no person held as a slave in one State under the laws thereof, escaping into another, shall, in consequence of any law or regulation therein, be discharged from his slavery, but shall be delivered up on claim of his owner. The laws of one State, whether they support slavery or any other institution, have no power in another State. Consequently, if a slave escapes into a Free State, he becomes free. This is the general rule of law. In virtue of it, thousands of slaves are now free on the soil of Canada. In virtue of it, a fugitive slave from South Carolina would be free in this State, were it not for this section in the Constitution. But this section declares that he shall not thereby become free, but shall be delivered up. Again, *the Constitution makes an exception from a general rule of law in favor of slavery.* It gives to slaveholders, and slave-laws, a power which the general rule of law does not give. It enables a South Carolina slaveholder to drag from the soil of Massachusetts a person whom the general rule of law pronounces free, solely because South Carolina laws declare the contrary. It makes the whole Union a vast hunting-ground for slaves! There is not a single spot from the Atlantic to the Pacific, from the St. John's to the Rio del Norte, or "wheresoe'er may be the fleeting boundary of this republic," on which a fugitive slave may rest, and his owner may not, in virtue of this clause, claim and retake him as his slave!

Art. 1, sec. 8: "Congress shall have power. . . . to provide for calling forth the militia. . . . to suppress insurrections."

Art. 4, sec. 4: "The United States shall guarantee to every State in this Union a republican form of government, and shall protect each of them against invasion; and, on application of the legislature or of the executive (when the legislature cannot be convened), against domestic violence."

All insurrections and *all* cases of domestic violence are here provided for. To constitute an insurrection within the meaning of the Constitution, there must be a rising against those laws which are recognized as such by the Constitution; and, to make out a case of domestic violence, the violence must be exerted against that right or power which is recognized by the Constitution as lawful. But, by Art. 4, sec. 2, the Constitution admits that some persons are legally slaves; else the clause itself must be entirely inoperative. Consequently, if these persons rise in rebellion, or commit acts of violence contrary to the laws which hold them in slavery, their rising constitutes an insurrection; such acts are acts of violence within the meaning of the Constitution, and consequently must be suppressed by the national power. And what insurrections were more likely to happen and more to be dreaded than slave-insurrections, and therefore more likely to have been provided for?

A Nation of Slaveholders

Slave-owners are not the only slaveholders. All persons who voluntarily assist or pledge themselves to assist in holding persons in slavery are slaveholders. *In sober truth, then, we are a nation of slaveholders!* for we have bound our whole national strength to the slave-owners, to aid them, if necessary, in holding their slaves in subjection!

VIEWPOINT 2

"The constitutionality of slavery can be made out only by disregarding the plain and common-sense reading of the Constitution itself."

The U.S. Constitution Does Not Support Slavery

Frederick Douglass (1817-1895)

Frederick Douglass was one of the foremost black leaders of his time. Born a slave, he escaped in 1838 and became a noted abolitionist speaker for William Lloyd Garrison's Massachusetts Anti-Slavery Society. His autobiography *The Narrative of the Life of Frederick Douglass* was first published in 1845. In 1847 he began publishing his own abolitionist newspaper, *The North Star.*

Douglass disagreed with Garrison and others about the U.S. Constitution's position on slavery. He believed that the Constitution was not necessarily proslavery, and that abolitionists should pursue political means, such as forming new political parties, to end slavery. In the following viewpoint, excerpted from *The Constitution of the United States: Is It Pro-Slavery or Anti-Slavery*, published in 1860, Douglass examines the key clauses of the Constitution that implicitly deal with slavery and the slave trade, and he argues that such clauses do not mean the Constitution prevents effective political action against slavery.

Because he believed political action against slavery was possible, Douglass disagreed with those abolitionists who advocated the dissolution of the United States and the removal of its Constitution. Dissolution, argued Douglass, would leave slaves in worse shape than before, beyond the power of the U.S. government to emancipate them.

Here then are the several provisions of the Constitution to which reference has been made. I read them word for word just as they stand in the paper, called the United States Constitution, Art. 1, sec. 2. "Representatives and direct taxes shall be apportioned among the several States which may be included in this Union, according to their respective numbers, which shall be determined by adding to the whole number of free persons, including those bound to service for a term of years, and excluding Indians not taxed, three-fifths of all other persons; Art. 1, sec. 9. The migration or importation of such persons as any of the States now existing shall think fit to admit, shall not be prohibited by the Congress prior to the year one thousand eight hundred and eight, but a tax or duty may be imposed on such importation, not exceeding ten dollars for each person; Art. 4, sec. 2. No person held to service or labour in one State, under the laws thereof, escaping into another shall, in consequence of any law or regulation therein, be discharged from such service or labour; but shall be delivered up on claim of the party to whom such service or labour may be due; Art. 1, sec. 8. To provide for calling forth the militia to execute the laws of the Union, suppress insurrections, and repel invasions." Here, then, are those provisions of the Constitution, which the most extravagant defenders of slavery can claim to guarantee a right of property in man. These are the provisions which have been pressed into the service of the human fleshmongers of America. Let us look at them just as they stand, one by one.

Constitutional Provisions

Let us grant, for sake of the argument, that the first of these provisions, referring to the basis of representation and taxation, does refer to slaves. We are not compelled to make that admission, for it might fairly apply to aliens—persons living in the country, but not naturalized. But giving the provisions the very worst construction, what does it amount to? I answer—It is a downright disability laid upon the slaveholding States; one which deprives those States of two-fifths of their natural basis of representation. A black man in a free State is worth just two-fifths more than a black man in a slave State, as a basis of political power under the Constitution. Therefore, instead of encouraging slavery, the Constitution encourages freedom by giving an increase of "two-fifths" of political power to free over slave States. So much for the three-fifths clause; taking it at its worst, it still leans to freedom, not to slavery; for, be it remembered that the Constitution nowhere forbids a coloured man to vote.

I come to the next, that which it is said guaranteed the continuance of the African slave trade for twenty years. I will also take

National Archives.

During the Civil War, Frederick Douglass recruited blacks for the Union Army and pushed for emancipation.

that for just what my opponent alleges it to have been, although the Constitution does not warrant any such conclusion. But, to be liberal, let us suppose it did, and what follows? why, this—that this part of the Constitution, so far as the slave trade is concerned, became a dead letter more than 50 years ago, and now binds no man's conscience for the continuance of any slave trade whatever. . . . But there is still more to be said about this abolition of the slave trade. Men, at that time [the Constitution was written], both in England and in America, looked upon the slave trade as the life of slavery. The abolition of the slave trade was supposed to be the certain death of slavery. Cut off the stream, and the pond will dry up, was the common notion at that time. . . . The American statesmen, in providing for the abolition of the slave trade, thought they were providing for the abolition of slavery. This view is quite consistent with the history of the times. All regarded slavery as an expiring and doomed system, destined to speedily disappear from the country. But, again, it should be remembered that this very provision, if made to refer to the African slave trade at all, makes the Constitution anti-slavery rather than for slavery, for it says to the slave States, the price you will have to pay for coming into the American Union is, that the slave trade, which you would carry on indefinitely out of the Union, shall be put an end to in twenty years if you come into the Union. Secondly, if it does apply, it expired by its own limitation more than fifty years ago. Thirdly, it is anti-slavery, because it looked to the abolition of slavery rather than to its perpetuity. Fourthly, it showed that the intentions of the framers of the Constitution were good, not bad. I think this is quite enough for this point.

I go to the "slave insurrection" clause, though, in truth, there is no such clause. The one which is called so has nothing whatever to do with slaves or slaveholders any more than your laws for the suppression of popular outbreaks has to do with making slaves of you and your children. It is only a law for suppression of riots or insurrections. But I will be generous here, as well as elsewhere, and grant that it applies to slave insurrections. Let us suppose that an anti-slavery man is President of the United States (and the day that shall see this the case is not distant) and this very power of suppressing slave insurrection would put an end to slavery. The right to put down an insurrection carries with it the right to determine the means by which it shall be put down. If it should turn out that slavery is a source of insurrection, that there is no security from insurrections while slavery lasts, why, the Constitution would be best obeyed by putting an end to slavery, and an anti-slavery Congress would do that very thing. Thus, you see, the so-called slaveholding provisions of the American Constitution, which a little while ago looked so formidable, are, after all, no defence or guarantee for slavery whatever.

Fugitive Slaves

But there is one other provision. This is called the "Fugitive Slave Provision." It is called so by those who wish to make it subserve the interest of slavery in America, and the same by those who wish to uphold the views of a party in this country. It is put thus in the speech at the City Hall [a speech attacking Douglass and his position on slavery and the Constitution]:

Let us go back to 1787, and enter Liberty Hall, Philadelphia, where sat in convention the illustrious men who framed the Constitution—with George Washington in the chair. On the 27th of September, Mr. Butler and Mr. Pinckney, two delegates from the State of South Carolina, moved that the Constitution should require that fugitive slaves and servants should be delivered up like criminals, and after a discussion on the subject, the clause, as it stands in the Constitution, was adopted. After this, in the conventions held in the several States to ratify the Constitution, the same meaning was attached to the words. For example, Mr. Madison (afterwards President), when recommending the Constitution to his constituents, told them that the clause would secure them their property in slaves. . . .

Now, what are the facts connected with this provision of the Constitution? You shall have them. It seems to take two men to tell the truth. It is quite true that Mr. Butler and Mr. Pinckney introduced a provision expressly with a view to the recapture of fugitive slaves: it is quite true also that there was some discussion on the subject—and just here the truth shall come out. These illustrious kidnappers were told promptly in that discussion that no such idea as property in man should be admitted into the Constitution. The speaker in question might have told you, and he would have told you but the simple truth, if he had told you that the proposition of Mr. Butler and Mr. Pinckney—which he leads you to infer was adopted by the convention that framed the Constitution—was, in fact, promptly and indignantly rejected by that convention. He might have told you, had it suited his purpose to do so, that the words employed in the first draft of the fugitive clause were such as applied to the condition of slaves, and expressly declared that persons held to "servitude" should be given up; but that the word "servitude" was struck from the provision, for the very reason that it applied to slaves. He might have told you that that same Mr. Madison declared that that word was struck out because the convention would not consent that the idea of property in men should be admitted into the Constitution. The fact that Mr. Madison can be cited on both sides of this question is another evidence of the folly and absurdity of making the secret intentions of the framers the criterion by which the Constitution is to be construed.

But it may be asked—if this clause does not apply to slaves, to whom does it apply? I answer, that when adopted, it applied to a very large class of persons—namely, redemptioners—persons who had come to America from Holland, from Ireland, and other quarters of the globe—like the Coolies to the West Indies—and had, for a consideration duly paid, become bound to "serve and labour" for the parties to whom their service and labour was due. It applies to indentured apprentices and others who had become bound for a consideration, under contract duly made, to serve and labour. To such persons this provision applies, and only to such persons. . . .

Slavery and the Law

In all matters where laws are taught to be made the means of oppression, cruelty, and wickedness, I am for strict construction. I will concede nothing. It must be shown that it is so nominated in the bond. The pound of flesh, but not one drop of blood. The very nature of law is opposed to all such wickedness, and makes it difficult to accomplish such objects under the forms of law. Law is not merely an arbitrary enactment with regard to justice, reason, or humanity. . . . The Supreme Court of the United States lays down this rule, and it meets the case exactly—"Where rights are infringed—where the fundamental principles of the law are overthrown—where the general system of the law is departed from, the legislative intention must be expressed with irresistible clearness." The same court says that the language of the law must be construed strictly in favour of justice and liberty. . . .

I set these rules down against those employed at the City Hall. To me they seem just and rational. I only ask you to look at the American Constitution in the light of them, and you will see with me that no man is guaranteed a right of property in man, under the provisions of that instrument. If there are two ideas more distinct in their character and essence than another, those ideas are "persons" and "property," "men" and "things." Now, when it is proposed to transform persons into "property" and men into beasts of burden, I demand that the law that contemplates such a purpose shall be expressed with irresistible clearness. The thing must not be left to inference, but must be done in plain English.

I know how this view of the subject is treated by the class represented at the City Hall. They are in the habit of treating the negro as an exception to general rules. When their own liberty is in question they will avail themselves of all rules of law which protect and defend their freedom; but when the black man's rights are in question they concede everything, admit everything for slavery, and put liberty to the proof. They reverse the common law usage, and presume the negro a slave unless he can prove himself free. I, on the other hand, presume him free unless he is proved to be otherwise.

Let us look at the objects for which the Constitution was framed and adopted, and see if slavery is one of them. Here are its own objects as set forth by itself:

> We, the people of these United States, in order to form a more perfect union, establish justice, ensure domestic tranquillity, provide for the common defence, promote the general welfare, and secure the blessings of liberty to ourselves and our prosperity [sic], do ordain and establish this Constitution for the United States of America.

The objects here set forth are six in number: union, defence, welfare, tranquillity, justice, and liberty. These are all good objects, and slavery, so far from being among them, is a foe of them all. But it has been said that negroes are not included within the benefits sought under this declaration. This is said by the slaveholders in America—it is said by the City Hall orator—but it is not said by the Constitution itself. Its language is "we the people;" not we the white people, not even we the citizens, not we the privileged class, not we the high, not we the low, but we the peo-

The Declaration of Independence Freed the Slaves

Lysander Spooner was a Massachusetts lawyer and abolitionist. In his book The Unconstitutionality of Slavery, *published in 1845 and excerpted here, he argues that the 1776 Declaration of Independence established in principle the freedom of all people. He argues that the U.S. Constitution fails to explicitly establish the legality of slavery, and thus all of its provisions that seem to support slavery are void.*

The declaration was certainly the constitutional law of this country for certain purposes. For example, it absolved the people from their allegiance to the English crown. . . . If, then, the declaration were the constitutional law of the country for that purpose, was it not also constitutional law for the purpose of recognizing and establishing, as law, the natural and inalienable right of individuals to life, liberty, and the pursuit of happiness? . . . . It is sufficient for our purpose, if it be admitted that this principle was the law of the country at that particular time, (1776)—even though it had continued to be the law for only a year, or even a day. For if it were the law of the country even for a day, it freed every slave in the country—(if there were, as we say there were not, any legal slaves then in the country). And the burden would then be upon the slaveholder to show that slavery had *since* been *constitutionally* established. And to show this, he must show an express *constitutional* designation of the particular individuals, who have since been made slaves. Without such particular designation of the individuals to be made slaves, (and not even the present constitutions of the slave States make any such designation) all constitutional provisions, purporting to authorize slavery, are indefinite, and uncertain in their application, and for that reason void.

ple; not we the horses, sheep, and swine, and wheel-barrows, but we the people, we the human inhabitants; and, if negroes are people, they are included in the benefits for which the Constitution of America was ordained and established. But how dare any man who pretends to be a friend to the negro thus gratuitously concede away what the negro has a right to claim under the Constitution? Why should such friends invent new arguments to increase the hopelessness of his bondage? This, I undertake to say, as the conclusion of the whole matter, that the constitutionality of slavery can be made out only by disregarding the plain and common-sense reading of the Constitution itself; by discrediting and casting away as worthless the most beneficent rules of legal interpretation; by ruling the negro outside of these beneficent rules; by claiming everything for slavery; by denying everything for freedom; by assuming that the Constitution does not mean what it says, and that it says what it does not mean; by disregarding the written Constitution, and interpreting it in the light of a secret understanding. It is in this mean, contemptible, and underhand method that the American Constitution is pressed into the service of slavery. They go everywhere else for proof that the Constitution is pro-slavery but to the Constitution itself. The Constitution declares that no person shall be deprived of life, liberty, or property without due process of law; it secures to every man the right of trial by jury, the privilege of the writ of habeas corpus—that great writ that put an end to slavery and slave-hunting in England—it secures to every State a republican form of government. Any one of these provisions, in the hands of abolition statesmen, and backed up by a right moral sentiment, would put an end to slavery in America. The Constitution forbids the passing of a bill of attainder: that is, a law entailing upon the child the disabilities and hardships imposed upon the parent. Every slave law in America might be repealed on this very ground. The slave is made a slave because his mother is a slave.

But to all this it is said that the practice of the American people is against my view. I admit it. They have given the Constitution a slaveholding interpretation. I admit it. They have committed innumerable wrongs against the negro in the name of the Constitution. Yes, I admit it all; and I go with him who goes farthest in denouncing these wrongs. But it does not follow that the Constitution is in favour of these wrongs because the slaveholders have given it that interpretation. . . .

Slavery and the Union

My argument against the dissolution of the American Union is this: It would place the slave system more exclusively under the control of the slaveholding States, and withdraw it from the power in the Northern States which is opposed to slavery. Slavery is essentially barbarous in its character. It, above all things else, dreads the presence of an advanced civilisation. It flourishes best where it meets no reproving frowns, and hears no condemning voices. While in the Union it will meet with both. Its hope of life, in the last resort, is to get out of the Union. I am, therefore, for drawing the bond of the Union more closely, and bringing the Slave States more completely under the power of the Free States. What they most dread, that I most desire. I have much confidence in the instincts of the slaveholders. They see that the Constitution will afford slavery no protection when it shall cease to be administered by slaveholders. They see, moreover, that if there is once a will in the people of America to abolish slavery, there is no word, no syllable in the Constitution to forbid that result. They see that the Constitution has not saved slavery in Rhode Island, in Connecticut, in New York, or Pennsylvania; that the Free States have increased from one up to eighteen in number, while the Slave

States have only added three to their original number. There were twelve Slave States at the beginning of the Government: there are fifteen now. There was one Free State at the beginning of the Government: there are eighteen now. The dissolution of the Union would not give the North a single advantage over slavery, but would take from it many. Within the Union we have a firm basis of opposition to slavery. It is opposed to all the great objects of the Constitution. The dissolution of the Union is not only an unwise but a cowardly measure—15 millions running away from three hundred and fifty thousand slaveholders.

Mr. Garrison and his friends tell us that while in the Union we are responsible for slavery. He and they sing out "No Union with slaveholders," and refuse to vote. I admit our responsibility for slavery while in the Union, but I deny that going out of the Union would free us from that responsibility. There now clearly is no freedom from responsibility for slavery to any American citizen short of the abolition of slavery. The American people have gone quite too far in this slaveholding business now to sum up their whole business of slavery by singing out the cant phrase, "No union with slaveholders." To desert the family hearth may place the recreant husband out of the presence of his starving children, but this does not free him from responsibility. If a man were on board a pirate ship, and in company with others had robbed and plundered, his whole duty would not be performed simply by taking the longboat and singing out "No union with pirates." His duty would be to restore the stolen property. The American people in the Northern States have helped to enslave the black people. Their duty will not have been done till they give them back their plundered rights. . . .

Reform, Not Revolution

My position now is one of reform, not of revolution. I would act for the abolition of slavery through the Government—not over its ruins. If slaveholders have ruled the American Government for the last fifty years, let the anti-slavery men rule the nation for the next fifty years. If the South has made the Constitution bend to the purposes of slavery, let the North now make that instrument bend to the cause of freedom and justice. If 350,000 slaveholders have, by devoting their energies to that single end, been able to make slavery the vital and animating spirit of the American Confederacy for the last 72 years, now let the freemen of the North, who have the power in their own hands, and who can make the American Government just what they think fit, resolve to blot out for ever the foul and haggard crime, which is the blight and mildew, the curse and the disgrace of the whole United States.

Viewpoint 3

"There are two clauses in the Constitution which point directly and specifically to the negro race as a separate class of persons, and show clearly that they were not regarded as a portion of the people or citizens of the Government they formed."

Constitutional Rights Do Not Extend to Ex-Slaves

Roger Taney (1777-1864)

Roger Taney was the chief justice of the U.S. Supreme Court from 1836 until his death in 1864. He had a long and distinguished public career and served as chief justice for longer than anyone else except his predecessor John Marshall. He is best remembered, however, for a single decision: the Dred Scott case of 1857.

The decision was thoroughly enmeshed in the national debate over slavery and the power of Congress to regulate it. Congress was involved in a bitter fight over the extension of slavery to the western territories. In the 1787 Northwest Ordinance and the 1820 Missouri Compromise, Congress had sought to limit slavery by forbidding its introduction in western territories north of certain latitudes, thus dividing the country into slave and free regions.

Dred Scott was a slave who had accompanied his master when he moved from Missouri, where slavery was allowed, to Illinois, a free state where slavery was outlawed. Shortly after they moved back to Missouri, his master died, and Scott sued the widow for his freedom on the grounds that his residence in a free state had ended his bondage. The case eventually made it to the federal court system and ultimately to the U.S. Supreme Court, where, by a seven-to-two vote, Scott lost his case for freedom.

The Dred Scott case involved three important issues. One was whether Scott's residence in a free state freed him from slavery. A second was the constitutionality of the Missouri Compromise, and whether Congress had the power to limit or regulate slavery. Taney ruled against Scott on both these matters. In so doing, he ruled that Congress had no power to regulate slavery in the territories and that the Missouri Compromise was unconstitutional.

The excerpts from Taney's opinion reprinted here concentrate on the third issue: whether Scott was a citizen of Missouri and thus able to sue in a federal court. Taney argues that slaves and their descendants were never meant to be part of the political community of citizens envisioned by the writers of the U.S. Constitution and that Scott had no legal standing as a U.S. citizen.

The Dred Scott decision, which Taney hoped would settle the national controversy over slavery, instead intensified it. Taney's reputation was severely tarnished by the case. Dred Scott was ultimately freed by his masters in 1857 and died in the same year. The decision itself was eventually nullified by the Thirteenth and Fourteenth Amendments to the U.S. Constitution.

The question is simply this: Can a negro, whose ancestors were imported into this country, and sold as slaves, become a member of the political community formed and brought into existence by the Constitution of the United States, and as such become entitled to all the rights, and privileges, and immunities, guarantied by that instrument to the citizen? One of which rights is the privilege of suing in a court of the United States in the cases specified in the Constitution.

Can Blacks Be Citizens?

It will be observed, that the plea applies to that class of persons only whose ancestors were negroes of the African race, and imported into this country, and sold and held as slaves. The only matter in issue before the court, therefore, is, whether the descendants of such slaves, when they shall be emancipated, or who are born of parents who had become free before their birth, are citizens of a State, in the sense in which the word citizen is used in the Constitution of the United States. And this being the only matter in dispute on the pleadings, the court must be understood as speaking in this opinion of that class only, that is, of those persons who are the descendants of Africans who were imported into this country, and sold as slaves. . . .

The Constitution has conferred on Congress the right to establish a uniform rule of naturalization, and this right is evidently exclusive, and has always been held by this court to be so. Consequently, no State, since the adoption of the Constitution, can by naturalizing an alien invest him with the rights and privileges secured to a citizen of a State under the Federal Government. . . .

The Bettmann Archive.

Dred Scott's struggle for freedom through the American court system lasted nine years.

It is very clear, therefore, that no State can, by any act or law of its own, passed since the adoption of the Constitution, introduce a new member into the political community created by the Constitution of the United States. It cannot make him a member of this community by making him a member of its own. And for the same reason it cannot introduce any person, or description of persons, who were not intended to be embraced in this new political family, which the Constitution brought into existence, but were intended to be excluded from it.

The question then arises, whether the provisions of the Constitution, in relation to the personal rights and privileges to which the citizen of a State should be entitled, embraced the negro African race, at that time in this country, or who might afterwards be imported, who had then or should afterwards be made free in any State; and to put it in the power of a single State to make him a citizen of the United States, and endue him with the full rights of citizenship in every other State without their consent? Does the Constitution of the United States act upon him whenever he shall be made free under the laws of a State, and raised there to the rank of a citizen, and immediately clothe him with all the privileges of a citizen in every other State, and in its own courts?

The court thinks the affirmative of these propositions cannot be maintained. And if it cannot, the plaintiff in error could not be a citizen of the State of Missouri, within the meaning of the Constitution of the United States, and, consequently, was not entitled to sue in its courts.

Members of the Political Body

It is true, every person, and every class and description of persons, who were at the time of the adoption of the Constitution recognised as citizens in the several States, became also citizens of this new political body; but none other; it was formed by them, and for them and their posterity, but for no one else. And the personal rights and privileges guarantied to citizens of this new sovereignty were intended to embrace those only who were then members of the several State communities, or who should afterwards by birthright or otherwise become members, according to the provisions of the Constitution and the principles on which it was founded. It was the union of those who were at that time members of distinct and separate political communities into one political family, whose power, for certain specified purposes, was to extend over the whole territory of the United States. And it gave to each citizen rights and privileges outside of his State which he did not before possess, and placed him in every other State upon a perfect equality with its own citizens as to rights of person and rights of property; it made him a citizen of the United States.

It becomes necessary, therefore, to determine who were citizens of the several States when the Constitution was adopted. And in order to do this, we must recur to the Governments and institutions of the thirteen colonies, when they separated from Great Britain and formed new sovereignties, and took their places in the family of independent nations. We must inquire who, at that time, were recognised as the people or citizens of a State, whose rights and liberties had been outraged by the English Government; and who declared their independence, and assumed the powers of Government to defend their rights by force of arms.

In the opinion of the court, the legislation and histories of the times, and the language used in the Declaration of Independence, show, that neither the class of persons who had been imported as slaves, nor their descendants, whether they had become free or not, were then acknowledged as a part of the people, nor intended to be included in the general words used in that memorable instrument.

It is difficult at this day to realize the state of public opinion in relation to that unfortunate race, which prevailed in the civilized and enlightened portions of the world at the time of the Declaration of Independence, and when the Constitution of the United States was framed and adopted. But the public history of every European nation displays it in a manner too plain to be mistaken.

An Inferior Race

They had for more than a century before been regarded as beings of an inferior order, and altogether unfit to associate with the white race, either in social or political relations; and so far inferior, that they had no rights which the white man was bound to respect; and that the negro might justly and lawfully be reduced to slavery for his benefit. He was bought and sold, and treated as an ordinary article of merchandise and traffic, whenever a profit could be made by it. This opinion was at that time fixed and universal in the civilized portion of the white race. It was regarded as an axiom in morals as well as in politics, which no one thought of disputing, or supposed to be open to dispute; and men in every grade and position in society daily and habitually acted upon it in their private pursuits, as well as in matters of public concern, without doubting for a moment the correctness of this opinion.

And in no nation was this opinion more firmly fixed or more uniformly acted upon than by the English Government and English people. They not only seized them on the coast of Africa, and sold them or held them in slavery for their own use; but they took them as ordinary articles of merchandise to every country where they could make a profit on them, and were far more extensively engaged in this commerce than any other nation in the world.

The opinion thus entertained and acted upon in England was naturally impressed upon the colonies they founded on this side of the Atlantic. And, accordingly, a negro of the African race was regarded by them as an article of property, and held, and bought and sold as such, in every one of the thirteen colonies which united in the Declaration of Independence, and afterwards formed the Constitution of the United States. The slaves were more or less numerous in the different colonies, as slave labor was found more or less profitable. But no one seems to have doubted the correctness of the prevailing opinion of the time.

The legislation of the different colonies furnishes positive and indisputable proof of this fact. . . .

They show that a perpetual and impassable barrier was in-

231

tended to be erected between the white race and the one which they had reduced to slavery, and governed as subjects with absolute and despotic power, and which they then looked upon as so far below them in the scale of created beings, that intermarriages between white persons and negroes or mulattoes were regarded as unnatural and immoral, and punished as crimes, not only in the parties, but in the person who joined them in marriage. And no distinction in this respect was made between the free negro or mulatto and the slave, but this stigma, of the deepest degradation, was fixed upon the whole race.

We refer to these historical facts for the purpose of showing the fixed opinions concerning that race, upon which the statesmen of that day spoke and acted. It is necessary to do this, in order to determine whether the general terms used in the Constitution of the United States, as to the rights of man and the rights of the people, was intended to include them, or to give to them or their posterity the benefit of any of its provisions.

The Declaration of Independence

The language of the Declaration of Independence is equally conclusive:

It begins by declaring that, "when in the course of human events it becomes necessary for one people to dissolve the political bands which have connected them with another, and to assume among the powers of the earth the separate and equal station to which the laws of nature and nature's God entitle them, a decent respect for the opinions of mankind requires that they should declare the causes which impel them to the separation."

It then proceeds to say: "We hold these truths to be self-evident: that all men are created equal; that they are endowed by their Creator with certain unalienable rights; that among them is life, liberty, and the pursuit of happiness; that to secure these rights, Governments are instituted, deriving their just powers from the consent of the governed."

The general words above quoted would seem to embrace the whole human family, and if they were used in a similar instrument at this day would be so understood. But it is too clear for dispute, that the enslaved African race were not intended to be included, and formed no part of the people who framed and adopted this declaration; for if the language, as understood in that day, would embrace them, the conduct of the distinguished men who framed the Declaration of Independence would have been utterly and flagrantly inconsistent with the principles they asserted; and instead of the sympathy of mankind, to which they so confidently appealed, they would have deserved and received universal rebuke and reprobation.

Yet the men who framed this declaration were great men—high in literary acquirements—high in their sense of honor, and incapable of asserting principles inconsistent with those on which they were acting. They perfectly understood the meaning of the language they used, and how it would be understood by others; and they knew that it would not in any part of the civilized world be supposed to embrace the negro race, which, by common consent, had been excluded from civilized Governments and the family of nations, and doomed to slavery. They spoke and acted according to the then established doctrines and principles, and in the ordinary language of the day, and no one misunderstood them. The unhappy black race were separated from the white by indelible marks, and laws long before established, and were never thought of or spoken of except as property, and when the claims of the owner or the profit of the trader were supposed to need protection.

This state of public opinion had undergone no change when the Constitution was adopted, as is equally evident from its provisions and language.

The U.S. Constitution

The brief preamble sets forth by whom it was formed, for what purposes, and for whose benefit and protection. It declares that it is formed by the *people* of the United States; that is to say, by those who were members of the different political communities in the several States; and its great object is declared to be to secure the blessings of liberty to themselves and their posterity. It speaks in general terms of the *people* of the United States, and of *citizens* of the several States, when it is providing for the exercise of the powers granted or the privileges secured to the citizen. It does not define what description of persons are intended to be included under these terms, or who shall be regarded as a citizen and one of the people. It uses them as terms so well understood, that no further description or definition was necessary.

But there are two clauses in the Constitution which point directly and specifically to the negro race as a separate class of persons, and show clearly that they were not regarded as a portion of the people or citizens of the Government they formed.

One of these clauses reserves to each of the thirteen States the right to import slaves until the year 1808, if it thinks proper. And the importation which it thus sanctions was unquestionably of persons of the race of which we are speaking, as the traffic in slaves in the United States had always been confined to them. And by the other provision the States pledge themselves to each other to maintain the right of property of the master, by delivering up to him any slave who may have escaped from his service, and be found within their respective territories. By the first above-mentioned clause, therefore, the right to purchase and hold this property is directly sanctioned and authorized for twenty years by the people who framed the Constitution. And by the second, they pledge themselves to maintain and uphold the right of the master in the manner specified, as long as the Government they then formed should endure. And these two provisions show, conclusively, that neither the description of persons therein referred to, nor their descendants, were embraced in any of the other provisions of the Constitution; for certainly these two clauses were not intended to confer on them or their posterity the blessings of liberty, or any of the personal rights so carefully provided for the citizen.

No one of that race had ever migrated to the United States voluntarily; all of them had been brought here as articles of merchandise. The number that had been emancipated at that time were but few in comparison with those held in slavery; and they were identified in the public mind with the race to which they belonged, and regarded as a part of the slave population rather than the free. It is obvious that they were not even in the minds of the framers of the Constitution when they were conferring special rights and privileges upon the citizens of a State in every other part of the Union.

Indeed, when we look to the condition of this race in the several States at the time, it is impossible to believe that these rights and privileges were intended to be extended to them.

It is very true, that in that portion of the Union where the labor of the negro race was found to be unsuited to the climate and unprofitable to the master, but few slaves were held at the time of the Declaration of Independence; and when the Constitution was adopted, it had entirely worn out in one of them, and measures had been taken for its gradual abolition in several others. But this change had not been produced by any change of opinion in relation to this race; but because it was discovered, from experience, that slave labor was unsuited to the climate and productions of these States: for some of the States, where it had ceased or nearly ceased to exist, were actively engaged in the slave trade, procuring cargoes on the coast of Africa, and transporting them for sale to those parts of the Union where their labor was found to be profitable, and suited to the climate and productions. And this traffic was openly carried on, and fortunes accumulated by it, without reproach from the people of the States where they resided. And it can hardly be supposed that, in the States where it was then countenanced in its worst form—that is, in the seizure and transportation—the people could have regarded those who were emancipated as entitled to equal rights with themselves.

And we may here again refer, in support of this proposition, to the plain and unequivocal language of the laws of the several States, some passed after the Declaration of Independence and before the Constitution was adopted, and some since the Government went into operation. . . .

Black Reactions to Dred Scott

The response of free blacks to the Dred Scott decision are typified by the following resolution of Robert Purvis, made during a black meeting at Israel Church, Philadelphia, and reprinted in The Liberator *on April 10, 1857.*

Whereas, the Supreme Court of the United States has decided in the case of Dred Scott that *people of African descent are not and cannot be citizens of the United States, and cannot sue in any of the United Sates courts* . . . and, *Whereas,* this Supreme Court is the constitutionally approved tribunal to determine all such questions; therefore,

Resolved, that this atrocious decision furnishes final confirmation of the already well-known fact that, under the Constitution and government of the United States, the colored people are nothing and can be nothing but an alien, disfranchised, and degraded class. . . .

Resolved, that to persist in supporting a government which holds and exercises the power, as distinctly set forth by a tribunal from which there is no appeal, to trample a class underfoot as an inferior and degraded race, is on the part of the colored man at once the height of folly and the depth of pusillanimity.

It would be impossible to enumerate and compress in the space usually allotted to an opinion of a court, the various laws, marking the condition of this race, which were passed from time to time after the Revolution, and before and since the adoption of the Constitution of the United States. In addition to those already referred to, it is sufficient to say, that Chancellor Kent, whose accuracy and research no one will question, states in the sixth edition of his Commentaries, (published in 1848, 2 vol., 258, note *b*,) that in no part of the country except Maine, did the African race, in point of fact, participate equally with the whites in the exercise of civil and political rights.

The legislation of the States therefore shows, in a manner not to be mistaken, the inferior and subject condition of that race at the time the Constitution was adopted. . . . It cannot be believed that the large slaveholding States regarded them as included in the word citizens, or would have consented to a Constitution which might compel them to receive them in that character from another State. . . .

No one, we presume, supposes that any change in public opinion or feeling, in relation to this unfortunate race, in the civilized nations of Europe or in this country, should induce the court to give to the words of the Constitution a more liberal construction in their favor than they were intended to bear when the instrument was framed and adopted. Such an argument would be altogether inadmissable in any tribunal called on to interpret it. If any of its provisions are deemed unjust, there is a mode prescribed in the instrument itself by which it may be amended; but while it remains unaltered, it must be construed now as it was understood at the time of its adoption. It is not only the same in words, but the same in meaning, and delegates the same powers to the Government, and reserves and secures the same rights and privileges to the citizen; and as long as it continues to exist in its present form, it speaks not only in the same words, but with the same meaning and intent with which it spoke when it came from the hands of its framers, and was voted on and adopted by the people of the United States. Any other rule of construction would abrogate the judicial character of this court, and make it the mere reflex of the popular opinion or passion of the day. This court was not created by the Constitution for such purposes. Higher and graver trusts have been confided to it, and it must not falter in the path of duty.

What the construction was at that time, we think can hardly admit of doubt. We have the language of the Declaration of Independence and of the Articles of Confederation, in addition to the plain words of the Constitution itself; we have the legislation of the different States, before, about the time, and since, the Constitution was adopted; we have the legislation of Congress, from the time of its adoption to a recent period; and we have the constant and uniform action of the Executive Department, all concurring together, and leading to the same result. And if anything in relation to the construction of the Constitution can be regarded as settled, it is that which we now give to the word "citizen" and the word "people."

And upon a full and careful consideration of the subject, the court is of opinion, that, upon the facts stated in the plea in abatement, Dred Scott was not a citizen of Missouri within the meaning of the Constitution of the United States, and not entitled as such to sue in its courts; and, consequently, that the Circuit Court had no jurisdiction of the case, and that the judgment on the plea in abatement is erroneous. . . .

Property Rights

The right of property in a slave is distinctly and expressly affirmed in the Constitution. The right to traffic in it, like an ordinary article of merchandise and property, was guarantied to the citizens of the United States, in every State that might desire it, for twenty years. And the Government in express terms is pledged to protect it in all future time, if the slave escapes from his owner. This is done in plain words—too plain to be misunderstood. And no word can be found in the Constitution which gives Congress a greater power over slave property, or which entitles property of that kind to less protection than property of any other description. The only power conferred is the power coupled with the duty of guarding and protecting the owner in his rights.

Upon these considerations, it is the opinion of the court that the act of Congress which prohibited a citizen from holding and owning property of this kind in the territory of the United States north of the line therein mentioned, is not warranted by the Constitution, and is therefore void; and that neither Dred Scott himself, nor any of his family, were made free by being carried into this territory; even if they had been carried there by the owner, with the intention of becoming a permanent resident.

We have so far examined the case, as it stands under the Constitution of the United States, and the powers thereby delegated to the Federal Government.

But there is another point in the case which depends on State power and State law. And it is contended, on the part of the plaintiff, that he is made free by being taken to Rock Island, in the State of Illinois, independently of his residence in the territory of the United States; and being so made free, he was not again reduced to a state of slavery by being brought back to Missouri.

Our notice of this part of the case will be very brief; for the principle on which it depends was decided in this court, upon much consideration, in the case of Strader et al, *v.* Graham, reported in 10th Howard, 82. In that case, the slaves had been taken from Kentucky to Ohio, with the consent of the owner, and afterwards brought back to Kentucky. And this court held that their *status* or condition, as free or slave, depended upon the laws of Kentucky, when they were brought back into that State, and not of Ohio; and that this court had no jurisdiction to revise the judgment of a State court upon its own laws. This was the point directly before the court, and the decision that this court had not jurisdiction turned upon it, as will be seen by the report of the case.

So in this case. As Scott was a slave when taken into the State of Illinois by his owner, and was there held as such, and brought back in that character, his *status*, as free or slave, depended on the laws of Missouri, and not of Illinois.

Viewpoint 4

"That [the Constitution] was made exclusively for the white race is, in my opinion, not only an assumption not warranted by anything in the Constitution, but contradicted by its opening declaration, that it was ordained and established by the people of the United States, for themselves and their posterity."

Constitutional Rights Do Extend to Ex-Slaves

Benjamin Robbins Curtis (1809-1874)

Benjamin Robbins Curtis was a Supreme Court justice from 1840 to 1857. He is most famous for his dissent on the Dred Scott case of 1857, a dissent which ultimately led to his resignation from the Court.

Dred Scott was a slave who had sued for his freedom on the grounds that he had resided in a state where slavery was outlawed. The Supreme Court, led by Chief Justice Roger Taney, ruled against him, partly on the basis that slaves and their descendants have no standing as citizens under the U.S. Constitution. In the following excerpts, Curtis challenges this reasoning. He argues that the Constitution contains no provisions excluding blacks from U.S. citizenship. He concludes that the states themselves have the power to determine citizenship, and that all citizens of the states are also citizens of the United States.

Curtis' opposition to the Dred Scott case was shared by America's free black population, abolitionists, and the new Republican party. The Dred Scott decision failed to resolve America's sectional crisis over slavery and helped pave the way to the Civil War.

The question is, whether any person of African descent, whose ancestors were sold as slaves in the United States, can be a citizen of the United States. If any such person can be a citizen, this plaintiff has the right to the judgment of the court that he is so; for no cause is shown by the plea why he is not so, except his descent and the slavery of his ancestors.

The first section of the second article of the Constitution uses the language, "a citizen of the United States at the time of the adoption of the Constitution." One mode of approaching this question is, to inquire who were citizens of the United States at the time of the adoption of the Constitution.

Citizens of the United States at the time of the adoption of the Constitution can have been no other than citizens of the United States under the Confederation. By the Articles of Confederation, a Government was organized, the style whereof was, "The United States of America." This Government was in existence when the Constitution was framed and proposed for adoption, and was to be superseded by the new Government of the United States of America, organized under the Constitution. When, therefore, the Constitution speaks of citizenship of the United States, existing at the time of the adoption of the Constitution, it must necessarily refer to citizenship under the Government which existed prior to and at the time of such adoption.

Without going into any question concerning the powers of the Confederation to govern the territory of the United States out of the limits of the States, and consequently to sustain the relation of Government and citizen in respect to the inhabitants of such territory, it may safely be said that the citizens of the several States were citizens of the United States under the Confederation.

Citizens of the States

That Government was simply a confederacy of the several States, possessing a few defined powers over subjects of general concern, each State retaining every power, jurisdiction, and right, not expressly delegated to the United States in Congress assembled. And no power was thus delegated to the Government of the Confederation, to act on any question of citizenship, or to make any rules in respect thereto. The whole matter was left to stand upon the action of the several States, and to the natural consequence of such action, that the citizens of each State should be citizens of that Confederacy into which that State had entered, the style whereof was, "The United States of America."

To determine whether any free persons, descended from Africans held in slavery, were citizens of the United States under the Confederation, and consequently at the time of the adoption of the Constitution of the United States, it is only necessary to

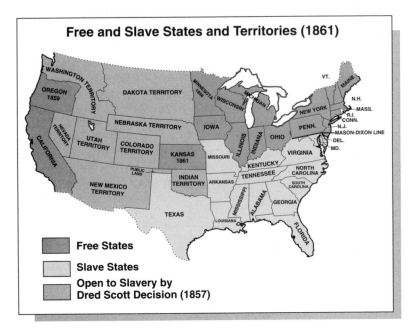

Free and Slave States and Territories (1861)

- Free States
- Slave States
- Open to Slavery by Dred Scott Decision (1857)

know whether any such persons were citizens of either of the States under the Confederation, at the time of the adoption of the Constitution.

Of this there can be no doubt. At the time of the ratification of the Articles of Confederation, all free native-born inhabitants of the States of New Hampshire, Massachusetts, New York, New Jersey, and North Carolina, though descended from African slaves, were not only citizens of those States, but such of them as had the other necessary qualifications possessed the franchise of electors, on equal terms with other citizens. . . .

Descendants of Slaves Are Citizens

An argument from speculative premises, however well chosen, that the then state of opinion in the Commonwealth of Massachusetts was not consistent with the natural rights of people of color who were born on that soil, and that they were not, by the Constitution of 1780 of that State, admitted to the condition of citizens, would be received with surprise by the people of that State, who know their own political history. It is true, beyond all controversy, that persons of color, descended from African slaves, were by that Constitution made citizens of the State; and such of them as have had the necessary qualifications, have held and exercised the elective franchise, as citizens, from that time to the present. . . .

The Constitution of New Hampshire conferred the elective

franchise upon "every inhabitant of the State having the necessary qualifications," of which color or descent was not one. . . .

That of New Jersey, to "all inhabitants of this colony, of full age, who are worth £50 proclamation money, clear estate."

New York, by its Constitution of 1820, required colored persons to have some qualifications as prerequisites for voting, which white persons need not possess. And New Jersey, by its present Constitution, restricts the right to vote to white male citizens. But these changes can have no other effect upon the present inquiry, except to show, that before they were made, no such restrictions existed; and colored in common with white persons, were not only citizens of those States, but entitled to the elective franchise on the same qualifications as white persons, as they now are in New Hampshire and Massachusetts. I shall not enter into an examination of the existing opinions of that period respecting the African race, nor into any discussion concerning the meaning of those who asserted, in the Declaration of Independence, that all men are created equal; that they are endowed by their Creator with certain inalienable rights; that among these are life, liberty, and the pursuit of happiness. My own opinion is, that a calm comparison of these assertions of universal abstract truths, and of their own individual opinions and acts, would not leave these men under any reproach of inconsistency; that the great truths they asserted on that solemn occasion, they were ready and anxious to make effectual, wherever a necessary regard to circumstances, which no statesman can disregard without producing more evil than good, would allow; and that it would not be just to them, nor true in itself, to allege that they intended to say that the Creator of all men had endowed the white race, exclusively, with the great natural rights which the Declaration of Independence asserts. But this is not the place to vindicate their memory. As I conceive, we should deal here, not with such disputes, if there can be a dispute concerning this subject, but with those substantial facts evinced by the written Constitutions of States, and by the notorious practice under them. And they show, in a manner which no argument can obscure, that in some of the original thirteen States, free colored persons, before and at the time of the formation of the Constitution, were citizens of those States. . . .

Did the Constitution of the United States deprive them or their descendants of citizenship?

That Constitution was ordained and established by the people of the United States, through the action, in each State, of those persons who were qualified by its laws to act thereon, in behalf of themselves and all other citizens of that State. In some of the States, as we have seen, colored persons were among those qualified by law to act on this subject. These colored persons were not only included in the body of "the people of the United States," by whom the Constitution was ordained and established, but in at least five of the States they had the power to act, and doubtless did act, by their suffrages, upon the question of its adoption. It would be strange, if we were to find in that instrument anything which deprived of their citizenship any part of the people of the United States who were among those by whom it was established.

No Provisions that Deprive Citizenship

I can find nothing in the Constitution which, *proprio vigore*, deprives of their citizenship any class of persons who were citizens of the United States at the time of its adoption, or who should be native-born citizens of any State after its adoption; nor any power enabling Congress to disfranchise persons born on the soil of any State, and entitled to citizenship of such State by its Constitution and laws. And my opinion is, that, under the Constitution of the United States, every free person born on the soil of a State, who is a citizen of that State by force of its Constitution or laws, is also a citizen of the United States.

I will proceed to state the grounds of that opinion.

The first section of the second article of the Constitution uses the language, "a natural-born citizen." It thus assumes that citizenship may be acquired by birth. . . .

The Constitution having recognised the rule that persons born within the several States are citizens of the United States, one of four things must be true:

First. That the Constitution itself has described what native-born persons shall or shall not be citizens of the United States; or,

Second. That it has empowered Congress to do so; or,

Third. That all free persons, born within the several States, are citizens of the United States; or,

Fourth. That it is left to each State to determine what free persons, born within its limits, shall be citizens of such State, and *thereby* be citizens of the United States.

If there be such a thing as citizenship of the United States acquired by birth within the States, which the Constitution expressly recognises, and no one denies, then these four alternatives embrace the entire subject, and it only remains to select that one which is true.

No Definition of Citizenship

That the Constitution itself has defined citizenship of the United States by declaring what persons, born within the several States, shall or shall not be citizens of the United States, will not be pretended. It contains no such declaration. We may dismiss the first alternative, as without doubt unfounded.

Has it empowered Congress to enact what free persons, born within the several States, shall or shall not be citizens of the United States?

Can Congress Create Privileged Classes?

Before examining the various provisions of the Constitution which may relate to this question, it is important to consider for a moment the substantial nature of this inquiry. It is, in effect, whether the Constitution has empowered Congress to create privileged classes within the States, who alone can be entitled to the franchises and powers of citizenship of the United States. If it be admitted that the Constitution has enabled Congress to declare what free persons, born within the several States, shall be citizens of the United States, it must at the same time be admitted that it is an unlimited power. If this subject is within the control of Congress, it must depend wholly on its discretion. For, certainly, no limits of that discretion can be found in the Constitution, which is wholly silent concerning it; and the necessary consequence is, that the Federal Government may select classes of persons within the several States who alone can be entitled to the political privileges of citizenship of the United States. If this power exists, what persons born within the States may be President or Vice President of the United States, or members of either House of Congress, or hold any office or enjoy any privilege whereof citizenship of the United States is a necessary qualification, must depend solely on the will of Congress. By virtue of it, though Congress can grant no title of nobility, they may create an oligarchy, in whose hands would be concentrated the entire power of the Federal Government.

It is a substantive power, distinct in its nature from all others; capable of affecting not only the relations of the States to the General Government, but of controlling the political condition of the people of the United States. Certainly we ought to find this power granted by the Constitution, at least by some necessary inference, before we can say it does not remain to the States or the people. I proceed therefore to examine all the provisions of the Constitution which may have some bearing on this subject.

Among the powers expressly granted to Congress is "the power to establish a uniform rule of naturalization." It is not doubted that this is a power to prescribe a rule for the removal of the disabilities consequent on foreign birth. To hold that it extends further than this, would do violence to the meaning of the term naturalization. . . .

Whether there be anything in the Constitution from which a broader power may be implied, will best be seen when we come

243

to examine the two other alternatives, which are, whether all free persons, born on the soil of the several States, or only such of them as may be citizens of each State, respectively, are thereby citizens of the United States. The last of these alternatives, in my judgment, contains the truth. . . .

It may be proper here to notice some supposed objections to this view of the subject.

The White Race

It has been often asserted that the Constitution was made exclusively by and for the white race. It has already been shown that in five of the thirteen original States, colored persons then possessed the elective franchise, and were among those by whom the Constitution was ordained and established. If so, it is not true, in point of fact, that the Constitution was made exclusively by the white race. And that it was made exclusively for the white race is, in my opinion, not only an assumption not warranted by anything in the Constitution, but contradicted by its opening declaration, that it was ordained and established by the people of the United States, for themselves and their posterity. And as free colored persons were then citizens of at least five States, and so in every sense part of the people of the United States, they were among those for whom and whose posterity the Constitution was ordained and established.

The Fourteenth Amendment

The Fourteenth Amendment to the Constitution was approved by Congress in 1866 and ratified by the states by 1868. Created to help protect the civil rights of newly freed slaves, it directly reversed by Dred Scott decision depriving blacks of citizenship in the United States.

Section 1. All persons born or naturalized in the United States and subject to the jurisdiction thereof, are citizens of the United States and of the State wherein they reside. No State shall make or enforce any law which shall abridge the privileges or immunities of citizens of the United States; or shall any State deprive any person of life, liberty, or property, without due process of law; nor deny to any person within its jurisdiction the equal protection of the laws.

Again, it has been objected, that if the Constitution has left to the several States the rightful power to determine who of their inhabitants shall be citizens of the United States, the States may make aliens citizens.

The answer is obvious. The Constitution has left to the States the determination what persons, born within their respective lim-

244

its, shall acquire by birth citizenship of the United States; it has not left to them any power to prescribe any rule for the removal of the disabilities of alienage. This power is exclusively in Congress.

It has been further objected, that if free colored persons, born within a particular State, and made citizens of that State by its Constitution and laws, are thereby made citizens of the United States, then, under the second section of the fourth article of the Constitution, such persons would be entitled to all the privileges and immunities of citizens in the several States; and if so, then colored persons could vote, and be eligible to not only Federal offices, but offices even in those States whose Constitutions and laws disqualify colored persons from voting or being elected to office.

But this position rests upon an assumption which I deem untenable. Its basis is, that no one can be deemed a citizen of the United States who is not entitled to enjoy all the privileges and franchises which are conferred on any citizen. That this is not true, under the Constitution of the United States, seems to me clear.

Citizens and Their Rights

A naturalized citizen cannot be President of the United States, nor a Senator till after the lapse of nine years, nor a Representative till after the lapse of seven years, from his naturalization. Yet, as soon as naturalized, he is certainly a citizen of the United States. Nor is any inhabitant of the District of Columbia, or of either of the Territories, eligible to the office of Senator or Representative in Congress, though they may be citizens of the United States. So, in all the States, numerous persons, though citizens, cannot vote, or cannot hold office, either on account of their age, or sex, or the want of the necessary legal qualifications. The truth is, that citizenship, under the Constitution of the United States, is not dependent on the possession of any particular political or even of all civil rights; and any attempt so to define it must lead to error. To what citizens the elective franchise shall be confided, is a question to be determined by each State, in accordance with its own views of the necessities or expediencies of its condition. What civil rights shall be enjoyed by its citizens, and whether all shall enjoy the same, or how they may be gained or lost, are to be determined in the same way. . . .

It may be further objected, that if free colored persons may be citizens of the United States, it depends only on the will of a master whether he will emancipate his slave, and thereby make him a citizen. Not so. The master is subject to the will of the State. Whether he shall be allowed to emancipate his slave at all; if so, on what conditions; and what is to be the political *status* of the freed man, depend, not on the will of the master, but on the will of the State, upon which the political *status* of all its native-born inhabitants depends. Under the Constitution of the United States, each State has retained this power of determining the political *status* of its native-born inhabitants, and no exception thereto can be found in the Constitution. And if a master in a slaveholding State should carry his slave into a free State, and there emancipate him, he would not thereby make him a native-born citizen of that State, and consequently no privileges could be claimed by such emancipated slave as a citizen of the United States. For, whatever powers the States may exercise to confer privileges of citizenship on persons not born on their soil, the Constitution of the United States does not recognise such citizens. As has already been said, it recognises the great principle of public law, that allegiance and citizenship spring from the place of birth. It leaves to the States the application of that principle to individual cases. It secured to the citizens of each State the privileges and immunities of citizens in every other State. But it does not allow to the States the power to make aliens citizens, or permit one State to take persons born on the soil of another State, and, contrary to the laws and policy of the State where they were born, make them its citizens, and so citizens of the United States. No such deviation from the great rule of public law was contemplated by the Constitution; and when any such attempt shall be actually made, it is to be met by applying to it those rules of law and those principles of good faith which will be sufficient to decide it, and not, in my judgment, by denying that all the free native-born inhabitants of a State, who are its citizens under its Constitution and laws, are also citizens of the United States.

It has sometimes been urged that colored persons are shown not to be citizens of the United States by the fact that the naturalization laws apply only to white persons. But whether a person born in the United States be or be not a citizen, cannot depend on laws which refer only to aliens, and do not affect the *status* of persons born in the United States. The utmost effect which can be attributed to them is, to show that Congress has not deemed it expedient generally to apply the rule to colored aliens. That they might do so, if thought fit, is clear. The Constitution has not excluded them. And since that has conferred the power on Congress to naturalize colored aliens, it certainly shows color is not a necessary qualification for citizenship under the Constitution of the United States. It may be added, that the power to make colored persons citizens of the United States, under the Constitution, has been actually exercised in repeated and important instances. (See the Treaties with the Choctaws, of September 27, 1830, art. 14; with the Cherokees, of May 23, 1836, art. 12;

Treaty of Guadalupe Hidalgo, February 2, 1848, art. 8.)

I do not deem it necessary to review at length the legislation of Congress having more or less bearing on the citizenship of colored persons. It does not seem to me to have any considerable tendency to prove that it has been considered by the legislative department of the Government, that no such persons are citizens of the United States. Undoubtedly they have been debarred from the exercise of particular rights or privileges extended to white persons, but, I believe, always in terms which, by implication, admit they may be citizens. Thus the act of May 17, 1792, for the organization of the militia, directs the enrollment of "every free, able-bodied, white male citizen." An assumption that none but white persons are citizens, would be as inconsistent with the just import of this language, as that all citizens are able-bodied, or males. . . .

Conclusions

The conclusions at which I have arrived on this part of the case are:

First. That the free native-born citizens of each State are citizens of the United States.

Second. That as free colored persons born within some of the States are citizens of those States, such persons are also citizens of the United States.

Third. That every such citizen, residing in any State, has the right to sue and is liable to be sued in the Federal courts, as a citizen of that State in which he resides.

Fourth. That as the plea to the jurisdiction in this case shows no facts, except that the plaintiff was of African descent, and his ancestors were sold as slaves, and as these facts are not inconsistent with his citizenship of the United States, and his residence in the State of Missouri, the plea to the jurisdiction was bad, and the judgment of the Circuit Court overruling it was correct.

I dissent, therefore, from that part of the opinion of the majority of the court, in which it is held that a person of African descent cannot be a citizen of the United States.

VIEWPOINT 5

"I believe this government cannot endure, permanently, half slave and half free."

Popular Sovereignty over Slavery Divides the Nation

Abraham Lincoln (1809-1865)

Abraham Lincoln is regarded by many as America's greatest president. On June 16, 1858, however, he was a relatively unknown lawyer from Illinois who had served one undistinguished term in Congress and who was seeking election to the U.S. Senate seat held by Stephen A. Douglas. He launched his election with the speech reprinted below, a speech which eventually led to the famous Lincoln-Douglas debates concerning slavery.

In this speech Lincoln reacts to recent events and laws that had greatly altered the slavery debate. The Compromise of 1850 and the 1854 Kansas-Nebraska Act had tried to promote the idea of "popular sovereignty"—allowing local settlers of the new territories to decide whether to legalize slavery. The 1857 Dred Scott decision had invalidated previous Congressional laws limiting slavery in the western territories. Douglas, who had been a sponsor of the Kansas-Nebraska Act, was an especially strong supporter of popular sovereignty.

Lincoln argues that these developments were part of an ominous trend that, if continued, would make slavery legal throughout the United States. He attacks the concept of popular sovereignty, stating that the decision to legalize or outlaw slavery had to be made on a national level—that the United States "cannot endure, permanently, half slave and half free."

Douglas won the 1858 senatorial campaign, but the national prominence Lincoln achieved played a key role in his 1860 election to president.

Mr. *President and Gentlemen of the Convention:*

If we could first know where we are and whither we are tending, we could better judge what to do and how to do it. We are now far into the fifth year since a policy was initiated with the avowed object and confident promise of putting an end to slavery agitation. Under the operation of that policy, that agitation has not only not ceased but has constantly augmented. In my opinion, it will not cease until a crisis shall have been reached and passed. "A house divided against itself cannot stand." I believe this government cannot endure, permanently, half slave and half free. I do not expect the Union to be dissolved; I do not expect the house to fall; but I do expect it will cease to be divided. It will become all one thing, or all the other. Either the opponents of slavery will arrest the further spread of it and place it where the public mind shall rest in the belief that it is in the course of ultimate extinction, or its advocates will push it forward till it shall become alike lawful in all the states, old as well as new, North as well as South.

Have we no tendency to the latter condition?

Let anyone who doubts carefully contemplate that now almost complete legal combination—piece of machinery, so to speak—compounded of the Nebraska doctrine and the Dred Scott decision. Let him consider, not only what work the machinery is adapted to do, and how well adapted, but also let him study the history of its construction and trace, if he can, or rather fail, if he can, to trace the evidences of design and concert of action among its chief architects, from the beginning.

The new year of 1854 found slavery excluded from more than half the states by state constitutions and from most of the national territory by congressional prohibition. Four days later commenced the struggle which ended in repealing that congressional prohibition. This opened all the national territory to slavery and was the first point gained.

But, so far, Congress *only* had acted; and an endorsement by the people, real or apparent, was indispensable to save the point already gained and give chance for more.

The Nebraska Bill

This necessity had not been overlooked, but had been provided for, as well as might be, in the notable argument of "squatter sovereignty," otherwise called "sacred right of self-government," which latter phrase, though expressive of the only rightful basis of any government, was so perverted in this attempted use of it

Library of Congress.

Abraham Lincoln was not an abolitionist, and as late as 1862 believed the best solution to slavery was for American blacks to be sent back to Africa.

as to amount to just this: That if any *one* man choose to enslave *another*, no *third* man shall be allowed to object. That argument was incorporated into the Nebraska Bill itself, in the language which follows:

> It being the true intent and meaning of this act not to legislate slavery into any territory or state, nor to exclude it therefrom, but to leave the people thereof perfectly free to form and regulate their domestic institutions in their own way, subject only to the Constitution of the United States.

Then opened the roar of loose declamation in favor of "squatter sovereignty" and "sacred right of self-government." "But," said opposition members, "let us amend the bill so as to expressly declare that the people of the territory may exclude slavery." "Not we," said the friends of the measure; and down they voted the amendment.

While the Nebraska Bill was passing through Congress, a law case, involving the question of a Negro's freedom, by reason of his owner having voluntarily taken him first into a free state and then into a territory covered by the congressional prohibition, and held him as a slave for a long time in each, was passing through the United States Circuit Court for the district of Missouri; and both Nebraska Bill and lawsuit were brought to a decision in the same month of May 1854. The Negro's name was Dred Scott, which name now designates the decision finally made in the case. Before the then next presidential election, the law case came to, and was argued in, the Supreme Court of the United States; but the decision of it was deferred until after the election. Still, before the election, Senator Trumbull, on the floor of the Senate, requested the leading advocate of the Nebraska Bill to state his opinion whether the people of a territory can constitutionally exclude slavery from their limits; and the latter answers: "That is a question for the Supreme Court."

The election came. Mr. Buchanan was elected, and the endorsement, such as it was, secured. That was the second point gained. The endorsement, however, fell short of a clear popular majority by nearly 400,000 votes, and so, perhaps, was not overwhelmingly reliable and satisfactory. The outgoing President, in his last annual message, as impressively as possible echoed back upon the people the weight and authority of the endorsement. The Supreme Court met again, did not announce their decision, but ordered a reargument.

The Dred Scott Decision

The presidential inauguration came, and still no decision of the Court; but the incoming President, in his inaugural address, fervently exhorted the people to abide by the forthcoming decision, whatever it might be. Then, in a few days, came the decision.

The reputed author of the Nebraska Bill finds an early occasion to make a speech at this capital endorsing the Dred Scott decision, and vehemently denouncing all opposition to it. The new President, too, seizes the early occasion of the Silliman letter to endorse and strongly construe that decision, and to express his astonishment that any different view had ever been entertained!

At length a squabble springs up between the President and the author of the Nebraska Bill, on the mere question of *fact*, whether the Lecompton constitution was or was not in any just sense made by the people of Kansas; and in that quarrel the latter declares that all he wants is a fair vote for the people, and that he cares not whether slavery be voted *down* or voted *up*. I do not understand his declaration, that he cares not whether slavery be voted down or voted up, to be intended by him other than as an apt definition of the policy he would impress upon the public mind—the principle for which he declares he has suffered so much and is ready to suffer to the end. And well may he cling to that principle! If he has any parental feeling, well may he cling to it. That principle is the only shred left of his original Nebraska doctrine.

Under the Dred Scott decision, "squatter sovereignty" squatted out of existence, tumbled down like temporary scaffolding; like the mold at the foundry, served through one blast and fell back into loose sand; helped to carry an election and then was kicked to the winds. His late joint struggle with the Republicans against the Lecompton constitution involves nothing of the original Nebraska doctrine. That struggle was made on a point—the right of a people to make their own constitution—upon which he and the Republicans have never differed.

Legal Machinery Supporting Slavery

The several points of the Dred Scott decision, in connection with Senator Douglas' "care not" policy, constitute the piece of machinery in its present state of advancement. This was the third point gained. The working points of that machinery are:

First, that no Negro slave, imported as such from Africa, and no descendant of such slave can ever be a citizen of any state in the sense of that term as used in the Constitution of the United States. This point is made in order to deprive the Negro, in every possible event, of the benefit of that provision of the United States Constitution which declares that "the citizens of each state shall be entitled to all the privileges and immunities of citizens in the several states."

Second, that, "subject to the Constitution of the United States," neither Congress nor a territorial legislature can exclude slavery from any United States territory. This point is made in order that individual men may fill up the territories with slaves, without danger of losing them as property, and thus enhance the chances of permanency to the institution through all the future.

Third, that whether the holding a Negro in actual slavery in a free state makes him free, as against the holder, the United States courts will not decide, but will leave to be decided by the courts of any slave state the Negro may be forced into by the master. This point is made, not to be pressed immediately but, if acquiesced in for awhile, and apparently endorsed by the people at an election, then to sustain the logical conclusion that what Dred Scott's master might lawfully do with Dred Scott in the free state of Illinois, every other master may lawfully do with any other one, or 1,000 slaves, in Illinois or in any other free state.

Auxiliary to all this, and working hand in hand with it, the Nebraska doctrine, or what is left of it, is to educate and mold public opinion, at least Northern public opinion, not to care whether slavery is voted down or voted up. This shows exactly where we now are; and partially, also, whither we are tending.

It will throw additional light on the latter to go back and run the mind over the string of historical facts already stated. Several things will now appear less dark and mysterious than they did when they were transpiring. The people were to be left "perfectly free," "subject only to the Constitution." What the Constitution had to do with it, outsiders could not then see. Plainly enough, now, it was an exactly fitted niche for the Dred Scott decision to afterward come in and declare the perfect freedom of the people to be just no freedom at all.

A Conspiracy?

Why was the amendment expressly declaring the right of the people voted down? Plainly enough, now, the adoption of it would have spoiled the niche for the Dred Scott decision. Why was the Court decision held up? Why even a senator's individual opinion withheld till after the presidential election? Plainly enough, now, the speaking out then would have damaged the "perfectly free" argument upon which the election was to be carried. Why the outgoing President's felicitation on the endorsement? Why the delay of a reargument? Why the incoming President's advance exhortation in favor of the decision? These things look like the cautious patting and petting of a spirited horse preparatory to mounting him when it is dreaded that he may give the rider a fall. And why the hasty after-endorsement of the decision by the President and others?

We cannot absolutely know that all these exact adaptations are the result of preconcert. But when we see a lot of framed timbers, different portions of which we know have been gotten out at different times and places and by different workmen—Stephen, Franklin, Roger, and James, for instance—and when we see these timbers joined together and see they exactly make the frame of a house or a mill, all the tenons and mortises exactly fitting, and all the lengths and proportions of the different pieces exactly adapted to their respective places, and not a piece too many or too few, not omitting even scaffolding, or, if a single piece be lacking, we see the place in the frame exactly fitted and prepared yet to bring such piece in—in such a case, we find it impossible not to believe that Stephen and Franklin and Roger and James all understood one another from the beginning, and all worked upon a common plan or draft drawn up before the first blow was struck.

Viewpoint 6

"It is no answer ... to say that slavery is an evil, and hence should not be tolerated. You must allow the people to decide for themselves whether it is a good or an evil."

Popular Sovereignty Should Decide Slavery

Stephen A. Douglas (1813-1861)

Stephen A. Douglas was a U.S. senator from Illinois from 1846 to 1861 and was a candidate for president in 1860. He is perhaps best remembered for his association and political rivalry with Abraham Lincoln.

The following viewpoint is taken from the opening speech Douglas gave in Chicago on July 9, 1858, during his reelection campaign against Lincoln. The campaign featured debates between the two candidates over the issue of slavery and especially whether slavery should be allowed to expand in the western territories. Douglas's position, expressed in this viewpoint, was "popular sovereignty"—that local communities of the territories themselves should decide whether to legalize slavery. This principle was central to the 1854 Kansas-Nebraska Act, a law Douglas sponsored, which said that the status of the Kansas and Nebraska territories regarding slavery should be decided by the local residents. In this speech, Douglas also defends the 1857 Dred Scott ruling. The court had ruled that blacks have no standing or rights under the U.S. Constitution, which, Douglas states, was made for the white race only.

Douglas defeated Lincoln in the 1858 senatorial election. Two years later, he received the Democratic party's nomination for president. The southern wing of the party was opposed to Douglas, however, in part because of statements he had made during

the Lincoln-Douglas debates concerning the territory's right to exclude slavery, and they nominated their own candidate. Douglas
lost the election to Lincoln, the candidate of the new Republican
party. Douglas subsequently worked in the Senate in support of
Lincoln and the Union. He had just completed a speaking tour of
the West urging people to support Lincoln when he died in 1861.

I regard the great principle of popular sovereignty as having
been vindicated and made triumphant in this land as a permanent rule of public policy in the organization of territories and the
admission of new states. Illinois took her position upon this principle many years ago. . . .

The great principle is the right of every community to judge
and decide for itself whether a thing is right or wrong, whether it
would be good or evil for them to adopt it; and the right of free
action, the right of free thought, the right of free judgment, upon
the question is dearer to every true American than any other under a free government. . . . It is no answer to this argument to say
that slavery is an evil, and hence should not be tolerated.

The People Must Decide

You must allow the people to decide for themselves whether it
is a good or an evil. You allow them to decide for themselves
whether they desire a Maine Liquor Law or not; you allow them
to decide for themselves what kind of common schools they will
have, what system of banking they will adopt, or whether they
will adopt any at all; you allow them to decide for themselves the
relations between husband and wife, parent and child, guardian
and ward; in fact, you allow them to decide for themselves all
other questions; and why not upon this question? Whenever you
put a limitation upon the right of any people to decide what laws
they want, you have destroyed the fundamental principle of self-
government.

Mr. Lincoln made a speech before that Republican Convention
which unanimously nominated him for the Senate—a speech evidently well prepared and carefully written in which he states the
basis upon which he proposes to carry on the campaign during
this summer. In it he lays down two distinct propositions which I
shall notice, and upon which I shall take a direct and bold issue
with him.

His first and main proposition I will give in his own language,
Scripture quotations and all. [*Laughter.*] I give his exact language:
"'A house divided against itself cannot stand.' I believe this gov-

ernment cannot endure, permanently, half *slave* and half *free*. I do not expect the Union to be *dissolved*; I do not expect the house to *fall*; but I do expect it to cease to be divided. It will become all one thing, or *all* the other."

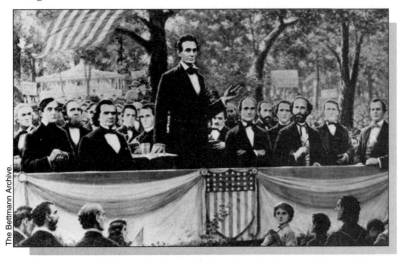

The Bettmann Archive.

A clean-shaven Abraham Lincoln makes his point during one of his well-known debates with Stephen A. Douglas. Douglas is seated on Lincoln's immediate right.

In other words, Mr. Lincoln asserts, as a fundamental principle of this government, that there must be uniformity in the local laws and domestic institutions of each and all the states of the Union; and he therefore invites all the nonslaveholding states to band together, organize as one body, and make war upon slavery in Kentucky, upon slavery in Virginia, upon the Carolinas, upon slavery in all of the slaveholding states in this Union, and to persevere in that war until it shall be exterminated.

He then notifies the slaveholding states to stand together as a unit and make an aggressive war upon the free states of this Union with a view of establishing slavery in them all; of forcing it upon Illinois, of forcing it upon New York, upon New England, and upon every other free state, and that they shall keep up the warfare until it has been formally established in them all.

In other words, Mr. Lincoln advocates boldly and clearly a war of sections, a war of the North against the South, of the free states against the slave states, a war of extermination to be continued relentlessly until the one or the other shall be subdued and all the states shall either become free or become slave.

Now, my friends, I must say to you frankly that I take bold, unqualified issue with him upon that principle. I assert that it is neither desirable nor possible that there should be uniformity in the local institutions and domestic regulations of the different states of this Union. . . .

The framers of the Constitution well understood that each locality, having separate and distinct interests, required separate and distinct laws, domestic institutions, and police regulations adapted to its own wants and its own condition; and they acted on the presumption, also, that these laws and institutions would be as diversified and as dissimilar as the states would be numerous and that no two would be precisely alike, because the interests of no two would be precisely the same. Hence, I assert that the great fundamental principle which underlies our complex system of state and federal governments contemplated diversity and dissimilarity in the local institutions and domestic affairs of each and every state then in the Union or thereafter to be admitted into the confederacy.

I therefore conceive that my friend Mr. Lincoln has totally misapprehended the great principles upon which our government rests. Uniformity in local and domestic affairs would be destructive of state rights, of state sovereignty, of personal liberty and personal freedom. Uniformity is the parent of despotism the world over, not only in politics but in religion. Wherever the doctrine of uniformity is proclaimed that all the states must be free or all slave, that all labor must be white or all black, that all the citizens of the different states must have the same privileges or be governed by the same regulations, you have destroyed the greatest safeguard which our institutions have thrown around the rights of the citizen.

How could this uniformity be accomplished if it was desirable and possible? There is but one mode in which it could be obtained, and that must be by abolishing the state legislatures, blotting out state sovereignty, merging the rights and sovereignty of the states in one consolidated empire, and vesting Congress with the plenary power to make all the police regulations, domestic and local laws, uniform throughout the limits of the republic. When you shall have done this, you will have uniformity. Then the states will all be slave or all be free; then Negroes will vote everywhere or nowhere; then you will have a Maine Liquor Law in every state or none; then you will have uniformity in all things, local or domestic, by the authority of the federal government. But, when you attain that uniformity, you will have converted these thirty-two sovereign, independent states into one consolidated empire, with the uniformity of disposition reigning triumphant throughout the length and breadth of the land.

From this view of the case, my friends, I am driven irresistibly to the conclusion that diversity, dissimilarity, variety in all our local and domestic institutions is the great safeguard of our liberties and that the framers of our institutions were wise, sagacious, and patriotic when they made this government a confederation of sovereign states, with a legislature for each, and conferred upon each legislature the power to make all local and domestic institutions to suit the people it represented, without interference from any other state or from the general Congress of the Union. If we expect to maintain our liberties, we must preserve the rights and sovereignty of the states; we must maintain and carry out that great principle of self-government incorporated in the compromise measures of 1850; endorsed by the Illinois legislature in 1851; emphatically embodied and carried out in the Kansas-Nebraska Bill, and vindicated this year by the refusal to bring Kansas into the Union with a constitution distasteful to her people.

The Dred Scott Case

The other proposition discussed by Mr. Lincoln in his speech consists in a crusade against the Supreme Court of the United States on account of the Dred Scott decision. On this question, also, I desire to say to you unequivocally that I take direct and distinct issue with him. I have no warfare to make on the Supreme Court of the United States, either on account of that or any other decision which they have pronounced from that bench. The Constitution of the United States has provided that the powers of government (and the constitution of each state has the same provision) shall be divided into three departments: executive, legislative, and judicial. The right and the province of expounding the Constitution and constructing the law is vested in the judiciary established by the Constitution. As a lawyer, I feel at liberty to appear before the Court and controvert any principle of law while the question is pending before the tribunal; but, when the decision is made, my private opinion, your opinion, all other opinions must yield to the majesty of that authoritative adjudication. . . .

Hence, I am opposed to this doctrine of Mr. Lincoln by which he proposes to take an appeal from the decision of the Supreme Court of the United States, upon this high constitutional question, to a Republican caucus sitting in the country. Yes, or any other caucus or town meeting, whether it be Republican, American, or Democratic. I respect the decisions of that august tribunal; I shall always bow in deference to them. I am a law-abiding man. I will sustain the Constitution of my country as our fathers have made it. I will yield obedience to the laws, whether I like them or not, as I find them on the statute book. I will sustain the judicial tribunals and constituted authorities in all matters within the pale of their jurisdiction as defined by the Constitution.

But I am equally free to say that the reason assigned by Mr. Lincoln for resisting the decision of the Supreme Court in the Dred Scott case does not in itself meet any approbation. He objects to it because that decision declared that a Negro descended from African parents, who were brought here and sold as slaves, is not, and cannot be, a citizen of the United States. He says it is wrong because it deprives the Negro of the benefits of that clause of the Constitution which says that citizens of one state shall enjoy all the privileges and immunities of citizens of the several states: in other words, he thinks it wrong because it deprives the Negro of the privileges, immunities, and rights of citizenship which pertain, according to that decision, only to the white man.

I am free to say to you that in my opinion this government of ours is founded on the white basis. It was made by the white man, for the benefit of the white man, to be administered by white men, in such manner as they should determine. It is also true that a Negro, an Indian, or any other man of inferior race to a white man should be permitted to enjoy, and humanity requires that he should have, all the rights, privileges, and immunities which he is capable of exercising consistent with the safety of society. I would give him every right and every privilege which his capacity would enable him to enjoy, consistent with the good of the society in which he lived.

But you may ask me: What are these rights and these privileges? My answer is that each state must decide for itself the nature and extent of these rights.

Illinois has decided for herself. We have decided that the Negro shall not be a slave, and we have at the same time decided that he shall not vote, or serve on juries, or enjoy political privileges. I am content with that system of policy which we have adopted for ourselves. I deny the right of any other state to complain of our policy in that respect, or to interfere with it, or to attempt to change it.

On the other hand, the state of Maine has decided that in that state a Negro man may vote on an equality with the white man. The sovereign power of Maine has the right to prescribe that rule for herself. Illinois has no right to complain of Maine for conferring the right of Negro suffrage, nor has Maine any right to interfere with or complain of Illinois because she has denied Negro suffrage. . . .

Thus you see, my fellow citizens, that the issues between Mr. Lincoln and myself. . . are direct, unequivocal, and irreconcilable. He goes for uniformity in our domestic institutions, for a war of sections, until one or the other shall be subdued. I go for the great principle of the Kansas-Nebraska Bill—the right of the people to decide for themselves.

VIEWPOINT 7

"The Union cause has suffered and is now suffering immensely from mistaken deference to Rebel slavery."

Freeing the Slaves Should Be the Primary War Aim

Horace Greeley (1811-1872)

Horace Greeley was a newspaper editor and political leader. He founded the influential *New York Tribune* in 1841 and edited it for more than thirty years. He supported the antislavery cause with his newspaper and as an early member of the Republican party. In 1872, he unsuccessfully ran for president.

The following viewpoint is taken from an open letter published in the August 19, 1862, edition of the *Tribune*. Greeley addressed the letter to President Abraham Lincoln during the Civil War. Lincoln had resisted calls to emancipate the slaves, believing it would hurt the Union cause by alienating slaveholding individuals and states that supported the Union. Greeley argues that the president should place a higher priority on freeing the slaves. He urges Lincoln to actively enforce the Confiscation Act, an 1862 law passed by Congress which called on the president to confiscate captured Confederate property, including slaves, and to put that property to use in the war effort. He accuses Lincoln of being too deferential to the slave states that had not seceded from the Union and to slavery sympathizers. Greeley concludes that the cooperation of freed slaves would be essential in winning the war against the Confederacy.

Dear Sir:

I do not intrude to tell you—for you must know already—that a great proportion of those who triumphed in your election, and of all who desire the unqualified suppression of the rebellion now desolating our country, are sorely disappointed and deeply pained by the policy you seem to be pursuing with regard to the slaves of Rebels. I write only to set succinctly and unmistakably before you what we require, what we think we have a right to expect, and of what we complain.

I. We require of you, as the first servant of the republic, charged especially and pre-eminently with this duty, that you EXECUTE THE LAWS. Most emphatically do we demand that such laws as have been recently enacted, which therefore may fairly be presumed to embody the public will and to be dictated by the *present* needs of the republic, and which, after due consideration, have received your personal sanction, shall by you be carried into full effect and that you publicly and decisively instruct your subordinates that such laws exist, that they are binding on all functionaries and citizens, and that they are to be obeyed to the letter.

II. We think you are strangely and disastrously remiss in the discharge of your official and imperative duty with regard to the emancipating provisions of the new Confiscation Act. Those provisions were designed to fight slavery with liberty. They prescribe that men loyal to the Union, and willing to shed their blood in her behalf, shall no longer be held, with the nation's consent, in bondage to persistent, malignant traitors, who for twenty years have been plotting and for sixteen months have been fighting to divide and destroy our country. Why these traitors should be treated with tenderness by you, to the prejudice of the dearest rights of loyal men, we cannot conceive.

Slavery the Cause of Treason

III. We think you are unduly influenced by the councils, the representations, the menaces, of certain fossil politicians hailing from the border Slave states. Knowing well that the heartily, unconditionally loyal portion of the white citizens of those states do not expect nor desire that slavery shall be upheld to the prejudice of the Union—for the truth of which we appeal not only to every Republican residing in those states but to such eminent loyalists as H. Winter Davis, Parson Brownlow, the Union Central Committee of Baltimore, and to the *Nashville Union*—we ask you to consider that slavery is everywhere the inciting cause and sustaining base of treason: the most slaveholding sections of Maryland and Delaware being this day, though under the Union flag, in full sympathy with the rebellion, while the free labor portions

The Bettmann Archive.

The New York Tribune, *the influential newspaper Horace Greeley (left) founded and edited, had a circulation of more than 200,000 in 1860.*

of Tennessee and of Texas, though writhing under the bloody heel of treason, are unconquerably loyal to the Union. . . .

It seems to us the most obvious truth that whatever strengthens or fortifies slavery in the border states strengthens also treason and drives home the wedge intended to divide the Union. Had you, from the first, refused to recognize in those states, as here, any other than unconditional loyalty—that which stands for the Union, whatever may become of slavery—those states would have been, and would be, far more helpful and less troublesome to the defenders of the Union than they have been, or now are.

No Time for Timidity

IV. We think timid counsels in such a crisis calculated to prove perilous, and probably disastrous. It is the duty of a government so wantonly, wickedly assailed by rebellion as ours has been to oppose force to force in a defiant, dauntless spirit. It cannot afford to temporize with traitors, nor with semi-traitors. . . .

V. We complain that the Union cause has suffered and is now suffering immensely from mistaken deference to Rebel slavery. Had you, sir, in your inaugural address, unmistakably given notice that in case the rebellion already commenced were persisted in and your efforts to preserve the Union and enforce the laws should be resisted by armed force, *you would recognize no loyal person as rightfully held in slavery by a traitor*, we believe the rebellion would therein have received a staggering if not fatal blow. At that moment, according to the returns of the most recent elections, the Unionists were a large majority of the voters of the Slave states. But they were composed in good part of the aged, the feeble, the wealthy, the timid—the young, the reckless, the aspiring, the adventurous had already been largely lured by the gamblers and Negro traders, the politicians by trade and the conspirators by instinct, into the toils of treason. Had you then proclaimed that rebellion would strike the shackles from the slaves of every traitor, the wealthy and the cautious would have been supplied with a powerful inducement to remain loyal. . . .

VI. We complain that the Confiscation Act which you approved is habitually disregarded by your generals, and that no word of rebuke for them from you has yet reached the public ear. Fremont's Proclamation and Hunter's Order favoring emancipation were promptly annulled by you; while Halleck's Number Three, forbidding fugitives from slavery to Rebels to come within his lines—an order as unmilitary as inhuman, and which received the hearty approbation of every traitor in America—with scores of like tendency, have never provoked even your remonstrance.

Refusing to Welcome Slaves

We complain that the officers of your armies have habitually repelled rather than invited the approach of slaves who would have gladly taken the risks of escaping from their Rebel masters to our camps, bringing intelligence often of inestimable value to the Union cause. We complain that those who *have* thus escaped to us, avowing a willingness to do for us whatever might be required, have been brutally and madly repulsed, and often surrendered to be scourged, maimed, and tortured by the ruffian traitors who pretend to own them. We complain that a large proportion of our regular Army officers, with many of the volunteers, evince far more solicitude to uphold slavery than to put down the rebellion.

And, finally, we complain that you, Mr. President, elected as a Republican, knowing well what an abomination slavery is and how emphatically it is the core and essence of this atrocious rebellion, seem never to interfere with these atrocities and never give a direction to your military subordinates, which does not appear to have been conceived in the interest of slavery rather than of freedom. . . .

VIII. On the face of this wide earth, Mr. President, there is not one disinterested, determined, intelligent champion of the Union cause who does not feel that all attempts to put down the rebellion and at the same time uphold its inciting cause are preposterous and futile; that the rebellion, if crushed out tomorrow, would be renewed within a year if slavery were left in full vigor; that Army officers who remain to this day devoted to slavery can at best be but halfway loyal to the Union; and that every hour of deference to slavery is an hour of added and deepened peril to the Union. I appeal to the testimony of your ambassadors in Europe. It is freely at your service, not at mine. Ask them to tell you candidly whether the seeming subserviency of your policy to the slaveholding, slavery-upholding interest is not the perplexity, the despair of statesmen of all parties, and be admonished by the general answer!

IX. I close as I began with the statement that what an immense majority of the loyal millions of your countrymen require of you is a frank, declared, unqualified, ungrudging execution of the laws of the land, more especially of the Confiscation Act. That act gives freedom to the slaves of Rebels coming within our lines, or whom those lines may at any time enclose—we ask you to render it due obedience by publicly requiring all your subordinates to recognize and obey it. The Rebels are everywhere using the late anti-Negro riots in the North, as they have long used your officers' treatment of Negroes in the South, to convince the slaves that they have nothing to hope from a Union success, that we mean in that case to sell them into a bitter bondage to defray the cost of the war.

Let them impress this as a truth on the great mass of their ignorant and credulous bondmen, and the Union will never be restored—never. We cannot conquer 10 million people united in solid phalanx against us, powerfully aided by Northern sympathizers and European allies. We must have scouts, guides, spies, cooks, teamsters, diggers, and choppers from the blacks of the South, whether we allow them to fight for us or not, or we shall be baffled and repelled.

As one of the millions who would gladly have avoided this struggle at any sacrifice but that of principle and honor, but who now feel that the triumph of the Union is indispensable, not only to the existence of our country but to the well-being of mankind, I entreat you to render a hearty and unequivocal obedience to the law of the land.

VIEWPOINT 8

"My paramount object in this struggle is to save the Union, and is not either to save or destroy slavery."

Preserving the Union Should Be the Primary War Aim

Abraham Lincoln (1809-1865)

Abraham Lincoln was president of the United States from 1861 to 1865. His presidency was dominated by the Civil War, in which eleven southern states attempted to secede from the United States and form a separate Confederacy, in large part to preserve the institution of slavery. Lincoln was noted for his single-minded devotion to preserving the Union. This focus was continually challenged during his presidency, both by abolitionists who considered him too mild on the subject of slavery, and by those who sought to end the Civil War by accepting the division and negotiating with the Confederacy.

Lincoln, although not an active abolitionist during his political career, was personally opposed to slavery, and during the first part of his term he tried to persuade the leaders of the southern slaveholding states which remained in the Union to plan for the gradual and compensated emancipation of their slaves. But he hesitated to issue a general proclamation abolishing slavery, believing that preserving the Union should take highest priority. Lincoln succinctly expresses his views in the following letter which he wrote on August 22, 1862, in reply to Horace Greeley's criticism of his war and antislavery policies.

Dear Sir:

I have just read yours of the 19th, addressed to myself through the *New York Tribune*. If there be in it any statements or assumptions of fact which I may know to be erroneous, I do not now and here controvert them. If there be in it any inferences which I may believe to be falsely drawn, I do not now and here argue against them. If there be perceptible in it an impatient and dictatorial tone, I waive it in deference to an old friend, whose heart I have always supposed to be right.

As to the policy I "seem to be pursuing," as you say, I have not meant to leave anyone in doubt.

The Union Must Be Saved

I would save the Union. I would save it the shortest way under the Constitution. The sooner the national authority can be restored, the nearer the Union will be "the Union as it was." If there be those who would not save the Union unless they could at the same time *save* slavery, I do not agree with them. If there be those who would not save the Union unless they could at the same time *destroy* slavery, I do not agree with them. My paramount object in this struggle *is* to save the Union, and is *not* either to save or destroy slavery. If I could save the Union without freeing *any* slave, I would do it; and if I could save it by freeing *all* the slaves, I would do it; and if I could do it by freeing some and leaving others alone, I would also do that.

What I do about slavery and the colored race I do because I believe it helps to save this Union; and what I forbear I forbear because I do *not* believe it would help to save the Union. I shall do *less* whenever I shall believe what I am doing hurts the cause, and I shall do *more* whenever I shall believe doing more will help the cause. I shall try to correct errors when shown to be errors; and I shall adopt new views so fast as they shall appear to be true views.

I have here stated my purpose according to my view of *official* duty, and I intend no modification of my oft-expressed *personal* wish that all men, everywhere, could be free.

Chapter 6

Two Historians Look Back at Slavery

Chapter Preface

Slavery in America ended in 1865 with the passage of the Thirteenth Amendment to the Constitution. Disagreements over slavery's legacy have not. Historians over the past hundred years have fiercely debated the nature of slavery, its impact on slaves and slave owners, and its significance to U.S. society as a whole.

Among other issues, historians have debated whether slavery was a profitable institution—one that necessitated a war to abolish it—or whether it was a dying system that would have eventually ended without warfare. They have disagreed over slavery's impact on the personality of slaves and their descendants. They have argued over the extent to which slaves succeeded in creating an autonomous community and culture independent of their masters. They have clashed over whether statistical historical evidence supports the slave owners' contention that slaves were better fed and housed than poor whites. All of these debates have attempted to shed light on what constituted the American slavery experience and how America's slavery past might still affect American lives today.

Historian Peter J. Parish asserts that many historiographical controversies contain truth on both sides:

> There is an almost irresistible tendency to define the issues in a series of excessively rigid dichotomies. It does not help to insist on the complete dominance of profit seeking over paternalism (or vice versa) in the thinking of the slave owners; the two were not mutually exclusive in slave owners' minds, whatever the demands logic or ideology may dictate to modern historians of slavery. . . . Among the slaves, unyielding rebelliousness or utter docility were both exceptions to the general rule; the great majority of slaves maneuvered in the broad ground between these extremes. The debate over the relative influence of the African heritage and the American environment in shaping slave culture has to accept sooner or later that a distinct Afro-American culture evolved from the intermingling of the two.

The truth about American slavery, Parish and many other historians conclude, lies within its contradictions. The slave child confronting her parents' powerlessness in the face of the master; the would-be slave runaway deterred by family obligations, Thomas Jefferson writing against slavery but keeping slaves of his own, the slave owner's boast of his slaves' loyalty while at the same time constantly fearing revolt; the genuine affection that could and did develop between owner and slave, who was both human

268

and property—all are part of the truth about slavery's legacy. "At the heart of all the contrasts and contradictions which surrounded slavery," writes Parish, "lay the greatest paradox of all—the existence of an expanding and deeply entrenched system of human bondage in the midst of a society which treasured freedom as its fundamental principle and its greatest glory."

The two viewpoints featured here deal with one manifestation of that central paradox of freedom and slavery in America—the U.S. Constitution. The Constitution, which begins with the words "We the people of the United States," had among its purposes "to promote the general Welfare and secure the Blessings of Liberty to ourselves and our Posterity." Yet slavery was to continue in the United States for another seven decades after its adoption. Should the Constitution—and the U.S. government and society it underpinned—be condemned as fundamentally flawed? What historical lessons can we learn by examining the making of the Constitution in light of modern understanding? The following two viewpoints examine these questions.

VIEWPOINT 1

"Racial segregation, discrimination, and degradation are no unanticipated accidents in this nation's history. They stem logically and directly from the legacy that the Founding Fathers bestowed upon contemporary America."

Slavery Left America with a Weak Moral Foundation

John Hope Franklin (1915-)

John Hope Franklin is a noted historian specializing in black history and the South. He has taught at Howard University, the University of Chicago, and Duke University. His books include *From Slavery to Freedom* and *The Emancipation Proclamation*.

The following viewpoint is taken from a lecture given at the University of Chicago in 1975, one year before America's bicentennial. Franklin examines the words and actions of America's founders during the American Revolution and the making of the U.S. Constitution. He notes that the founders preached liberty while they maintained the institution of slavery. Franklin argues that the failure to end slavery at America's founding left a dubious moral legacy and contributed to racial problems which continue to plague the nation to this day.

As we approach the bicentennial of the independence of the United States, it may not be inappropriate to take advantage of the perspective afforded by these last two centuries. Such a perspective should enable us to understand the distance we have traveled and where we are today. . . .

In the effort to create an "instant history" with which we could live and prosper, our early historians intentionally placed our early national heroes and leaders beyond the pale of criticism. From the time that Benjamin Franklin created his own hero in "Poor Richard" and Mason L. Weems created the cherry tree story about George Washington, it has been virtually impossible to regard our Founding Fathers as normal, fallible human beings. And this distorted image of them has not only created a gross historical fallacy, but it has also rendered it utterly impossible to deal with our past in terms of the realities that existed at the time.

Serious Mistakes

To put it another way, our romanticizing about the history of the late 18th century has prevented our recognizing the fact that the Founding Fathers made serious mistakes that have greatly affected the course of our national history from that time to the present.

In 1974 we observed the bicentennial of the first Continental Congress, called to protest the new trade measures invoked against the colonies by Great Britain and to protest the political and economic measures directed particularly against the colony of Massachusetts. In a sense these measures were, indeed, intolerable as the colonists were forced to house British soldiers stationed in their midst, and Quebec was given political and economic privileges that appeared to be clearly discriminatory against the thirteen colonies.

But were these measures imposed by the British more intolerable than those imposed or, at least, sanctioned by the colonists against their own slaves? And yet, the colonists were outraged that the mother country was denying them their own freedom—the freedom to conduct their trade as they pleased.

It was not that the colonists were unaware of the problem of a much more basic freedom than that for which they were fighting in London. First of all, they knew of the 1772 decision of Lord Mansfield in the Somerset case, in which slavery was outlawed in Britain on the compelling ground that human bondage was "too odious" in England without specific legislation authorizing it. Although the colonists did have the authorization to establish and maintain slavery, Lord Mansfield's strictures against slavery could not have been lost on them altogether.

Secondly, and even more important, the slaves themselves were already pleading for their own freedom even before the first Continental Congress met. In the first six months of 1773 several slaves in Massachusetts submitted petitions to the General Court "praying to be liberated from a State of slavery." In the following year scores of other slaves, denying that they had ever forfeited the blessings of freedom by any compact or agreement to become slaves, asked for their freedom and for some land on which each of them "could sit down quietly under his own fig free." The legislature of the Massachusetts Colony debated the subject of slavery in 1774 and 1775, but voted simply that "the matter now subside."

Three Considerations

But the matter would neither die nor subside. As the colonists plunged into war with Great Britain, they were faced with the problem of what to do about Negro slavery. The problem presented itself in the form of urgent questions. First, should they continue to import slaves?

This was a matter of some importance to British slave trading interests who had built fortunes out of the traffic in human beings and to colonists who feared that new, raw recruits from the West Indies and Africa would be more of a problem than a blessing. Most of the colonies opposed any new importations, and the Continental Congress affirmed the prohibition in April, 1776.

Secondly, should the colonists use black soldiers in their fight against Britain? Although a few were used in the early skirmishes of the war, a pattern of exclusion of blacks had developed by the time that independence was declared. In July, 1775, the policy had been set forth that recruiters were not to enlist any deserter from the British army, "nor any stroller, negro, or vagabond."

Then, late in the year the British welcomed all Negroes willing to join His Majesty's troops, and promised to set them free in return. The colonists were terrified, especially with the prospect of a servile insurrection. And so the Continental Congress shortly reversed its policy and grudgingly admitted blacks into the Continental Army.

The final consideration, as the colonists fought for their own freedom from Britain, was what would be the effect of their revolutionary philosophy on their own slaves. The colonists argued in the Declaration of Independence that they were oppressed; and they wanted their freedom. Thomas Jefferson, in an early draft, went so far as to accuse the King of England of imposing slavery on them; but more "practical" heads prevailed, and that provision was stricken from the Declaration.

Even so, the Declaration said "All men are created equal." "Black men as well as white men?" some wondered. Every man had an inalienable right to "life, liberty, and the pursuit of happiness." "Every black man as well as every white man?" some could well have asked.

How could the colonists make distinctions in their revolutionary philosophy? They either meant that *all* men were created
equal or they did not mean it at all. They either meant that *every*
man was entitled to life, liberty, and the pursuit of happiness, or
they did not mean it at all.

To be sure, some patriots were apparently troubled by the contradictions between their revolutionary philosophy of political
freedom and the holding of human beings in bondage. Abigail
Adams, the wife of John Adams, admitted that there was something strange about their fighting to achieve and enjoy a status
that they daily denied to others. Patrick Henry, who had cried
"Give me liberty or give me death," admitted that slavery was
"repugnant to humanity;" but not terribly repugnant, for he continued to hold blacks in bondage. So did George Washington and
Thomas Jefferson and George Mason and Edmund Randolph and
many others who signed the Declaration of Independence or the
federal Constitution. They simply would not or could not see
how ridiculous their position was.

And where the movement to emancipate the slaves took hold,
as in New England and in some of the Middle Atlantic states,
slavery was not economically profitable anyway. Consequently, if
the patriots in those states were genuinely opposed to slavery,
they could afford the luxury of speaking against it. But in neither
of the Continental Congresses nor in the Declaration of Independence did the Founding Fathers take an unequivocal, categorical
stand against slavery. Obviously, human bondage and human
dignity were not as important to them as their own political and
economic independence.

Black Protests

The Founding Fathers were not only compelled to live with
their own inconsistency but they also had to stand convicted before the very humble group which they excluded from their political and social fellowship. In 1777 a group of Massachusetts
blacks told the whites of that state that every principle which im-
pelled America to break with England "pleads stronger than a
thousand arguments" against slavery. In 1779 a group of Connecticut slaves petitioned the state for their liberty, declaring that
they "groaned" under the burdens and indignities they were required to bear.

In 1781 Paul Cuffe and his brother, two young enterprising
blacks, asked Massachusetts to excuse them from the duty of paying taxes, since they "had no influence in the election of those
who tax us." And when they refused to pay their taxes, those
who had shouted that England's taxation without representation
was tyranny, slapped the Cuffe brothers in jail!

Avoiding the Fundamental Issue

Nathan Irvin Huggins was W.E.B. Du Bois Professor of History and Afro-American Studies at Harvard University. In the preface for the revised edition of his book, Black Odyssey, *he argues that America's Founding Fathers erred in ignoring the contradictions between their ideals and the reality of slavery.*

The Founding Fathers, in their conception and framing of a more perfect union, did not address frankly and openly, in any of their official documents, the conspicuous fact of racial slavery. As far as race and slavery were concerned—both primary facts of their life and times—the Founding Fathers preferred to avoid the deforming mirror of truth.

It is as if the Founders hoped to sanitize their new creation, ridding it of a deep and awful stain. If the evil were not mentioned or seen, it would be as if it were not there at all. By burying the most flagrant contradiction to all their values, there would remain an ideal and perfect monument to republicanism. The nation would, in time, become somehow as pure in fact as in idea.

It was, however, a bad way to start. It encouraged the belief that American history—its institutions, its values, its people—was one thing and that racial slavery and oppression were a different story. Nothing so embarrassing, however, nothing so fundamentally contradictory to the social ethos, can be kept at a discrete distance for long. It will intrude, and rudely.

Thus, when the colonists emerged victorious from their war with England, they had both their independence *and* their slaves. It seemed to matter so little to most of the patriots that the slaves themselves had eloquently pointed out their inconsistencies or that not a few of the patriots themselves saw and pointed out their own fallacious position. It made no difference that 5,000 blacks had joined in the fight for independence, only to discover that *real* freedom did not apply to them. The agencies that forged a national policy against England—the Continental Congresses and the government under the Articles of Confederation—were incapable of forging—or unwilling to forge—a national policy in favor of human freedom.

It was not a propitious way to start a new nation, especially since its professions were so different from its practices and since it presumed to be the model for other new world colonies that would, in time, seek their independence from the tyranny of Europe.

Having achieved their own independence, the patriots exhibited no great anxiety to extend the blessings of liberty to those among them who did not enjoy it. They could not altogether ignore the implications of the revolutionary philosophy, however. As early as 1777 the Massachusetts legislature had under consideration a measure to prohibit "the practice of holding persons in Slavery." Three years later the new constitution of that state declared that "all men are born free and equal." Some doubtless hoped that those high sounding words would mean more in the Constitution of Massachusetts than they had meant in the Declaration of Independence.

Her neighbors, however, were more equivocal, with New Hampshire, Connecticut and Rhode Island vacillating, for one reason or another, until another decade had passed. Although Pennsylvania did abolish slavery in 1780, New York and New Jersey did no better than prepare the groundwork for gradual emancipation at a later date.

One may well be greatly saddened by the thought that the author of the Declaration of Independence and the commander of the Revolutionary army and so many heroes of the Revolution were slaveholders. Even more disheartening, if such is possible, is that those *same* leaders and heroes were not greatly affected by the philosophy of freedom which they espoused. At least they gave no evidence of having been greatly affected by it.

Slavery Entrenched

Nor did they show any great magnanimity of spirit, once the war was over and political independence was assured. While northerners debated the questions of how and when they would free their slaves, the institution of human bondage remained as deeply entrenched as ever—from Delaware to Georgia. The only area on which there was national agreement that slavery should be prohibited was the area east of the Mississippi River and north of the Ohio River—the Northwest Territory. The agreement to prohibit slavery in that area, where it did not really exist and where relatively few white settlers lived, posed no great problem and surely it did not reflect a ground swell for liberty.

Meanwhile the prohibition, it should be noted, did not apply to the area south of the Ohio River, where slaveholders were more likely to settle anyway! This clearly shows that the Founding Fathers were willing to "play" with the serious question of freedom, thus evincing a cynicism that was itself unworthy of statesmanship.

Nor is one uplifted or inspired by the attitude of the Founding Fathers toward the slave trade, once their independence was secured. In the decade following independence the importation of slaves into the United States actually increased over the previous decade as well as over the decade before the War for Independence began. Far from languishing, the institution of slavery was prospering and growing. In its deliberations between 1781 and 1789 the Congress of the Confederation barely touched on the question of slavery or the slave trade. There was, to be sure, some concern over the capture of slaves; and the Congress gave some attention to a Quaker petition against the trade, but it took no action.

On the whole the nation did not raise a hand against it. The flurry of activity in the states, which led to the prohibition of slave importations in some of them and a temporary cessation of the trade in others, had the effect of misleading many people into thinking that slavery's hold on the nation was weakening.

The Constitution

That this was far from the actual situation became painfully clear when the delegates gathered in Philadelphia in 1787 to write a new Constitution. In the discussion over the slave trade only practical and economic considerations held sway. Humane considerations simply were not present. Maryland and Virginia tended to oppose the slave trade simply because they were overstocked and were not anxious to have any large importations into their midst. South Carolina and Georgia, where the death rate in the rice swamps was high and where slaveholders needed new recruits to develop new areas, demanded an open door for slave dealers.

And who rushed to the rescue when South Carolina demanded concessions on the question of the slave trade? It was Oliver Ellsworth of Connecticut, who observed that a provision in the Constitution against the slave trade would be "unjust towards South Carolina and Georgia. Let us not intermeddle," he said. "As population increases, poor laborers will be so plenty as to render slaves useless." It is impossible to conceive that such temporizing on the part of a leading colonist would have been tolerated in the late dispute with England.

Could the new national government that was designed to be strong have *anything* to say regarding slavery and the slave trade in the states? Elbridge Gerry of Massachusetts answered that it could not. It only had to refrain from giving direct sanction to the system.

Perhaps this is the view that seemed to silence the venerable Benjamin Franklin. The oldest and easily one of the most respected members of the Constitutional Convention, Franklin brought with him a strong resolution against the slave trade that had been entrusted to him by the Pennsylvania Abolition Society. Although he was one of the most frequent speakers at the Convention, he never introduced the resolution. With faint hearts such as Gerry's and Franklin's there is little wonder that South Carolina and Georgia were able to have their own way in wording the provision that declared that the slave trade could not be prohibited for another twenty years. One need only to look at the slave importation figures between 1788 and 1808 to appreciate how much advantage was taken of this generous reprieve.

The Founding Fathers did no better when it came to counting slaves for purposes of representation and taxation. Northerners, who regarded slaves as property, insisted that for the purpose of representation they could not be counted as people. Southern slaveholders, while cheerfully admitting that slaves were property, insisted that they were also people and should be counted as such. It is one of the remarkable ironies of the early history of this democracy that the very men who had shouted so loudly that all men were created equal could not now agree on whether or not persons of African descent were men at all.

The irony was compounded when, in the so-called major compromise of the Constitution, the delegates agreed that a slave was three-fifths of a man, meaning that five slaves were to be counted as three persons. The magic of racism can work magic with the human mind. One wonders whether Catherine Drinker Bowen had this in mind when she called her history of the Constitutional Convention *The Miracle at Philadelphia.*

If slaveholders feared possible insurrections by their slaves, they were no less apprehensive about the day-to-day attrition of the institution caused by slaves running away. They wanted to be certain that the Constitution recognized slaves as property and that it offered protection to that property, especially runaways. Significantly, there was virtually no opposition to the proposal that states give up fugitive slaves to their owners. The slave owners had already won such sweeping constitutional recognition of slavery that the fugitive slave provision may be regarded as something of an anti-climax. There was, as Roger Sherman of Connecticut pointed out, as much justification for the public seizure and surrendering of a slave as there was for the seizure of a horse. Thus, a slave, who was only three-fifths of a man, was to be regarded in this connection as no more than a horse!

And the Constitution required that slaves who ran away were not to enjoy the freedom that they had won in their own private war for independence, but were to be returned to those who claimed title to them. Consequently, there was a remarkable distinction between fighting for one's political independence, which the patriots expected to win, and did, and fighting for one's freedom from slavery, which these same patriots made certain that the slaves would not win.

Criticizing Our Leaders

At the outset it was observed that we tend to shy away from making criticisms or judgments of those who occupy the seats of the mighty. This is not good either for ourselves or the institutions and way of life we seek to foster. If we would deal with our past in terms of the realities that existed at the time, it becomes necessary for us to deal with our early leaders in their own terms, namely, as frail, fallible human beings, and—at times—utterly indifferent to the great causes they claimed to serve.

We may admire them for many things: their courage and bravery in the military struggle against Britain; their imaginative creativity in forging a new instrument of government; and their matchless service to a cause that captured the imagination of people around the world.

It does not follow, however, that we should admire them for betraying the ideals to which they gave lip service, for speaking eloquently at one moment for the brotherhood of man and in the next moment denying it to their black brothers who fought by their side in their darkest hours of peril, and for degrading the human spirit by equating five black men with three white men or equating a black man with a horse!

We are concerned here not so much for the harm that the Founding Fathers did to the cause which they claimed to serve as for the harm that their moral legacy has done to every generation of their progeny. Having created a tragically flawed revolutionary doctrine and a Constitution that did *not* bestow the blessings of liberty on its posterity, the Founding Fathers set the stage for every succeeding generation of Americans to apologize, compromise, and temporize on those principles of liberty that were supposed to be the very foundation of our system of government and way of life.

That is why the United States was so very apprehensive when Haiti and most of the other Latin American countries sought to wipe out slavery the moment they received their political independence. The consistency of those nations was alien to the view of the United States on the same question.

That is why the United States failed to recognize the existence of the pioneer republics of Haiti and Liberia until this nation was in the throes of a great civil war and sought to "use" these countries for colonizing some blacks. Earlier recognition would have implied an equality in the human family that the United States was unwilling to concede.

That is why this nation tolerated and, indeed, nurtured the cultivation of a racism that has been as insidious as it has been pervasive.

Slavery and Racism

Racial segregation, discrimination, and degradation are no unanticipated accidents in this nation's history. They stem logically and directly from the legacy that the Founding Fathers be-

278

stowed upon contemporary America. The denial of equality in the year of independence led directly to the denial of equality in the era of the bicentennial of independence. The so-called compromises in the Constitution of 1787 led directly to the arguments in our own time that we can compromise equality with impunity and somehow use the Constitution as an instrument to preserve privilege and to foster inequality. It has thus become easy to invoke the spirit of the Founding Fathers whenever we seek ideological support for the social, political and economic inequities that have become a part of the American way.

It would be perverse indeed to derive satisfaction from calling attention to the flaws in the character and conduct of the Founding Fathers. And it would be irresponsible to do so merely to indulge in whimsical iconoclasm.

But it would be equally irresponsible in the era of the bicentennial of independence not to use the occasion to examine our past with a view to improving the human condition.

An appropriate beginning, it would seem, would be to celebrate our origins for what they were—to honor the principles of independence for which so many patriots fought and died. It is equally appropriate to be outraged over the manner in which the principles of human freedom and human dignity were denied and debased by those same patriots. Their legacy to us in this regard cannot, under any circumstances, be cherished or celebrated. Rather, this legacy represents a continuing and dismaying problem that requires us all to put forth as much effort to overcome it as the Founding Fathers did in handing it down to us.

VIEWPOINT 2

"In their accommodation to slavery, the Founders limited and confined it and carefully withheld any indication of moral approval."

America's Founders Recognized the Dilemma of Slavery

Herbert J. Storing (1928-1977)

Herbert J. Storing was a professor of government at the University of Chicago from 1956 to 1977, and at the time of his death was professor of government and director of the Program on the Presidency of the White Burkett Miller Center for Public Affairs at the University of Virginia in Charlottesville. A noted authority on the nation's founding period and on the American constitutional system, Storing's works include *The Complete Anti-Federalist* and *Black American Political Thought, What Country Have I?*

In the following viewpoint Storing refutes the argument made by John Hope Franklin and others that the nation's founders left the United States a fundamentally flawed legacy because of their failure to abolish slavery. Storing notes that this idea was paradoxically shared by nineteenth-century abolitionists who wished to abolish the U.S. Constitution and by Chief Justice Roger Taney, author of the Dred Scott decision which ruled that the Constitution legitimized slavery. Storing argues that this view of the founders fails to give them credit for recognizing the injustice of slavery. Both the Declaration of Independence and the Constitution, Storing argues, contain the seeds for the eventual abolition of slavery. The United States should still be proud of its founding documents and the ideals they express, he concludes.

"It is refreshing," said one of the dissenters in the case of *Dred Scott v. Sandford*, "to turn to the early incidents of our history and learn wisdom from the acts of the great men who have gone to their account." It is a common opinion today, however, that, admirable as the American Founders may be in other respects, in their response to the institution of Negro slavery their example is one to be lived down rather than lived up to. A good expression of this opinion has recently come from the distinguished American historian John Hope Franklin. We need to face the fact, Franklin contends, that the Founders "betray[ed] the ideals to which they gave lip service." They failed to take an unequivocal stand against slavery. They regarded "human bondage and human dignity" as less important than "their own political and economic independence." They spoke "eloquently at one moment for the brotherhood of man and in the next moment den[ied] it to their black brothers." They "degrad[ed] the human spirit by equating five black men with three white men." The moral legacy of the Founders is shameful and harmful:

> Having created a tragically flawed revolutionary doctrine and a Constitution that did *not* bestow the blessings of liberty on its posterity, the Founding Fathers set the stage for every succeeding generation of American to apologize, compromise, and temporize on those principles of liberty that were supposed to be the very foundation of our system of government and way of life.

This view of the American Founding—that the Founders excluded the Negroes from the "rights of man" expressed in the Declaration of Independence and sanctioned slavery and Negro inferiority in the Constitution—is a view that the radical Abolitionists, from whom John Hope Franklin descends, share with their proslavery antagonists. Indeed, one of the best, and surely most authoritative, expressions of this view came in the opinion of Chief Justice Taney in the famous Supreme Court case of *Dred Scott v. Sandford* in 1857, in which the Supreme Court, for the second time in its history, held an act of Congress unconstitutional and in which Taney tried to secure once and for all the place of slavery under the Constitution. I want to examine Taney's carefully worked-out reasoning, for there one can confront most clearly what is today the dominant opinion about the Founders and slavery.

Dred Scott

Dred Scott was a slave owned by a Doctor Emerson, a surgeon in the U.S. Army. In 1834 Scott was taken by his master from Missouri to Rock Island, Illinois, where they lived for about two years, and from there to Fort Snelling in the federal "Louisiana territory," where they lived for another couple of years before returning to Missouri. On Emerson's death Scott tried to purchase his freedom from Mrs. Emerson. Failing in that, he sued in the Missouri courts for his freedom, on the ground that he had become free by virtue of his residence in a free state and a free territory. He won in the lower court, but the decision was reversed on appeal. The Supreme Court of Missouri, abandoning eight Missouri precedents and departing from the then almost universal adherence of Southern courts to the principle "once free, always free," held that, whatever his condition in Illinois and in federal territory, Scott was a slave upon his return to Missouri.

On Mrs. Emerson's remarriage, Scott became the property of her brother, John Sandford, a citizen of New York; and this enabled Scott to sue for his freedom in federal court under the provision of the Constitution that gives federal courts jurisdiction in cases between citizens of different states. He lost in the lower court and appealed to the Supreme Court, which in 1857 finally handed down its opinion—or rather its opinions, for all nine justices expressed their opinions, most at considerable length. I will be concerned here only with the opinion "of the court" given by Chief Justice Taney. . . .

According to Taney, the Founders assumed the legitimacy of slavery; and back of that was a universal opinion of the inferiority of the Negro race. Negroes "had for more than a century before been regarded as beings of an inferior order; and altogether unfit to associate with the white race, either in social or political relations; and so far inferior, that they had no rights which the white man was bound to respect; and that the negro might justly and lawfully be reduced to slavery for his benefit." "No one thought," Taney said, "of disputing" such opinions. Negroes "were never thought of or spoken of except as property."

Only on such a basis, it seemed to Taney, could the framers of the Declaration of Independence be absolved from utter hypocrisy. They *said* that "all men are created equal and are endowed by their Creator with certain unalienable rights." Yet they were, many of them, slaveholders; and they certainly did not destroy slavery. But there was no hypocrisy, because the writers of the Declaration "perfectly understood the meaning of the language they used, and how it would be understood by others; and they knew it would not, in any part of the civilized world, be supposed to embrace the negro race, which, by common consent, had been excluded from civilized governments and the family of nations, and doomed to slavery." The men of that age (that is, the white men) simply did not regard Negroes as included among the "all men" who are, according to the Declaration of Independence, "created equal"; and, Taney concluded, "no one misunderstood them."

This whole argument—and I repeat, it is identical to the common view today—is a gross calumny on the Founders. The truth is almost the exact opposite of Taney's account. The Founders understood quite clearly that Negroes, like men everywhere, were created equal and were endowed with unalienable rights. They did not say that all men were actually secured in the *exercise* of their rights or that they had the power to provide such security; but there was no doubt about the *rights*. Far from it being true that "negroes were never thought of except as property," not only Negroes but slaves were very frequently spoken of and treated as persons. All of the Constitutional provisions relating to slaves, for example, refer to them as persons. And while slaves were typically deprived of *civil* rights, they were regarded as persons under criminal law. As rational and, to some degree, morally responsible human beings, they were held capable of committing crimes, and they were protected by the law—in principle and surprisingly often in practice—against crimes committed against them. In the first three or four decades of our history, the injustice of slavery was very generally acknowledged, not merely in the North but in the South and particularly in Southern courts.

Since this is likely to be unfamiliar territory to most readers, let me give a couple of examples.

In 1820 the Superior Court in Mississippi was confronted with the question, there being no positive legislation covering the matter, whether the killing of a slave was murder under the common law. The court held that it was; and this was the usual view of Southern courts that considered this question. The Mississippi judge began by emphasizing that "because individuals may have been deprived of many of their rights by society, it does not follow that they have been deprived of all their rights." The slave "is still a human being, and possesses all those rights, of which he is not deprived by the positive provisions of the law." Since the common law definition of murder is the taking away the life of a reasonable creature with malice aforethought and since a slave is a reasonable being, such a killing of a slave is murder.

Slavery and Natural Law

Slavery is the creature, Southern as well as Northern judges said again and again, of positive law only; it has no support in natural law or in transcendent principles of justice. Yet slavery existed; it was lawful in the Southern states. Even when the judges were giving effect to the positive law of slavery (which they had a clear duty to do), they typically acknowledged the injustice of the institution. . . .

Indeed, contrary to Taney's claim that no one questioned the legitimacy of slavery, nothing was more common than Southern

Mixed Feelings on Slavery

Don E. Fehrenbacher is professor emeritus of history and American studies at Stanford University. His book The Dred Scott Case: Its Significance in American Law and Politics *won a Pulitzer prize in history. He writes in the book* Slavery and Its Consequences *of the mixed feelings the people at the 1787 Constitutional Convention had about slavery, mirroring the sentiments of American society at that time.*

When the Constitutional Convention assembled in the spring of 1787, slavery was firmly established in the five southernmost states and more than a trivial presence in most of the others. There were, in the nation as a whole, two slaves for every nine free persons and, in the South, two slaves for every four free persons. . . .

At the same time, slavery was an institution under severe scrutiny, both as a matter of conscience and as a matter of public interest. Many Americans were finding it difficult to square slaveholding with the principles of Christianity, and many were troubled by the contrast between the celebration of human freedom in the Declaration of Independence and the presence of human servitude throughout so much of the Republic. A number of antislavery societies had been organized and could claim some of the nation's leading citizens as members. Abolition had begun in the northern states and was expected to prevail eventually at least as far south as Delaware. Virginia and Maryland had revised their laws in such a way as to facilitate private manumission. Every state except Georgia had taken some kind of action proscribing, inhibiting, or suspending the importation of slaves from abroad. And while the Convention was in session, Congress passed the Northwest Ordinance prohibiting slavery in all federal territory north of the Ohio River.

Yet these gains for freedom, though by no means insignificant, were all on the periphery of American slavery and scarcely touched the central problem, which was the massive concentration of more than 600,000 slaves in the five southern states. No one in the Convention and no one else of any standing in the country favored a frontal attack on that problem. Racial considerations alone were enough to make universal emancipation difficult even to visualize. Among American political leaders of the time, antislavery sentiment was widespread and evidently sincere, but never intense enough to become a prime motive force. Proslavery sentiment, though less prevalent and seldom categorically acknowledged, was more tenacious, being firmly rooted in economic and social interest. The Convention, viewed as an entity, had mixed feelings about slavery and did not consider itself charged with any power or duty to settle the destiny of the institution. Many delegates, to be sure, seem to have believed or hoped that somehow in the flow of time slavery would disappear, and the imprint of that expectation is plainly visible in the document that they finally approved.

judges giving public utterance to the excruciating agony of trying to reconcile the law that protected slavery with the principle of justice that condemns it. One of the most interesting of these cases is an 1820 North Carolina case, *State v. Mann*, where the court held that a master cannot commit a legal battery upon his slave. The court had held earlier that a white person could be punished for assault and battery against someone else's slave. But the law cannot protect the slave, Judge Ruffin held, against his master, even in case of a wanton, cruel, senseless beating. Ruffin was offered by counsel the analogy of parent and child or master and apprentice, where the authority of the superior is limited and supervised by law. He reluctantly, but surely correctly, rejected the analogy on the ground that the end of these relations is the good and happiness of the child or the apprentice, whereas in U.S. slavery the end is nothing but the profit of the master. It is the wrongness of slavery that makes it impossible to limit it. "We cannot allow the right of the master to be brought into discussion in the courts of justice." To question that right is to deny it, and that cannot be the business of a judge in a slave state. "The slave, to remain a slave, must be made sensible that there is no appeal from his master. . . . I most freely confess sense of the harshness of this proposition; I feel it as deeply as any man can; and as a principle of moral right every person in his retirement must repudiate it. But in the actual condition of things it must be so. There is no remedy. . . . It constitutes the curse of slavery to both the bond and free portion of our population. But it is inherent in the relation of master and slave."

I should add that twenty years later, nevertheless, Ruffin upheld a conviction of murder in the case of an especially brutal, but probably not premeditated, killing by a master of his own slave.

Another kind of case that was common in the Southern courts was like *Dred Scott*; it arose where a person who had been a slave but who had been taken to reside in a free state and then returned to a slave state sued in the courts of the latter for his freedom. As I have said, in such a case the Southern courts held (at least until the 1840s or 1850s) that such a person was free. Once the chains of slavery enforced by positive law are broken, they can never be restored.

A slave, Lydia, was taken in 1807 by her master from Missouri to free Indiana, where he registered her as his servant under Indiana's gradual emancipation law. He sold his right to her, but when her new master brought her back to Missouri, the court there upheld her claim to freedom. The rights of her master had been destroyed in Indiana, "and we are not aware of any law of this state which can or does bring into operation the right of slavery when once destroyed." Can it be thought, the judge asked, that "the noxious atmosphere of this state, without any express law for the purpose, clamped upon her newly forged chains of slavery, after the old ones were destroyed? For the honor of our country, we cannot for a moment admit, that the bare treading of its soil, is thus dangerous, even to the degraded African."

Slavery a Curse

The American Founders and their immediate descendants, North and South, not only believed in but emphasized the wrongness of slavery, at the same time that they wrestled with the fact of slavery and the enormous difficulty of getting rid of it. It was a fact; it seemed for the time being a necessity; but it was a curse—the curse of an unavoidable injustice. . . .

Taney held that Congress cannot prohibit slavery in federal territory: "an Act of Congress which deprives a citizen of the United States of his liberty or property, merely because he came himself or brought his property into a particular Territory of the United States, and who had committed no offense against the laws, could hardly be dignified with the name of due process of law." Nor, Taney contended (and this is crucial and the point on which Taney abandoned both federal and state precedents) is there any difference between property in slaves and other property. In fact, he said, "the right of property in a slave is distinctly and expressly affirmed in the Constitution." These words are striking: if one had to think of two adverbs that do *not* describe the way the Constitution acknowledged slavery, he could not do better than "distinctly and expressly."

No form of the word *slave* appears in the Constitution, and one would not know from the text alone that it was concerned with slavery at all. Today's beginning law students, I am told, are generally not aware that there are three provisions of the Constitution relating to slavery. This is testimony to the skill with which the framers wrote. Some concessions to slavery were thought to be necessary in order to secure the Union, with its promise of a broad and long-lasting foundation for freedom; the problem was to make the minimum concessions consistent with that end, to express them in language that would not sanction slavery, and so far as possible to avoid blotting a free Constitution with the stain of slavery. Frederick Douglass described it this way:

> I hold that the Federal Government was never, in its essence, anything but an anti-slavery government. Abolish slavery tomorrow, and not a sentence or syllable of the Constitution need be altered. It was purposely so framed as to give no claim, no sanction to the claim, of property in man. If in its origin slavery had any relation to the government, it was only as scaffolding

286

to the magnificent structure, to be removed as soon as the building was completed.

"Scaffolding" catches the intention exactly: support of slavery strong enough to allow the structure to be built, but unobtrusive enough to fade from view when the job was done.

The Constitution

Let us look at the provisions. Article I, sec. 2(3) provides, in a masterpiece of circumlocution:

> Representatives and direct Taxes shall be apportioned among the several States which may be included within this Union, according to their respective Numbers, which shall be determined by adding to the whole Number of free Persons, including those bound to Service for a Term of Years, and excluding Indians not taxed, three fifths of all other Persons.

"All other Persons" are slaves. Thus in counting population for purposes of determining the number of representatives and also apportioning land and poll taxes, five slaves count as three free persons. What this provision signifies in principle is extremely complex, and I will not exhaust the matter here. The question came up in the Constitutional Convention in the course of a debate over whether numbers or wealth is the proper basis of representation. That issue was resolved, or avoided, by use of Madison's suggestion that numbers are in fact a good index to wealth. In the case of slaves, however, that is not so clear, partly because the productivity of slaves is thought to be lower than that of free men, so some kind of discount seemed appropriate. This line of reasoning is supported by recalling that the three-fifths rule originated under the Articles of Confederation as a way of apportioning population for purposes of laying requisitions on the states. Suggestions that the three-fifths rule implies a lack of full humanity in the slave, while not without some basis, are wide of the main point. The three-fifths clause is more a way of measuring wealth than of counting human beings represented in government; wealth can claim to be the basis for apportioning representation and is of course the basis for apportioning direct taxes. Given the limited importance of direct taxation, the provision was understood to be a bonus for the Southern slave states. That gives the common argument against the three-fifths clause an unusual twist. While it may be that the provision "degrades the human spirit by equating five black men [more correctly, five slaves] with three white men," it has to be noted that the Southerners would have been glad to count slaves on a one-for-one basis. The concession to slavery here was not in somehow paring the slave down to three-fifths but in counting him for as much as three-fifths of a free person.

Regarding the second constitutional provision relating to slavery, Justice Taney said, "the right to trade in [slave property], like an ordinary article of merchandise and property, was guaranteed to the citizens of the United States, in every State that might desire it, for twenty years." Clearly this is a major concession to slavery. It protects not merely an existing slave population but the creation of new slaves. Practically, it allowed a substantial augmentation of the slave population and thus, of course, of the slave problem. Yet the concession is less than Taney suggests. Even on the basis of Taney's account, one might wonder why the slave trade is guaranteed only to those citizens "in every State that might desire it" rather than to all citizens; and one would surely ask why this guarantee was limited to twenty years. These qualifications suggest that there is something that is *not* ordinary about this particular article of merchandise and property. When we look at the clause itself, this suggestion is reinforced. The clause reads: "The Migration or Importation of such Persons as any of the States now existing shall think proper to admit, shall not be prohibited by the Congress prior to the year one thousand eight hundred and eight, but a tax or duty may be imposed on such Importation, not exceeding ten dollars for each Person" (Art. I, sec. 9[1]). We note that the form is not a guarantee of a right but a postponement of a power to prohibit. Moreover we see, what Taney neglects to point out, that the postponement of federal power to prohibit applies only to the states "now existing." We have here, apparently, a traditional or vested right or interest, which is to be preserved for a time but which Congress need not allow to spread to new states. The clause, fairly interpreted, gives a temporary respite to an illicit trade; the presumption was that Congress would, after twenty years, forbid this trade (as it would not and perhaps could not prohibit trade in ordinary articles of merchandise), and in fact Congress did so.

The Fugitive Slave Clause

Finally, to quote Taney again, "the government in express terms is pledged to protect [slave property] in all future times, if the slave escapes from his owner." Here is another major concession. It is a clear case of a new legal right of slavery—there was nothing like it under the Articles of Confederation. It amounts, moreover, to a kind of nationalization of slave property, in the sense that everyone in a free state has an obligation to assist in the enforcement, so far as fugitive slaves are concerned, of the institution of slavery. It is not surprising that this clause turned out to be the most intensely controversial of the three provisions dealing with slavery. Yet it was hardly noticed in the Northern ratification conventions. The fugitive slave clause in the Constitution, like its model in the Northwest Ordinance which outlawed slavery in the Northwest Territory, was the price of a broader freedom. And the price was grudgingly, at least narrowly, defined. Here are what Taney called "plain words—too plain to be misunderstood": "No Person held to Service or Labour in one State, under the Laws thereof, escaping into another, shall, in Consequence of any Law or Regulation therein, be discharged from such Service or Labour, but shall be delivered up on Claim of the Party to whom such Service or Labour may be due" (Art. IV, sec. 2[3]). Whether or not these words are plain, they were carefully chosen. . . .

Supposing that a concession to return fugitive slaves had to be made, it is hard to see how it could have been made in any way that would have given less sanction to the idea that property in slaves has the same moral status as other kinds of property.

The Founders did acknowledge slavery; they compromised with it. The effect was in the short run probably to strengthen it. Perhaps they could have done more to restrict it, though the words of a Missouri judge express what the Founders thought they were doing and, I think, probably the truth. "When the States assumed the rights of self-government, they found their citizens claiming a right of property in a miserable portion of the human race. Sound national policy required that the evil should be restricted as much as possible. What they could, they did." "As those fathers marked it," Lincoln urged on the eve of the Civil War, "so let it be again marked, as an evil not to be extended, but to be tolerated and protected only because of and so far as its actual presence among us makes that toleration and protection a necessity." Slavery was an evil to be tolerated, allowed to enter the Constitution only by the back door, grudgingly, unacknowledged, on the presumption that the house would be truly fit to live in only when it was gone, and that it would ultimately be gone.

In their accommodation to slavery, the Founders limited and confined it and carefully withheld any indication of moral approval, while they built a Union that they thought was the greatest instrument of human liberty ever made, that they thought would lead and that did in fact lead to the extinction of Negro slavery. It is common today to make harsh reference to the irony of ringing declarations of human rights coming from the pens of men who owned slaves. But I think that Professor Franklin is wrong when he says that "they simply would not or could not see how ridiculous their position was." They saw it all right, and they saw better than their critics how difficult it was to extricate themselves from that position in a reasonably equitable way. But they saw, too, a deeper irony: these masters knew that they were writing the texts in which their slaves would learn their rights.

For Further Study

Chapter One

1. Why do you think both Samuel Sewall and Joseph Saffin cite passages in the Bible to support their arguments? Who is more persuasive in his use of these arguments? Why?

2. Lord Dunmore and the *Virginia Gazette* editorialist both attempt to argue that they are for the slaves' best interest. What concerns or motivations might they have other than concern for the slaves' welfare? Which viewpoint do you find more credible on this issue? Why?

3. What examples of racial prejudice do you find in the viewpoints in chapter one? Are the opponents of slavery, such as Samuel Sewall and David Cooper, devoid of racism? How can you tell? What opinions toward blacks do they express?

4. How did the American Revolution and its philosophy of natural rights affect the argument over slavery? In comparing the viewpoints of David Cooper and Theodore Parsons, do you think the developments surrounding U.S. independence strengthened the case for the abolition of slavery?

Chapter Two

1. What kinds of supporting evidence does Theodore Dwight Weld use to support his assertions on the nature of slavery? What evidence does George McDuffie cite?

2. What examples of emotive language do you find in the viewpoints of George McDuffie, Theodore Dwight Weld, Peter Randolph, and others? How do the rhetorical flourishes help or hinder the points they are making?

3. Nehemiah Adams, Peter Randolph, Mary Reynolds, and Millie Evans all use personal experience and observation to support their views. What strengths and limitations do they have as witnesses to slavery? Which person do you believe makes the most objective witness? The most credible witness?

4. What would you say are the three main points used by both George McDuffie and Nehemiah Adams in support of slavery. What are the three main points of the antislavery viewpoints by Peter Randolph and Theodore Dwight Weld?

Chapter Three

1. How do the life experiences of Jupiter Hammon and Henry Garnet differ? How might these differences account for their opposite opinions concerning slave revolution?

2. How would you characterize Nat Turner, based on what is said in the viewpoints? What additional information or evidence, if any, do you believe is necessary for a conclusive description?

3. Does the fact that John Floyd privately expressed antislavery sentiments change the significance of his argument before the state legislature in viewpoint five? Why or why not?

4. How does William Lloyd Garrison reconcile his defense of Nat Turner with his philosophy of nonviolence? Are his arguments convincing?

Chapter Four

1. Both St. George Tucker and Robert Goodloe Harper support the colonization of freed slaves. What reasons do they provide for this proposal? Is racism a factor? Explain your answer.

2. How different are the writing styles of the abolitionists William Lloyd Garrison and Lydia Maria Child? What differing beliefs on how best to achieve abolition might underlie these dissimilarities in style?

3. Which authors in this chapter focus on the practical costs and benefits of emancipation? Which focus on moral aspects?

Chapter Five

1. According to William I. Bowditch, which sections of the Constitution support slavery? How does Frederick Douglass explain away those sections?

2. How does Roger Taney reconcile slavery with the Constitution and the Declaration of Independence? Are his arguments logical? Explain.

3. Are Abraham Lincoln's views on slavery, as revealed in the two viewpoints in this book, consistent with each other? Are they consistent with the Emancipation Proclamation, issued in 1863, which freed the slaves in the Confederacy but not in the Union?

Chapter Six

1. Do you think John Hope Franklin's assessment of the nation's

founders is fair? Why or why not? Is it appropriate to judge them by today's standards? Explain your answer.

2. Which viewpoints in this book could John Hope Franklin use to support his position? Which viewpoints could Herbert J. Storing cite as evidence for his view?

General Questions

1. What common themes are prevalent in the viewpoints defending slavery? Which arguments become more important over the two hundred or so years of slavery? Which become less important? Why do you think this change in emphasis occurs?

2. Do the viewpoints in this book shed any light on the question of whether racism was a cause or an effect of slavery in America? Explain.

Chronology

1619 First blacks arrive in British North America. Their precise status is unclear, but they probably were indentured servants.

1638 First blacks are brought into New England.

1641 Massachusetts becomes the first colony to mention slavery in its legal code.

1660 Virginia House of Burgesses passes first colonial laws detailing permanent chattel slavery for black Virginians.

1661 The English colony of Barbados adopts a comprehensive slave code.

1663 Carolina is organized as a proprietary colony. The Fundamental Constitution of Carolina, drafted by John Locke, permits slavery in the colony. First notable slave rebellion in colonial America occurs in Gloucester, Virginia.

1676 Bacon's Rebellion occurs in Virginia. Landowners, convinced that the government is not offering them adequate protection from Indian raids, establish their own rowdy antigovernment campaign under the leadership of wealthy planter Nathaniel Bacon. Because his "troops," who indiscriminately kill both friendly and hostile Indians, are comprised not only of white landowners but also of former indentured servants and freed slaves, Virginians feel the threat of an integrated, possibly class-based challenge to the powers that be. Bacon's unruly rebellion leads Virginia lawmakers to tighten the slave system.

1688 Friends (Quakers) in Germantown, Pennsylvania, draft the earliest antislavery document in America.

1700 Samuel Sewall writes *The Selling of Joseph*, the first antislavery tract published and distributed in the colonies.

1732 The colony of Georgia is established. It originally banned slavery, but within a few years the ban was rescinded.

1739 Stono Rebellion takes place in South Carolina. The first major slave uprising, it begins when twenty slaves gather near the Stono River, south of Charleston. With stolen weapons, they kill local storekeepers and white families before being captured by the militia. Those blacks not killed on the spot are later executed.

1764 James Otis Jr., in his pamphlet *The Rights of the British Colonies Asserted and Proved*, suggests that natural law means that all people, black and white, are born free and equal.

1773 Massachusetts slaves petition the state legislature for their freedom.

1775 First abolition society in America is organized by Philadelphia Quakers. Lord Dunmore, Royal Governor of Virginia, issues a proclamation offering freedom to male slaves who join British forces. George Washington responds by ordering Revolutionary War recruiting officers to accept free blacks.

1776   Thomas Jefferson pens the Declaration of Independence, with its reference to "all men" being created equal. In the 1850s, Lincoln, among others, will make much of the fact that the word "white" was not inserted before "men" in this founding statement of American freedom.

1777   John Laurens of South Carolina drafts a plan to employ slaves as soldiers in the American Revolution and to promise them freedom. The plan is repeatedly rejected by the South Carolina legislature.

In its new state constitution, Vermont becomes the first state of the now independent colonies to abolish slavery. Pennsylvania follows suit in 1780. In a series of cases during the 1780s, Massachusetts courts rule that slavery is unconstitutional. Rhode Island and Connecticut provide for gradual emancipation beginning in 1784. New York and New Jersey make similar rulings in 1799 and 1804, respectively.

1782   Virginia passes legislation permitting private manumissions of slaves.

1783   The Treaty of Paris, ending the American Revolution, is signed. Included in this treaty are provisions requiring the British to return captured slaves to the United States.

1787   Thomas Jefferson drafts the Northwest Ordinance, which bans slavery in the territory acquired from the British in the American Revolution. This is the first federal action against the institution of slavery and an important precedent for Lincoln and other "free soilers" of the 1850s.

1787-   The United States Constitution is drafted and ratified. It includes
1788   three references to the institution of slavery, although the word *slavery* is never used: The slave trade is to be extended for twenty years; a fugitive slave provision is included; and the three-fifths compromise is devised, stating that slaves are to be counted as three-fifths of persons for purposes of representation and direct taxation.

1790   Congress passes a law limiting naturalization to white aliens.

1791   Benjamin Banneker, a free black surveyor and astronomer, sends a copy of his latest almanac to Thomas Jefferson to prove to Jefferson that black mental powers are greater than Jefferson presumes them to be.

1792   Congress acts to limit the militia to white male citizens.

1793   A federal Fugitive Slave Act is passed; it provides for the return of slaves who have escaped across state boundaries.

A revolution of mulattos and blacks is carried out in the French colony of Saint Domingue (Haiti). European rule there is overthrown under the leadership of a mulatto, Toussaint L'Overture.

Eli Whitney invents the cotton gin, producing an increased demand for slaves.

1794 Blacks in Philadelphia and Baltimore found societies that eventually become the African Methodist Episcopal Church.

First national abolition society, the American Convention for the Promoting of the Abolition of Slavery, is founded.

1800 The Gabriel Prosser rebellion in Virginia begins and ends. Prosser, a blacksmith who placed himself in the tradition of the French and Haitian revolutions, plans to attack Richmond on the night of August 30, 1800. Heavy rains delay the plot. Whites then learn of the plot from their slaves. The major conspirators, including Prosser, are eventually captured and hanged.

1807 Without significant opposition, Congress passes legislation that officially closes the slave trade as of January 1, 1808.

1817 The American Colonization Society is founded by members of the American elite, including James Madison. It seeks to return free blacks to Africa despite objections from free blacks themselves.

1819 Slavery returns to the national political stage when Missouri residents petition Congress for admission to the Union as a slave state.

1821 The Missouri Compromise is passed. It allows Congress to admit two new states, Missouri (slave) and Maine (free), to preserve the balance of slave and free states in the Senate. The legislation also deals with slavery west of Missouri by drawing a line (at 36° 30' north latitude) to the Pacific Ocean, north of which line would be no slavery and south of which slavery could exist.

1822 The Denmark Vesey conspiracy is foiled by black informers; Vesey and other conspirators are arrested and executed.

1827 Birth of a militant, free black newspaper, *Freedom's Journal*.

1829 Officials in Cincinnati drive as many as two thousand blacks from the city by enforcing a city ordinance requiring cash bonds from blacks to ensure good behavior.

Walker's Appeal, a militant pamphlet published by David Walker calling for slave rebellion, is distributed throughout the country, causing controversy in the South.

1830 First free black national convention is held in the United States. It evidences the growth of a small black middle class in the North.

1831 William Lloyd Garrison breaks with the moderate abolitionists and publishes the first issue of the *Liberator*, which will be a major weapon against slavery for thirty-five years.

Nat Turner's rebellion takes place in Virginia. On August 22, 1931, Turner, a preacher with a tendency toward mysticism, leads a group of black rebels in a series of raids that take the lives of some sixty whites, male and female, young and old. About two hundred blacks, including Turner, also lose their lives as a result of this revolt.

1833 The American Anti-Slavery Society is founded in Philadelphia by those abolitionists, including William Lloyd Garrison, who favor an immediate and unconditional end to slavery.

The state of South Carolina (with the open approval of the U.S.

postmaster general) begins to intercept and destroy abolitionist literature sent into the state.

Slavery is abolished in the British Empire.

1836 Congress adopts the "gag rule," which automatically tables all abolitionist petitions, thereby effectively preventing Congressional debate on the issue.

1837 Abolitionist editor Elijah Lovejoy is murdered in Alton, Illinois, by an anti-abolitionist mob intent on sacking his office.

1838 Frederick Douglass escapes from slavery in Maryland and arrives in New York City to begin a life of freedom and abolition activism.

1839 The most famous shipboard slave revolt occurs on the Spanish slave ship *Amistad*. John Quincy Adams argues on behalf of the African rebels before the U.S. Supreme Court; they are eventually freed.

1840 The Liberty Party is founded, indicating that abolitionism has changed its tactics from outside agitation to direct political action.

The American Anti-Slavery Society splits in a disagreement over tactics.

1841 Lydia Child assumes editorship of the official voice of the American Anti-Slavery Society, the *National Anti-Slavery Standard*; she is the first woman to achieve that position.

1844 For the second and last time, the Liberty Party fields a presidential candidate; he wins enough votes to deny the election to Henry Clay, thus bringing to power James K. Polk. Under Polk's presidency, the Mexican War begins raising anew the question of the expansion of slavery.

Largely because of the work of former president John Quincy Adams, Congress repeals its gag rule.

1845- The annexation of Texas and the U.S. victory in the Mexican War
1848 spurs debate on whether newly acquired territories should permit slavery. The Wilmot Proviso is proposed, calling for no slavery in any territory acquired during the Mexican War. While it passes the House, it fails repeatedly in the Senate.

1847 Frederick Douglass establishes his own newspaper, *North Star*, in which he advocates not only immediate abolition of slavery, but women's suffrage as well.

1849 Harriet Tubman escapes to Philadelphia from slavery in Maryland. She later returns south nineteen times to help more than three hundred slaves escape.

A major race riot occurs in Philadelphia. Mobs storm black churches, set them on fire, and kill those inside. It is the fifth anti-black riot in that city since 1832, leading Frederick Douglass to state that no black person is safe in the United States, south or north.

1850 The Compromise of 1850 is fashioned: California is admitted to the Union as a free state; a tougher Fugitive Slave Law is enacted; the slave trade is halted in the District of Columbia; and popular sovereignty is declared in the territories of New Mexico and Utah.

1852   Harriet Beecher Stowe writes *Uncle Tom's Cabin*, which indicts not only slavery but Northern complicity in it. Still, the book is an immediate popular success in the North; it causes great alarm in the South.

1854   The Kansas-Nebraska Act is passed, voiding the Missouri Compromise and possibly extending slavery into territories north of 36°30′ latitude under the doctrine of popular sovereignty, a policy that gives citizens of these territories the power to determine whether their territories will be slave or free.

The Republican Party is founded. While not an abolitionist organization, it stands firmly against the expansion of slavery into any new American territories.

1855-
1859   Seven northern states pass personal liberty laws designed to interfere with the Fugitive Slave Act by providing legal counsel to and requiring jury trials for alleged fugitives.

1857   Hinton Rowan Helper, a nonslaveholding Southerner, publishes *The Impending Crisis*, a book attacking slavery.

George Fitzhugh publishes *Cannibals All! Or Slaves Without Masters*, in which he favorably compares the lot of the slave with that of the exploited northern factory worker. Fitzhugh, a Southerner, is a major proponent of the "positive good" theory of slavery.

The *Dred Scott* decision is handed down. The incendiary Supreme Court decision declares that blacks are not citizens and that neither the states nor the federal government can prevent the extension of slavery.

1858   The Lincoln-Douglas debates take place in Illinois where Democrat Stephen Douglas's Senate seat is at stake. Also at stake is the issue of slavery expansion, as Lincoln argues for free soil and Douglas offers popular sovereignty.

1859   White abolitionist John Brown's raid on Harpers Ferry takes place. Designed to lead to a general slave uprising, it ends in failure and in Brown's execution.

The slave ship, *Clothilde*, lands the last U.S. illegal cargo of slaves in Mobile, Alabama.

1860   *November:* Abraham Lincoln is elected U.S. president.

1860   *December:* South Carolina begins the South's secession from the Union, which culminates in February of 1861 in the establishment of the Confederacy.

1861   The Civil War begins.

Congress passes the first Confiscation Act, which removes slaves from the owner's possession if those slaves are used for "insurrectionary purposes."

1862   President Lincoln proposes that the states individually consider emancipation. He also asks Congress to promise financial aid to any state that enacts emancipation legislation.

Congress passes the second Confiscation Act, which confiscates the property of those who support the Confederate rebellion, even if that support is limited to the paying of taxes to the Confederate government.

Lincoln issues the Emancipation Proclamation, which formally frees the slaves in those states that have seceded from the Union but does not free those slaves in the slave states that have remained loyal to the Union.

1864 Lincoln decides to lend his support to the idea of a constitutional amendment ending slavery. Such a proposal is included in the Republican Party platform for the 1864 presidential election.

1865 The Thirteenth Amendment, ending slavery, is ratified.

Bibliography

Historical Studies

Robert Abzug, *Passionate Liberator: The Life of Theodore D. Weld and the Dilemma of Reform*. New York: Oxford University Press, 1978. A biography of one of the leading evangelical abolitionists and husband of abolitionist-feminist Angelina Grimke.

Herbert Aptheker, *American Negro Slave Revolts*. New York: International Publishers, 1965. A study, from a Marxist perspective, of the major rebellions against the institution of slavery.

John Blassingame, *The Slave Community*. New York: Oxford University Press, 1979. A general history of slavery employing original slave sources to understand the slave system and the lives lived by the slaves within it.

David Brion Davis, *The Problem of Slavery in Western Culture*. New York: Oxford University Press, 1988. An intellectual history of slavery and of the European and American decisions to import slavery to the New World.

Carl Degler, *The Other South*. New York: Harper and Row, 1974. A history of dissent in the antebellum South. Dissenters include critics of slavery and of secession.

Martin Duberman, ed., *The Antislavery Vanguard*. Princeton, NJ: Princeton University Press, 1965. A collection of essays by leading historians of the abolitionist movement.

Stanley Elkins, *Slavery: A Problem in American Institutional Life*. Chicago: University of Chicago Press, 1976. A controversial intellectual history of slavery which contends that the system in the American South was so harsh that Sambo was real, that the slave became infantilized by the system, and that the plantation was comparable to a Nazi concentration camp.

Donald E. Fehrenbach, *Prelude to Greatness*. Palo Alto, CA: Stanford University Press, 1962. An examination of the political career of Abraham Lincoln during the 1850s when he did not hold public office, but when he began to publicly wrestle with the related issues of slavery and slave expansion.

Robert Fogel and Stanley Engerman, *Time on the Cross*. University Press of America, 1985. Another history of slavery, controversial because of its quantitative approach. It argues that the slave system was not as harsh as previous studies have contended.

Eric Foner, *Free Soil, Free Labor, Free Men*. New York: Oxford University

Press, 1970. A history of the origins of the Republican party, which opposed the expansion, but not the immediate abolition, of slavery.

George B. Forgie, *Patricide in the House Divided*. New York: Norton, 1981. A psychological interpretation of Abraham Lincoln that stresses his relationship to the Founding Fathers, as well as the significance of the attitudes of the Founders in the debate over slavery and slave expansion.

Elizabeth Fox-Genovese, *Within the Plantation: Black and White Women of the Old South*. Chapel Hill: University of North Carolina Press, 1988. Examines the dynamics of the lives of women across racial lines in a society dominated economically and politically by men.

John Hope Franklin, *From Slavery to Freedom*. New York: Knopf, 1979. A fine single-volume general history of black America.

William Freehling, *Road to Disunion*. New York: Oxford University Press, 1990. A general history of the internal turmoil within the South over the issues of slavery and secession.

Lawrence Friedman, *Gregarious Saints: Self and Community in American Abolitionism, 1830-1870*. New York: Cambridge University Press, 1982. An intellectual history of the abolitionist movement.

Eugene Genovese, *Roll, Jordan, Roll*. New York: Random House, 1976. An institutional history of slavery that emphasizes the concept of paternalism as a mechanism for understanding how the slaves acquired room to maneuver within the slave system.

Herbert Gutman, *The Black Family in Slavery and Freedom, 1750-1925*. New York: Random House, 1977. A comparative and quantitative history of the evolution of the black family under conditions of both slavery and freedom.

Michael Holt, *The Political Crisis of the 1850s*. New York: Wiley, 1978. A political history of the decade prior to the Civil War, with an emphasis on the differences between the Lower South and Upper South on the related questions of slave expansion and secession.

Harry Jaffa, *Crisis of the House Divided*. Chicago: University of Chicago Press, 1982. A history of the political and intellectual background to the Lincoln-Douglas debates, as well as a history of the debates themselves. Jaffa is highly critical of Douglas and full of praise for Lincoln.

Robert W. Johannsen, *Stephen A. Douglas*. New York: Oxford University Press, 1973. A major biography of a leader of the Democratic party of the 1850s who was also an advocate of popular sovereignty and a leading opponent of Abraham Lincoln and the Free-Soil Republicans.

Winthrop Jordan, *White over Black*. New York: Norton, 1977. An illuminating history of American racial attitudes from the precolonial period through the early national period.

Aileen Kraditor, *Means and Ends in American Abolitionism*. New York: Ivan Dee, 1989. A history of the debates over strategy within the abolitionist movement.

Gerda Lerner, *The Grimke Sisters from South Carolina.* Schocken Press, 1967. A dual biography of two daughters of slaveholders who converted to abolitionism.

Lawrence Levine, *Black Culture and Black Consciousness.* New York: Oxford University Press, 1980. A history of the impact of slavery on black America during and after the demise of the institution itself.

Leon Litwack, *Been in the Storm So Long.* New York: Random House, 1980. A history of the death of slavery and the birth of freedom in the days and months before and after the end of the Civil War. It stresses the problems faced by ex-slaves and their abilities to cope with the demands of freedom.

John Lofton, *Insurrection in South Carolina: The Turbulent World of Denmark Vesey.* Yellow Springs, OH: Antioch Press, 1964. A history of the Denmark Vesey conspiracy.

August Meier and Elliot Rudwick, *From Plantation to Ghetto.* New York: Hill and Wang, 1976. A general survey of black history.

Edmund Morgan, *American Slavery, American Freedom.* New York: Norton, 1975. An intellectual and institutional history of the fateful and collective decisions to bring slavery to seventeenth-century Virginia.

Gerald Mullin, *Flight and Rebellion: Slave Resistance in Eighteenth-Century Virginia.* New York: Oxford University Press, 1972. A history of various forms of slave resistance in one of the most significant slave colonies, including the open rebellion of Gabriel Prosser.

Russel Nye, *Fettered Freedom: Civil Liberties and the Slave Controversy, 1830-1860.* East Lansing: Michigan State University Press, 1964. A history of the threat presented by slavery and the slavocracy to republican government and republican ideas.

Stephen B. Oates, *Fires of Jubilee.* New York: Harper and Row, 1975. A brief history of the short but bloody rebellion of Nat Turner.

Stephen B. Oates, *With Malice Toward None.* New York: New American Library, 1981. The best recent single-volume biography of Abraham Lincoln.

Jane and William Pease, *They Who Would Be Free: Blacks' Search for Freedom, 1830-1861.* New York: Atheneum, 1974. A history of black abolitionism, stressing the differing conceptions of freedom between white and black abolitionists.

Ulrich B. Phillips, *American Negro Slavery.* New York: D. Appleton, 1918. The best of the earliest general histories of slavery written by professional historians, it discusses paternalism in a way that is more sympathetic to the slaveholders than to the slaves.

Benjamin Quarles, *Black Abolitionists.* New York: Oxford University Press, 1969. The first general history of this important group, it also contributes greatly to our understanding of Frederick Douglass, who was the leading black abolitionist.

George P. Rawick, *From Sundown to Sunup: The Making of the Black Community*. Westport, CT: Greenwood Publishing Company, 1972. A history that makes extensive use of the slave narratives gathered by the Work Projects Administration.

Donald Robinson, *Slavery in the Structure of American Politics, 1765-1820*. New York: Harcourt, Brace, Jovanovich, 1971. A political history of the role of slavery in the Revolutionary War period.

Willie Lee Rose, *Slavery and Freedom*. New York: Oxford University Press, 1982. A series of essays on slavery and the aftermath of slavery, including numerous book reviews of important recent histories of the institution.

William Scarborough, *The Overseer: Plantation Management in the Old South*. Baton Rouge: Louisiana State University Press, 1966. A history of the crucial figure on many plantations, namely the individual between the slaves and the slaveowner.

Richard Sewell, *Ballots for Freedom: Anti-Slavery Politics, 1837-1861*. New York: Oxford University Press, 1976. A political history of the evolution of the abolitionist movement in the direction of mainstream politics rather than outside agitation.

Kenneth Stampp, *The Imperiled Union*. New York: Oxford University Press, 1980. A collection of essays on the road to the Civil War by one of the leading historians of the pre-Civil War South.

Kenneth Stampp, *The Peculiar Institution*. New York: Vintage Books, 1956. The first general history of slavery to challenge the Phillips interpretation of the "peculiar institution" (the phrase is not Stampp's but was in usage during the antebellum period).

Robert Starobin, *Industrial Slavery in the Old South*. New York: Oxford University Press, 1970. A history of an often overlooked dimension of slavery and a rebuttal to those who would argue that slavery would have died out as the soil that nourished it became exhausted.

James B. Stewart, *Holy Warriors*. New York: Hill and Wang, 1976. A brief but important general survey of the abolitionist movement.

Sterling Stuckey, *Slave Culture*. New York: Oxford University Press, 1987. A bottom-up history of slavery that emphasizes the culture the slaves created rather than the efforts to impose white culture on them.

Larry Tise, *Proslavery: A History of the Defense of Slavery in America, 1701-1840*. Athens: University of Georgia Press, 1987. An intellectual history that stresses the movement toward the "positive good" defense of slavery.

Richard Wade, *Slavery in the Cities: The South, 1820-1860*. New York: Oxford University Press, 1964. A history of another overlooked feature of the slave system.

Peter H. Wood, *Black Majority: Negroes in Colonial South Carolina from 1670 Through the Stono Rebellion*. New York: Knopf, 1974. A history of slavery in the colony that contained the highest percentage of slaves at the time of the Civil War.

C. Vann Woodward, *American Counterpoint*. Boston: Little, Brown, 1971. A collection of essays on slavery and racism by one of the leading historians of the American South.

Document Collections and Other Important Primary Sources

John Spencer Bassett, ed., *The Southern Plantation Overseer as Revealed in His Letters*. Northampton, MA: Smith College, 1925. A collection of letters written by those who actually ran many of the large Southern plantations on a daily basis.

John Blassingame, ed., *Slave Testimony: Two Centuries of Letters, Speeches, Interviews, and Autobiographies*. Baton Rouge: Louisiana State University Press, 1977. A valuable collection from a wide variety of popular sources.

B. A. Botkin, *Lay My Burden Down: A Folk History of Slavery*. Chicago: University of Chicago Press, 1945. A collection of slave narratives gathered by the Federal Writers Project of the WPA during the New Deal.

James Breeden, ed., *Advice Among Masters: The Ideal in Slave Management in the Old South*. Westport, CT: Greenwood Press, 1980. A collection that stresses how important masters thought it was to resort to coercion to maintain their authority.

Richard M. Dorson, ed., *American Negro Folktales*. Greenwich, CT: Fawcett Publications, 1967. An important source for those interested in examining the history of American slavery from the point of view of the slaves themselves.

Philip Foner, ed., *The Voice of Black America*. New York: Simon and Schuster, 1972. A general anthology of slave and post-slave sources.

Jack P. Greene, ed., *The Diary of Colonel Landon Carter of Sabine Hall, 1752-1778*. Charlottesville: University Press of Virginia, 1965. This two-volume diary is the best single-published source for studying slavery during the colonial period.

Frances Anne Kemble, *Journal of a Resident on a Georgia Plantation in 1838-1839*. New York: Harper and Brothers, 1863. Kemble recorded her impressions of the slave system while she was the wife of Pierce Butler, a Georgia slaveholder.

James McPherson, ed., *Blacks in America: Bibliographical Essays*. Garden City, NY: Doubleday, 1971. Contains sources for original documents relating to slavery that have been collected in anthologies.

Robert M. Myers, ed., *Children of Pride*. New Haven, CT: Yale, 1984. A collection of letters of the Charles Colcock Jones family that does much to illuminate the relationship between slave and master on the plantation of well-educated Southern slaveholders.

Willie Lee Rose, ed., *A Documentary History of Slavery in North America*. New York: Oxford University Press, 1976. A monumental collection of sources covering the colonial, early national, and general nineteenth-century history of slavery.

William Scarborough, ed., *The Diary of Edmund Ruffin*. Baton Rouge: Louisiana State University Press, 1972. The diary of one of the leading advocates of secession, who was given the honor of firing the first shot on Fort Sumter, thereby igniting the Civil War.

Robert Starobin, ed., *Denmark Vesey: The Slave Conspiracy of 1822*. Englewood Cliffs, NJ: Prentice Hall, 1970. A collection of sources concerning the background to the failed revolution in South Carolina.

Henry I. Tragle, *The Southampton Slave Revolt of 1831: A Compilation of Source Material*. Amherst, MA: Amherst University Press, 1971. Documents relating to the Nat Turner rebellion of 1831.

C. Vann Woodward, ed., *Mary Chestnut's Civil War*. New Haven, CT: Yale University Press, 1981. The diary of a Southern woman who examines the impact of slavery, secession, and the Civil War on herself and her South.

Norman Yetman, *Voices from Slavery*. New York: Holt, Rinehart, and Winston, 1970. Another collection of the WPA slave narratives with extensive commentary on their general usefulness for the student of slavery.

Black Autobiographies from the Slavery Era

Sam Aleckson, *Before the War, and After the Union*. (1929)

Robert Anderson, *From Slavery to Affluence*. Hemingford, NE: The Hemingford Ledge, 1927.

Henry Bibb, *Narrative of the Life and Adventures of Henry Bibb, an American Slave*. (1849)

William Wells Brown, *Narrative of William W. Brown, A Fugitive Slave*. New York: Johnson Reprint Corporation, 1970.

Henry Clay Bruce, *The New Man. Twenty-Nine Years a Slave. Twenty-Nine Years a Free Man*. Miami: Mnemosune Publishing Co., 1895.

Louis Hughes, *Thirty Years a Slave*. (1897)

Elizabeth Keckley, *Behind the Scenes*. (1868)

Jermaine Wesley Loguen, *The Reverend J.W. Loguen, as a Slave and as a Freedman*. (1859)

Solomon Northrup, *Twenty Years a Slave*. (1853)

Austin Steward, *Twenty-Two Years a Slave, and Forty Years a Freedman*. Reading, MA: Addison-Wesley Publishing Company, 1969.

Jacob Stroyer, *My Life in the South*. (1890)

White Autobiographies from the Slavery Era

Letitia Burwell, *Plantation Reminiscences.* (1878)

Victoria Virginia Clayton, *White and Black Under the Old Regime.* Freeport, NY: Books for Libraries Press, 1899.

J.G. Clinkscales, *On the Old Plantation.* New York: Negro University Press, 1916.

Rebecca Latimer Felton, *Country Life in Georgia in the Days of My Youth.* New York: Arno Press, 1980.

Robert Q. Mallard, *Plantation Life Before Emancipation.* Richmond, VA: Whittet and Shepard, 1892.

Susan Dabney Smedes, *Memorials of a Southern Planter.* Baltimore: Cushing and Bailey, 1887.

Jane Grey Swisshelm, *Half A Century.* Chicago: Jansen, McClung, 1880.

Norman Wood, *The White Side of a Black Subject.* New York: Negro University Press, 1896.

Index

SOUTHEASTERN COMMUNITY COLLEGE LIBRARY

3 3255 00034 5620